C A S E S

CASES IN

Total Quality Management

Manufacturing and Services

Jay H. Heizer
Professor of Business Administration
Jesse H. Jones Chair in Business Administration
Texas Luthern College

Jay Nathan
Professor of Management
College of Business Administration
St. Johns University

Acquisitions Editor/Developmental Editor: Andrea Shaw
Team Director: John Szilagyi
Production Editor: Kelly Keeler
Production House: DPS Associates, Inc.

1 2 3 4 5 PN 0 9 8 7 6

Printed in the United States of America

ISBN: 0-789-50694-7

Library of Congress Cataloging-in-Publication Data

Heizer, Jay H.
    Cases in total quality management: manufacturing and services/
Jay Heizer and Jay Nathan.
        p.   cm.
    ISBN 0-789-50694-7
    1. Total quality management—Case studies.   2. Manufactures-
-Management—Case studies.   3. Service industries—Management—Case
studies.   I. Nathan, Jay.   II. Title.
HD62.15.H45   1997   96-49669
658.5′62—dc21   CIP

I(T)P
International Thomson Publishing

South-Western College Publishing is an ITP Company. The ITP trademark is used under license.

With love to our families

Kay, Donna, Kira, and Janée
—*Jay Heizer*

Radha, Shyam, and Shila
—*Jay Nathan*

C O N T E N T S

Total Quality Management (TQM) is sweeping across the world. Virtually all economic sectors throughout the world are now participating in the TQM crusade. In this casebook, we have tried to select cases that provide a sense of the breadth and depth of that crusade by including cases from a variety of sectors, as well as cases that go from the TQM vision to the application of TQM tools.

The case contributors have our thanks for their contributions to the TQM crusade. As you can see from the cases, progress is being made in various economic sectors worldwide. The case authors are to be congratulated for their contributions to that effort in both the academic and practitioner spheres. In many of our discussions with the contributors, we noted their excitement and commitment to the discipline. We hope this selection of cases reflects that excitement and commitment.

We have found our TQM journey a delight and hope you and your students will also enjoy the journey and these cases.

Feedback to either of us at the addresses below is most welcome.

Jay Heizer
Texas Lutheran University
Sequin, Texas 78155
(210) 372-6056 (office)
(210) 372-8096 (fax)
Internet:
heizer_j@txlutheran.edu

Jay Nathan
St. John's University
Jamaica, New York 11439
(718) 990-1879 (office)
(718) 380-3803 (fax)
Internet:
nathanj@sjuvm.stjohns.edu

I N T R O D U C T I O N

The cases were selected to represent a wide variety of applications. They represent manufacturing and services and many phases of the TQM effort. Hopefully the following discussions of the cases, appendices, teaching notes, and the data disk will aid you in selecting and presenting the cases that your students will find an exciting learning experience.

ORGANIZATION OF THE BOOK

The cases are organized in four sections:

- Quality Planning: Vision and Implementation
- Building TQM Culture and Management Systems
- Tools of TQM
- Advanced Tools of TQM

The cases range from brief to 20 page cases requiring substantial analysis. They are generally organized within each section to be progressively more challenging. The cases are typically discussed in some detail in the teaching notes. You may find a review of these notes helpful prior to making any assignments.

The Table of Contents also contains a few notes on each case to provide an initial orientation.

All the cases should be approached as case material prepared as the basis for class discussion rather than to illustrate either effective or ineffective handling of the situation. However, some of the cases do represent substantial advances for the organizations depicted in the case.

Teaching Notes

A separate book of teaching notes is available. Most of the teaching notes were prepared by the case authors; consequently they often provide some insight that might not otherwise be available.

Many of the teaching notes include additional questions and possible student projects, as well as background and solutions.

Data Disk

A data disk is available to adopters to ease the data manipulation for those cases where the data input can be onerous.

Videos

Two videos are available to adopters: one video for *Tom's of Maine* and another for *The Saturn Project*.

Appendices

While this casebook is not intended to be used without supplemental material, such an approach may be possible. The appendices do provide several teaching aids. Among those are:

Appendix A: A now classic outline of a widely used problem-solving process. Some have attributed this process to Ford Motor Company and later to Motorola, but the original source is unknown.

Appendix B: A brief review of the eight classic tools of TQM.

Appendix C: A very nice introduction to design of experiments by Darwin J. Davis and Vincent A. Mabert.

Appendix D: A discussion of natural and assigned variation.

Appendix E: A discussion of natural and assigned variation in the context of machine capability by Joseph R. Carter and Thomas E. Vollmann.

Appendix F: A discussion of Control Chart Calculations by Joseph R. Carter and Thomas E. Vollmann.

Appendix G: Control Chart Factors

Appendix H: Cumulative Binomial Probabilities

Appendix I: Baldrige Award Criteria Framework

Appendix J: Baldrige Examination Items and Point Value

ACKNOWLEDGMENTS

The cases presented in this text are the result of the contributions made by a number of people with a variety of perspectives on TQM. The authors thank each of them for their contributions to TQM and the cases presented here. Those authors are:

Timothy M. Bergquist
Jeanne Busemeyer
Mike Carnell
Joseph R. Carter
Thomas Y. Choi
Dan Ciampa
Gary Cone
Ed Conn
Darwin J. Davis
Dave Dipre
Harold Dyck
Sean Ennis
Brian Fynes
Sue Greenfeld
Mikel J. Harry
Janelle Heineke
George A. Johnson
Marilyn S. Jones
Jerry Kinard

Frederick R. Klug
Ashok Kumar
Vincent A. Mabert
Curtis P. McLaughlin
Jim Morris
Jaideep Motwani
Robert Orwig
George Peters
Kenneth D. Ramsing
Elizabeth Schubert
Kit N. Simpson
Victor E. Sower
George H. Thompson
Joanne Tokle
Thomas E. Vollmann
Lawrence A. Ward
Steven C. Wheelwright
Gary J. Zenz

Many individuals encouraged us and provided assistance in bringing this project to completion. Our thanks go to: Larry Mauer, Dean, College of Business Administration; Pat Lyons, Chair, Department of Management; and Doris Berritto, Word Processing Center at St. John's University; Nick Lockard, Chair, Business Administration; and Leonard Schulze, Vice President of Academic Affairs at Texas Lutheran University; DeVilla Williams, Editor at Course Technology; and Andrea Shaw at South-Western College Publishing. We also thank Christy Van Gelderen for outstanding clerical support.

PART I

Quality Planning:

Vision and

Implementation

Consumer Products, Inc.

At Consumer Products, Inc., the new head of engineering and asset planning (in charge of the strategy, building, maintenance, and renovation of all of this company's manufacturing and distribution facilities) had been handed a strategy from predecessors to continue the building of a distribution network based on large, automated central warehouse and distribution centers. The cost of these regional facilities and the software and hardware to manage and keep them linked together was extremely high, more than that of any other building program in the company's history. The analysis done by the company's own industrial engineers and distribution people, as well as by outside experts, showed that economies of scale and down-the-road efficiencies made this economical in the long run. Still, it didn't seem quite right to "Chet" (all names in this case history are disguised). The dollar cost was enormous. Some of the automated equipment that had been planned for was untested. The task of linking and communicating between these megadistribution centers was daunting. It all caused Chet to rethink the whole idea. He benchmarked other companies. He read. He questioned. Time was running out. His bosses were pressuring him to stay with the schedule and move ahead.

At a convention of his company's dealers, he heard a presentation on Just-In-Time, the philosophy of speed, flexibility, and elimination of the steps in manufacturing processes that do not add value. "Storing something doesn't add value. Counting it doesn't, either. Inventory is merely potentially useful product waiting to add value," he heard. He also heard of hard-to-believe cost savings that had resulted in other companies by thinking small and avoiding automation's inflexibility.

The germ of an idea began to form. If this could work in a plant, why not in a distribution center? In a network of distribution centers? "What is our business anyway," he reasoned, "if not, a local business." It is the drug store manager and grocery store manager who are our customers and it is they who determine our shelf space, in large part. How are megadistribution centers going to better serve them? Can we do better by having our product closer to customers rather than in larger warehouses hundreds of miles away? Where's the added value of that to the customer? Why not a system where the product goes right from our plants to the customer? When do we need to have inventory?

He began talking about this emerging image with division presidents and high-ranking staff people. He was asked to make presentations. He used only two slides for much of these sessions.

The first showed the current system and the path the product took. In the upper right corner was a sketch of a manufacturing plant. From it a line led to

Source: Adapted from Dan Ciampa, *Total Quality: A User's Guide for Implementation,* Addison-Wesley Publishing Company, Reading, MA, 1992, pp. 127–132.

the sketch of a tractor-trailer truck. From that, a line led to a warehouse. Then another truck, and a line to a larger warehouse. Another truck. And so on, until the product eventually arrived at a point on the lower left corner at a sketch of a customer's store. He then showed his second slide. It was the same as the first except that several of the lines connecting the sketches and two of the trucks and three of the warehouses had black crosses drawn over them. It was the best way Chet knew of conveying his picture and getting others to understand it, as well.

What emerged from this line of reasoning over time is a distribution strategy made up of small, low-cost, local warehouses geared to fast response. Interim warehouses and the transportation and communication costs that come with large, centralized systems are largely eliminated under Chet's strategy.

While Chet was coming up with a new picture of a distribution system, John, one of the division presidents, became committed to establishing an employee involvement effort. He had become convinced that getting employees involved and pushing responsibility to lower levels was a big part of revitalizing his division, which had slipped in volume and profit in recent years. John had brought in outside educators to "teach" employee involvement. He wasn't satisfied with the results. He began talking about it himself. Still, he felt there was something missing. Something was needed to give life to the employee involvement effort that he had become so committed to.

He attended one of Chet's presentations and became intrigued by the vast potential for cost savings that could come from such a distribution scheme. He began testing Chet and his countercultural scheme. Was it merely a pie-in-the-sky dream or was there really something to it? The more he delved into the idea of a dramatically shortened product-distribution pipeline, the more viable it seemed. The savings were real.

John also realized, though, that this sort of system required a change in the mindset of managers and employees and in the way that they went about doing their work. But making it happen could mean the difference between getting his division back on track financially and being behind budget for the next fiscal year.

Kevin had assumed the CEO role in this corporation a year before Chet began formulating the new product-pipeline strategy. He had risen quickly through the managerial ranks and, with each managerial assignment, had been known for increasing market share, repairing relationships with customers when necessary, and generating strong customer loyalty. He had been dismayed at other divisions' lack of attention to the customer when he assumed the CEO role; he was also disturbed at the lack of connection with the customer on the part of staff directors and managers at the corporate office. He began talking about the customer constantly, asking questions at staff meetings and middle managers' presentations about what impact the proposed new program would have on the customer. He began asking what value to the customer was provided by some of the staff departments that existed at the corporate office. He began to be thought of by employees as a customer-oriented leader. His questions and the obvious intensity of his conviction regarding the customer's importance began to have an effect. But Kevin wasn't satisfied. More had to be done.

At a staff meeting of his division presidents and senior staff, the topic of the new distribution system was discussed in detail. All the senior staff had heard Chet's presentation, and the two slides he used were by now well known throughout the company. John, the division president, endorsed it. The only challenge, he said, was how to change the current thinking of employees so that it would work. Kevin had been thinking about the new distribution system, too. A decision had to be made to go one way or the other. The first and more traditional strategy with its promised economies of scale or the new, more radical one. He liked the new one. He liked its simplicity and Chet's argument that if large chunks of activity were eliminated, cost would be eliminated as well. But each time he thought about Chet's idea, what excited Kevin the most was its potential for fast response to a customer; much faster, at least theoretically, than the current one or the one proposed for large megadistribution sites. That sort of speed could be a decided competitive advantage and boost market share. He knew from customer surveys and meetings with customers that what mattered to them was getting the right product when they needed it, not later, and not before (so that they had to carry the inventory). Local warehouses could make that easier. He also recognized the potential for the corporate staff groups to be part of this program and through that involvement, to become more in tune with customers and their needs.

Kevin recognized the danger of taking a stand one way or the other at this point. He was a persuasive enough leader that his subordinates might go along with his idea but yet not be committed. By encouraging conversation and the formation of two different positions, they could also perhaps emerge with a better and more well-thought-through solution. He encouraged John to talk more about this; and he probed to find out how deeply committed to this new system John really was. As John talked, things began to gel in Kevin's mind. He knew of John's frustration at not being able to get a real and robust employee involvement effort off the ground. He also began to see how a pilot program in John's area could answer several questions.

"John, hold on a minute," Kevin said. "You've talked about the cost savings and simplicity of this new system and Chet is certainly convincing, but we don't have any real evidence this will happen."

After reciting some of Chet's analysis and adding some of his own on the potential impact in his division, John said, "And, Kevin, I *believe* in this thing."

"But how can it be implemented? In order for this to work it will require people working differently than they do now. Getting the people in the field committed to it is the key."

John sat up and leaned forward in his chair. "The way to make that happen is to give them responsibility for thinking it through. If we have small, local warehouses we won't need another layer of managers. They can be run by self-managed teams. The responsibility can be the clerk's or the route-truck driver's to make this a success. That will save cost as well as get people involved. Let's let the people who will be affected the most get at this idea. Let's push it down to them. If they get committed to it they'll implement it."

The more John talked the more convincing he became. "There's no question this is going to have a positive impact on our share in the market, too. I have store chains in my division that get out of stock frequently. Others that sell out on some of our products and not others. Others stock out at odd times."

"Bingo," Kevin thought, "the customer connection."

"So, John, let me go a step further. This distribution system can gain us share if we can use it to respond faster than our competition. It will also be less expensive to operate. The way to make it happen is to get people at the local levels involved in really thinking this through, get them to tell us if this really makes sense and how to make it happen. Is that what we're saying?"

The entire group talked through the pluses and minuses of this notion for the rest of that meeting and over the next couple of weeks. At their next meeting, two weeks later, Kevin started off by saying,

"I've been thinking a lot about our discussion of the pipeline concept and market share over the last couple of weeks, as I know each of you have. It has made me step back and ask more fundamental questions. 'What kind of place do we want to create around here? Is it a place where decisions get pushed down that are as important as our distribution strategy or where we make all the decisions in this room? Is it one where our decisions are based on the impact on a grocery store manager? Is it one that really wants to listen to our customers? Is it one that is willing to step out and do something different?' We have to get clear on that first. When we are all in the same spot about the kind of place we want this company to be, then these important, strategic decisions are going to be easier to make, and they'll make a lot more sense to our employees. Once we do this we should come back to this decision about a distribution system and see which option most helps us get to where we want to be."

Another spirited discussion followed. An off-site meeting took place soon after to focus on Kevin's core question, "What kind of place do we want to create . . . ?"

DISCUSSION QUESTIONS

1. Help Kevin answer the question . . . "What kind of place do we want to create?"
2. How does answering Question 1 address the vision and implementation of Total Quality Management (TQM)?
3. How should this vision be conveyed to the customers of Consumer Products, Inc.?
4. What might be the appropriate measures for evaluating implementation of the vision?

Total Quality Management at Robert W. Baird & Co.

R obert W. Baird & Co., founded in Milwaukee, Wisconsin in 1919, is one of the nation's oldest and largest regionally headquartered investment bankers, serving individuals, corporations, municipalities, and institutional investors. Baird has been a member of the Northwestern Mutual Life Insurance Co. family of companies since 1982. Northwestern Mutual Life is also headquartered in Milwaukee and is the third largest insurance company in the world. In addition to the headquarters in Milwaukee, Baird has over 55 branch offices in 10 states. About half are in Wisconsin and most of the rest are in the Midwest (**Exhibit 1**). Baird has grown both internally and by taking over small investment firms in order to gain market share and good locations. The last two years have been Baird's most profitable ever. As of December 31, 1993, Baird had $453 million in assets with revenues of over $210 million. Recent success has led management to invest in the long-term future of Baird. One way of doing this has been the Total Quality Management (TQM) program.

THE SURVEYS

In 1992, Baird retained the consulting firm of Gray-Judson-Howard (G-J-H) to lead the TQM process, which started in April with an internal written survey regarding the problems and needs of the associates. This was sent to all Baird associates. The lead consultant also met with managers in small groups and conducted studies of the cost of quality, asking staff how much of their time was spent correcting problems. The first TQM workshop, conducted on June 13, 1992, was designed to build awareness of the TQM process, based on associates' responses to the surveys.

The consultants also surveyed three types of clients. These surveys were developed after conducting focus groups with clients in the Milwaukee and Madison, WI, and Grand Rapids, MI markets. The first external survey was mailed to a broad base, by location and type, of 4,000 active Baird clients. This produced a healthy 49% response rate. The second involved a set of telephone interviews with 300 Baird clients who have made fewer than two transactions in the last 24 months. A final set of phone interviews focused a sample of the

Source: Frederick R. Klug under the direction of Curtis P. McLaughlin, University of North Carolina at Chapel Hill.

1,200 accounts closed in 1992. These four surveys gave a reliable base of information regarding the needs of both clients and associates.

The most important findings of the client surveys were that:

1. Overall, client satisfaction was very high (**Exhibit 2**).

   - 88% indicated high satisfaction with their Investment Officer Relationship
   - 87% indicated high satisfaction with Baird Services
   - 81% indicated high satisfaction with Baird Products

2. Clients age 65 and over expressed the highest overall satisfaction with their Investment Officer (IO) Relationship, while younger clients, age 44 and under, expressed the lowest satisfaction with the overall quality of Baird's services (**Exhibit 3**).
3. Referrals are the leading source of new clients, yet 56% of respondents who said they would give a referral have never been asked for a referral (**Exhibits 4** and **5**).
4. The three most important factors that drive clients' perception of service from an Investment Officer are problem-solving ability, looking out for clients' interests first, and understanding clients' investment needs (**Exhibit 6**).
5. Only 10% of respondents had a "significant" problem within the past year. Yet, of the respondents who had a problem, 41% were dissatisfied with how their problems were handled due to issues such as poor follow-up, "getting the runaround," or not having the problem resolved within a reasonable amount of time.

A two-day workshop to set the foundation for a TQM plan, led by G-J-H, was held May 7 and May 8, 1993, to go over the fundamentals of TQM, review the results of the surveys, and develop "Opportunities for Improvement." The workshop was attended by 45 associates, including senior management, all department heads, and representatives from Baird's Branch Advisory Council. Top management expressed its support for TQM throughout the process. Fred Kasten, President and CEO, commented on the workshop, "We have a strong culture in place. However, we need to improve the communication of our culture with all of our associates. Our culture also embraces change in the way we serve our clients which is what TQM is all about. The right kind of change. This is a very exciting time in the development of our firm and I'm very pleased so many people are anxious to participate and help." This was quoted, together with supporting statements from other senior managers, in a May 1993 management newsletter to all Baird Associates.

With this support from top management, a three-pronged TQM plan was developed. These involved (1) redefining Baird's mission statement to give Baird direction, (2) creating Baird "University" as a training ground for associates, and (3) creating three quality teams to address key opportunities for improvement.

THE MISSION STATEMENT

One major step in TQM planning was to reexamine and redefine the mission statement to better communicate to the associates what Baird is all about. Management intended to reflect Baird's belief in satisfying client needs through creativity, teamwork and, most importantly, integrity. The new and improved mission statement was communicated, in memo form, to all associates in October, 1993.

The Mission of Robert W. Baird & Co. Incorporated is "to understand and anticipate our individual, institutional, investment banking and investment management clients' financial service needs. We will provide innovative and appropriate solutions and implement those solutions promptly and accurately. Baird's success will be measured by how effectively we achieve excellence in client satisfaction, develop our associates, create a climate conducive to continuous improvement and provide value to our shareholders."

In addition, associates would be expected to conduct themselves according to Principles revolving around the following topics: Integrity, Client Satisfaction, People, Consultative Sales, Communication, Teamwork, Growth, Balance, Community Involvement, and Stability. These Principles are expanded and defined in **Exhibit 7**.

"BAIRD UNIVERSITY"

As a direct result of the internal survey to all associates, the second part of the TQM plan was a formalized program, offering training in industry and developmental skills, called "Baird University." Courses would concentrate on the following:

- Quality Team Training
- Management Training
- Telephone Communication Skills
- Supervisory Training
- Investment Officer Training
- Associate Orientation
- Industry Overview
- Interpersonal Communication Skills
- Customer Service Skills
- Advanced Investment Officer Programs

ORIENTATION

Initially, training would focus on an orientation program for new associates and also on strengthening management skills. The orientation program would include videos, slides, a tour of Baird, and a presentation by senior management. This program would also provide a basic overview, presented monthly, of the securities industry so that both new and experienced associates would have a valuable knowledge base for the kind of work they will be doing. In addition, a program would be offered for associates in management positions based on The Wilson Learning Corporation's "Leadership Management" program, which emphasizes characteristics of good leadership and includes feedback to managers from their associates.

QUALITY TEAMS

The third part of the TQM plan was the development of three Quality Teams. Two of the teams focused on clients while the other team focused on Baird associates. The members of each team, all from within the firm, come from diverse backgrounds. All the team members were trained by an outside consultant.

Client Problem Handling and Resolution

This team was assembled because the survey pointed out that out of the 10% of people who had problems, nearly half were very disappointed with the way the problem was handled. As in any business, one unhappy client can cause tremendous damage to the reputation of a firm by telling everyone he or she knows about being handled poorly. In the beginning, the team focused on individual clients; discussing the process of handling problems, resolving them, and finding the cause of the problems in the most efficient and thorough way possible.

Client Satisfaction

Although the surveys found high levels of client satisfaction, this team concentrated on finding ways to measure client satisfaction on a regular basis. The team considered individual investors, institutional and investment banking, and asset management clients. Client satisfaction was recognized as the key to building long-term relationships with clients. This team's actions and its proposal to management are discussed later in more detail to illustrate further the approach used at Baird.

Associate Recognition

This team was, in part, a response to the results of the internal survey of all Baird associates. Top management realized that people are the key assets of Baird and that it is important to recognize and appreciate them. The team's main goal was to look at ways to recognize and reward associates for outstanding contributions.

THE CLIENT SATISFACTION TEAM

This team's mission was the following: "To develop a procedure whereby client (i.e., Individual, Institutional, Investment Banking, and Investment Management) satisfaction is measured and reported to management on a regular basis." Management believed that the measurement of customer satisfaction could be one of Baird's most powerful profit-building tools. If this process is done well, the team expects Baird to realize several expected benefits and results, including:

- Improved client satisfaction
- Enhanced current relationships
- A means of obtaining referrals from satisfied customers
- Assistance with product development
- Improved customer service
- Identification of new market opportunities

On August 3 and 4, 1993, G-J-H conducted a team training workshop for the twelve team members. The outline of the workshop for Tuesday, August 3, 1993 was Team-Building:

- Managing Diversity: Meyers-Briggs
- Team Exercise: The Game
- Baird Client Satisfaction Issues
- Discussion: Mission and Project Scope

For Wednesday, August 4, 1993, the Action Plan was:

- Communications
- Tasks, Roles and Assignments

The team's Scope of Effort was presented by the consultant facilitator as a Time Frame of six weeks, meeting weekly, if possible.
Recommendations were expected to address:

- Development of a survey/report card to be sent to all or to random active clients to measure their satisfaction.
- Development of a "process" for how often surveys are mailed, who they are sent to, and by whom they are sent.
- Potential costs of such a survey, including how surveys will be tabulated and by whom.
- How results will be reported and how action should be taken to leverage the findings.

The consultants also suggested that the team might want to investigate how competitors and non-competitors monitor client satisfaction (e.g., Wheat First, Raymond James, General Motors, etc.).

The Process

Four basic steps were followed by the Client Satisfaction Team: (1) basic information was collected, (2) a survey was developed, (3) a feedback process was formulated, and (4) a plan to implement the program was developed.
First, both internal and external information was collected. The internal research determined, from a sample of 21 high-performing Investment Officers (IOs), how they measured client satisfaction and what types of measurement they would prefer to see implemented. Most IOs measured client satisfaction very informally by using numbers of transfers and referrals, performance, and the amount of repeat business. Some just measured with their intuition. IO's feelings about mailers were mixed. About half favored personal surveys done by the IOs directly with the client.
The IOs were also asked what they discuss when they have annual reviews with their top clients. This information was used to help develop the survey. The team also surveyed outside firms who were fellow members of the SIA-PR roundtable on how they measure client satisfaction. The team report displayed forms developed by Scott & Stringfellow Investments, McDonald & Company Securities, Wheat First Securities/Butcher & Singer, Edward D. Jones & Co., Robert Thomas Securities, Inc., and others outside the industry such as Lexis. While some of this information was helpful, the team found no indication of how or whether these firms used the information they had gathered.
The team also found that the Baird branch office in Holland, Michigan was already surveying all of its clients by mail every six months. This included a letter from the Branch Manager, a Projected Funds Needed to Retire statement, and a survey called an Investment Needs Update. The latter asked about the client's desire for an update meeting, and a rating of Baird versus its competition as better or worse on the following eight items:

- Staff friendliness and willingness to help
- Knowledge, skill level, and training of staff
- Record-keeping accuracy

- Timeliness in processing transactions
- Fixing and resolving problems
- Overall clarity of statements and correspondence
- Relative quality and service experience

The clients were also asked about their interest in some 20 Baird investment products, services and seminars. Then the clients were asked to rate their IOs on some ten items, again using a five-point scale, and offered the chance to give an open-ended answer to the question, "What could we do to better meet or exceed your expectations of us?"

The ten items questioned asked about the IOs were:

1.	Knowledge of investments and financial markets	1	2	3	4	5
2.	Quality of financial advice	1	2	3	4	5
3.	Friendliness and willingness to listen	1	2	3	4	5
4.	Availability and accessibility to listen	1	2	3	4	5
5.	Timeliness in returning phone calls	1	2	3	4	5
6.	Understanding of your investment goals	1	2	3	4	5
7.	Taking time to give clear, concise explanations	1	2	3	4	5
8.	Looking out for your interests first	1	2	3	4	5
9.	Problem solving ability	1	2	3	4	5
10.	Overall quality of service	1	2	3	4	5

It was clear that much of the ambivalence about a regular survey was related to the topic of IO evaluation by customers. For example, the Executive Summary of the team's final report listed ten "broad areas of concern" which had to be addressed in their deliberations. The first was "Elimination of the possible 'top-down' threat to individual investment officers. The link between customer satisfaction, referrals, and commissions must be communicated." The second was "Development of appropriate measurement format that would *not* compromise the contact officer's *individual* relationship with the client." The fourth cited "Identification of parties affected by eventual measurement policy, e.g., client, contact officer, management and operations, and their competing interests or *needs (whether actual or perceived)*."

The second phase of the team effort was developing a survey. The Executive Summary of the team report notes concern about "Multiple Choice" vs. "Essay" formats (No. 3); properly identifying changing client *needs* over time, before focusing on satisfaction measures (No. 5); meeting the unique information needs of various departments, particularly public and corporate finance (No. 6). The team decided that Baird should be able to measure several factors with different combinations of surveys used for different clients. However, the team adopted the strategy that "The initial focus of the survey would be on the areas previously identified within the *Gray, Judson & Howard study*. These include broad areas of relationships, problem solving, knowledge, and attitudes, rather than concentrate on minutia such as fees, record-keeping, statement format, etc." (No. 9). **Exhibit 8** shows the survey which was proposed for use with Baird's individual investment clients.

The next step in the development of the client satisfaction plan was how to process the information into meaningful feedback. The team report's Executive Summary emphasized the need to have a Response Team in place before the survey went out (No. 7), but also recognized that the firm would have to decide on the appropriate "marginal rate of return on remedial efforts."

The team recommended that the information be analyzed by:

- Demographics
- Investment Officer
- Branch
- Region
- Trading Areas
- Service Areas

The results would then be measured relative to either an internal or an external benchmark. This would require the development of Baird's own standards of measurement and performance. (No. 10 in the Executive Summary). Finally, the information needed to filter down the organization to the right people (**Exhibit 9**). The team also acknowledged that "A second phase of the client satisfaction survey might be considered that would specifically measure the effectiveness of Baird's response to an identified area of dissatisfaction. Data from this survey could be utilized to further tailor the effectiveness of our follow-up methods" (No. 8).

The final step was to determine a plan for the implementation of this process, so that as many associates as possible could be positively influenced by the new client satisfaction measurement plan. First, the plan would be reviewed by an IO test group in order to deal with associates' concerns and refine parts of the implementation. Then client focus groups would be used to better refine survey questions and define survey instruments. Third, a test sample would be used to test the validity of the data gathered. Finally, a company wide buy-in program would be initiated as a part of "Baird University" to educate all Baird associates to be part of the process.

The Keys to Success

In the end, the team identified four main ingredients, or keys to success, in implementing such a measurement system. The first was flexibility. They considered it very important that the process allow each type of client to be surveyed in an appropriate manner. There must be an effective blend of types of questions as well as the types of surveys used. The second key was that the system must provide a consistent, ongoing measurement of client satisfaction. Thus, data processing had to be simple and new data must be comparable to previous data. Third, while this program was a tool for management's use, everyone must benefit from its implementation. Finally, it was important that the clients understand that the program is designed to better serve them, rather than being a marketing ploy to increase Baird's bottom line. **Exhibit 10** shows how these four points were expressed in the Final Thoughts section of the team's report.

Exhibit 1 Baird Offices

HEADQUARTERS
Milwaukee, Wisconsin

BRANCHES

Florida
Clearwater
Naples
Tampa

Illinois
Chicago
Lake Forest
Moline
Peoria
Rockford
Winnetka

Indiana
Indianapolis
Richmond
South Bend
Terre Haute
Valparaiso

Iowa
Cedar Rapids
Des Moines

Michigan
Big Rapids
Cascade
Grand Rapids
Holland
Kalamazoo
Ludington
Muskegon

Minnesota
Bloomington
Minneapolis

Nebraska
Omaha

Ohio
Columbus

Texas
Dallas

Baird Asset Management
Appleton
Milwaukee
Tampa Bay

Wisconsin
Metropolitan Milwaukee
 Downtown
 Brookfield
 Mayfair
 North Shore
 Southridge
Appleton
Beloit
Eau Claire
Fond du Lac
Green Bay
Janesville
Kenosha
LaCrosse
Madison/Downtown
Madison/West
Manitowoc
Neenah
Oconomowoc
Oshkosh
Racine
Sheboygan
Sister Bay
Stevens Point
Sturgeon Bay
Tomah
Wausau
West Bend

Exhibit 2 Satisfaction Opportunities

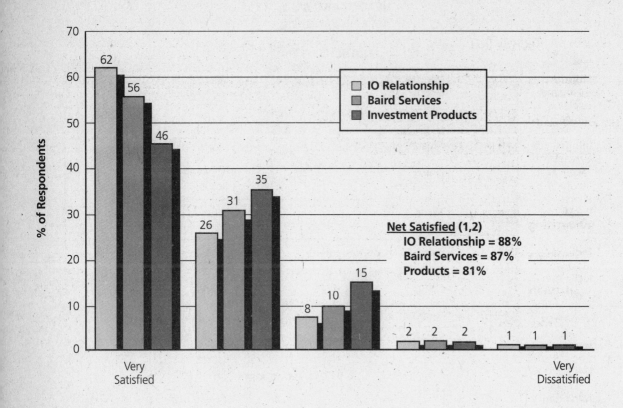

Exhibit 3 Identifying Key Age Differences

44 years and under	Ages 45 to 64	65 years and over
• More service-oriented • More demanding • Higher expectations	• More IO-focused • Demanding higher performance	• Relationship-oriented • More satisfied • Less diverse needs

	Relative	Absolute		Relative	Absolute		Relative	Absolute
Quality of IO Services	100	.29	Satisfaction with IO Relationship	100	.34	Satisfaction with IO Relationship	100	.44
Quality of Firm's Services	82	.23	Quality of IO Services	82	.28			
Satisfaction with IO Relationship	68	.20						

Exhibit 4 Referrals Are Leading Source of New Clients

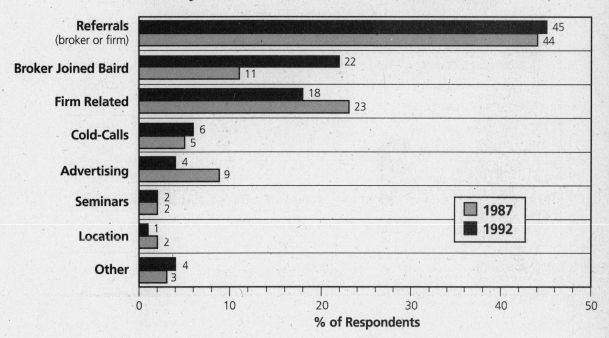

"What led you to first contact Robert W. Baird & Co.?"

	% of Respondents
Referrals (broker or firm)	45 / 44
Broker Joined Baird	22 / 11
Firm Related	18 / 23
Cold-Calls	6 / 5
Advertising	4 / 9
Seminars	2 / 2
Location	1 / 2
Other	4 / 3

1987
1992

Exhibit 5 Baird Has a Significant Opportunity

"If asked, would you make a recommendation?"

Has your Baird Investment Officer asked you to recommend him/her to a friend, relative, or business associate?	Would Recommend (1, 2)	Maybe (3)	Would Not Recommend (4, 5)
Yes	25%	3%	1%
No	56%	9%	6%

81% Total

Exhibit 6 Identifying Key IO Skills

	Relative Importance	Absolute Importance
➡ **Problem-solving ability**	100	.2089
➡ **Looking out for clients' interests first**	100	.2080
➡ **Understanding clients' investment needs**	84	.1754
Knowledge of investments & financial markets	48	.1011
Quality of financial advice	45	.0950
Availability & accessibility	40	.0842
Gives clear explanations	36	.0758
Friendliness & willingness to listen	33	.0691
Timeliness in returning calls	24	.0500

These nine factors "explain" 73% of the observed differences in clients' perceptions of service quality.

Exhibit 7 Baird's Principles

- **Integrity** is irreplaceable. We will strive to uphold the highest standards of business conduct in all dealings with our clients and associates.

- **Client Satisfaction** is our primary goal. We believe that in all of our endeavors, the clients' interests come first.

- **People** are our most important asset. We are committed to hiring the best people and to encourage individual growth through training, recognition and respect for each other.

- **Consultative Sales** are the by-product of leadership. It is not sufficient to simply take our clients' orders. Our goal is to fully understand their needs and to deliver complete financial solutions, building long-term relationships in the process.

- **Communication** is critical to our success. Clear, direct and frequent communication creates an atmosphere of understanding, confidence, and trust with our clients and associates.

- **Teamwork** is essential. Optimal client satisfaction can only be obtained when all Baird associates coordinate their efforts.

- **Growth** is the direct result of providing quality, value-added client services. Growth comes naturally from doing things right and always being in a position to take advantage of opportunities—be they new people, new skills, new geography, or new business.

- **Balance** is the key to success. By providing a broad range of products and services, we and our clients are able to diversify and insulate against the cyclical nature of securities markets. Equally important is the balance in our personal lives, giving appropriate consideration to business and family needs.

- **Community Involvement** is strongly encouraged. It is our opportunity to give something back to the communities in which we live and work.

- **Stability** is the result of our efforts. Stability of people, culture, and capital has served our clients, associates and shareholders very well over the long term.

Exhibit 8 Draft Cover Letter and Questionnaire

Month, 1994

Dear Baird Client:

    This is a personal request for your help. To
ensure that we are providing you with the finest
investment products and personalized service, we
would like about 10 minutes of your time to fill
out the enclosed questionnaire.

    Why are we conducting this survey? Very sim-
ply, to gather information that will help us
improve the quality of service and the products.

    Please note that this questionnaire may be
returned in complete anonymity; you have the
option to identify yourself or your Baird
Investment Officer. Whether or not you include
your name or that of your Investment Officer, we
ask that you answer each question as candidly as
possible. Your thoughts and input are invaluable
in our efforts to provide you with the highest
quality investment services.

    After you have completed the questionnaire,
please put it in the enclosed postage-paid envelope and drop it in the mail within a week. It
will be sent to ABC Research, an independent consulting firm which will keep your answers strictly
confidential.

    Thank you very much. Your time and help are
greatly appreciated.

                        Sincerely,

                        G. Frederick Kasten, Jr.

Exhibit 8 Draft Cover Letter and Questionnaire, continued

Overall Satisfaction with Baird

The following questions refer to your overall level of satisfaction with the quality and value of investment products and services you are receiving from Robert W. Baird & Co. In responding to each question, please compare Baird as a firm to other investment firms that you typically deal with including other brokerage firms, mutual fund companies, banks, and insurance companies.

Overall, how satisfied are you with the performance of your investment products with Baird?

Very Satisfied			Very Dissatisfied	
1	2	3	4	5
☐	☐	☐	☐	☐

Overall, how satisfied are you with the quality of services that you are receiving from Baird?

Very Satisfied			Very Dissatisfied	
1	2	3	4	5
☐	☐	☐	☐	☐

With how many other Investment Officers or brokerage firms do you maintain accounts? *(Check one box.)*

☐ Baird Only   ☐ Baird + 1 Other   ☐ Baird + 2 Others   ☐ Baird + 3 or more

Which firm do you consider to be your *primary investment firm*? _____

How would you rate Baird in the following areas compared to other financial service companies that you deal with? *(Please check one box for each of the statements below.)*

	Baird Is Much Better			Baird Is Much Worse	
	1	2	3	4	5
1) Staff friendliness and willingness to help	☐	☐	☐	☐	☐
2) Knowledge, skill level, and training of staff	☐	☐	☐	☐	☐
3) Record-keeping accuracy	☐	☐	☐	☐	☐
4) Timeliness in processing transactions	☐	☐	☐	☐	☐
5) Fixing and resolving problems	☐	☐	☐	☐	☐
6) Overall clarity of statements and correspondence	☐	☐	☐	☐	☐
7) Relative fairness of fees and service charges	☐	☐	☐	☐	☐
8) Overall quality and service experience	☐	☐	☐	☐	☐

How would you grade Baird's ability to provide you with advice and service related to the following types of investment products? *(Please check one box for each of the products below.)*

	Excellent			Poor		Never Heard of It
	1	2	3	4	5	
1) Common Stocks (Publicly Traded)	☐	☐	☐	☐	☐	☐
2) Preferred Stocks	☐	☐	☐	☐	☐	☐
3) Municipal Bonds	☐	☐	☐	☐	☐	☐
4 US Treasury Bills, Notes, Bonds	☐	☐	☐	☐	☐	☐
5) Mortgage-Backed Securities	☐	☐	☐	☐	☐	☐
6) Corporate Bonds	☐	☐	☐	☐	☐	☐
7) Relative fairness of fees and service charges	☐	☐	☐	☐	☐	☐
8) Overall quality and service experience	☐	☐	☐	☐	☐	☐
9) Money Market Funds	☐	☐	☐	☐	☐	☐
10) Certificates of Deposit (CDs)	☐	☐	☐	☐	☐	☐
11) Annuities	☐	☐	☐	☐	☐	☐
12) Unit Investment Trusts	☐	☐	☐	☐	☐	☐

Exhibit 8 Draft Cover Letter and Questionnaire, continued

Is there anything in particular about the service you receive from Baird that you really like or that you really dislike?

_____

_____

Is there anything about your financial or investment needs that we should tell your Investment Officer?

_____

_____

Are there any investment services that you need that you would like Baird to provide?

_____

_____

Your Baird Investment Officer

The following questions refer to your overall level of satisfaction with the services you are receiving from your Baird Investment Officer. Please remember your answers are strictly confidential.

How would you rate your Investment Officer in the following areas? *(Please check one box for each of the statements below.)*

	Excellent				Poor
	1	2	3	4	5
1) Knowledge of investments and financial markets	☐	☐	☐	☐	☐
2) Quality of financial advice	☐	☐	☐	☐	☐
3) Friendliness and willingness to listen	☐	☐	☐	☐	☐
4) Availability & accessibility to listen	☐	☐	☐	☐	☐
5) Timeliness in returning phone calls	☐	☐	☐	☐	☐
6) Understanding your investment goals	☐	☐	☐	☐	☐
7) Taking time to give clear, concise explanations	☐	☐	☐	☐	☐
8) Looking out for your interests first	☐	☐	☐	☐	☐
9) Problem solving ability	☐	☐	☐	☐	☐
10) Overall quality of service	☐	☐	☐	☐	☐

How satisfied are you with the frequency of contact you have with your Investment Officer?

Very Satisfied				Very Dissatisfied
1	2	3	4	5
☐	☐	☐	☐	☐

How frequently would you like to hear from your Baird Investment Officer? *(Check Box)*

☐ Once a week or more often.   ☐ Once a quarter.   ☐ Once a year.
☐ Once a month.   ☐ Twice a year.   ☐ Other: (specify) _____

Has your Investment Officer ever asked you to recommend him/her to a friend, relative, or business associate?

☐ Yes   ☐ No

If asked, would you recommend your Baird Investment Officer to a friend, relative, or business associate?

Enthusiastically				Not at All
1	2	3	4	5
☐	☐	☐	☐	☐

Overall, how satisfied are you with your relationship with your Baird Investment Officer?

Very Satisfied				Very Dissatisfied
1	2	3	4	5
☐	☐	☐	☐	☐

Exhibit 8 Draft Cover Letter and Questionnaire, concluded

About Yourself

The final set of questions is for background purposes only. All responses that you give will be kept strictly confidential.

1. What is your age?

   ❏ Less than 25 years   ❏ 35 to 44 years   ❏ 55 to 64 years   ❏ 75 years or older
   ❏ 25 to 34 years   ❏ 45 to 54 years   ❏ 65 to 74 years

2. Are you . . .

   ❏ Male   ❏ Female

3. Are you . . . *(Check one)*

   ❏ Employed full-time   ❏ Self-employed   ❏ Homemaker
   ❏ Employed part-time   ❏ Retired

4. Is your spouse employed outside the home?

   ❏ Yes   ❏ No

5. Which of the following income groups best describes your total household income before taxes in 1993?

   ❏ Under $25,000   ❏ $75,000 to $100,000
   ❏ $25,000 to $40,000   ❏ $100,000 to $150,000
   ❏ $40,000 to $60,000   ❏ $150,000 to $250,000
   ❏ $60,000 to $75,000   ❏ $250,000 or more

6. Which of the following best describes the total amount you have invested in all forms of financial instruments, such as stocks, bonds, mutual funds, annuities, IRAs, money market funds, and CDs?

   ❏ Under $20,000   ❏ $75,000 to $100,000
   ❏ $20,000 to $30,000   ❏ $100,000 to $150,000
   ❏ $30,000 to $40,000   ❏ $150,000 to $250,000
   ❏ $40,000 to $50,000   ❏ $250,000 to $500,000
   ❏ $50,000 to $75,000   ❏ $500,000 and above

7. What is your zip code? _____

Optional Information:

   Your Name: _____

   Your Investment Officer: _____

Thank you very much for taking time to complete this questionnaire. As a result of this survey, we hope to continue the Baird tradition of providing the best in investment products and the highest quality financial services.

Exhibit 9 Client Satisfaction Measurement Feedback

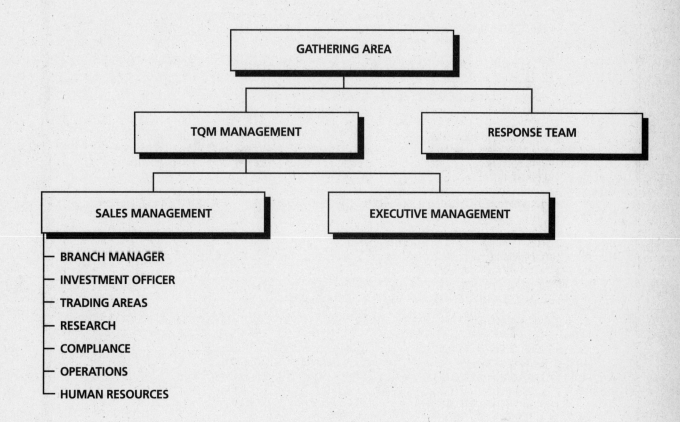

Exhibit 10 Final Thoughts

The implementation of Client Satisfaction Measurement will require total commitment and involvement of **Executive Management**. The long-term success of Client Satisfaction Measurement will require:

- Commitment and participation by management
- Centralized policy making
- Communication (two-way) with both internal and external publics
- Coordination of all efforts toward defined goals and objectives.

The first task, and a continuing one, of earning strong support and holding that support is most important. Unless support is earned, there will be conflict, friction and frustration, not coordination and cooperation. Firm management must send a strong consistent message of its involvement and commitment.

Baird Investment Officers must feel they have the "choice" but want to participate because of the opportunity of:

- Having a better understanding of client's needs
- Further development of client relationships
- Development of new relationship—referrals
- Availability of data to use in managing business
- Improvement of customer service.

Baird's clients are at the center of this process. Both Robert W. Baird and its clients will benefit from this process (via enhanced quality of service and products) and should be included in the feedback loop. If we fail to effectively communicate our underlying intent—to better meet our client's needs—then we risk the client interpreting our efforts as an exercise that is being undertaken for our benefit, rather than for theirs.

It is important to understand that this is an ongoing process that can/may constantly be changed to meet needs and desires of all elements (publics) involved.

One of the most significant findings to come out of the recent TQM research was the high level of satisfaction our clients reported receiving from their Baird Investment Officers. This information should not be overlooked and could be used as a benchmark for future measurement. Future surveys and feedback systems can provide valuable information on improving or developing new services.

Signetics Corporation: Implementing a Quality Improvement Program (Abridged)

Early in September, 1980, Dr. Tom Endicott, manager of the PPM (parts per million) program for Signetics' Automotive Products Division, was reviewing several technical problems related to a key customer contract. Six months earlier, Signetics had reached agreement with a major automotive manufacturer to supply several million integrated circuits (ICs) to customer design and specification over the next few years. The unique aspects of this contract were its specification of a PPM program that included feedback to Signetics as a supplier and increasingly tighter receiving inspection requirements for the number of allowable defects per million parts shipped (parts per million).

Such a contract was a major change from the traditional contracts entered into by Signetics. It represented a significant commitment to improve quality and to work together with the customer to identify and correct the quality problems that might arise. The open-ended nature of such an agreement had made Signetics nervous, but increasing competitive pressures caused management to conclude that the attractiveness of the new business outweighed the risks. **Exhibit 1** contains some of Signetics' preliminary estimates of the requirements associated with the PPM proposal. While things were generally going well on this particular contract and quality levels were already exhibiting noticeable improvement after only a few short months, Endicott now found himself confronting a set of tough decisions. Somehow his decisions would have to be consistent with the contract, feasible (given the company's resources), and financially acceptable both to Signetics and its customer.

COMPANY BACKGROUND

Signetics Corporation was founded in Sunnyvale, California, in 1961. It was the first company in the world established for the sole purpose of designing, manufacturing, and selling ICs. By 1980 Signetics had become the sixth largest U.S. semiconductor company and it offered one of the broadest lines of ICs in the industry. Since 1972, the company had experienced a compound annual growth rate of 26%.

Source: Steven C. Wheelwright, Copyright ©.1992 by the Board of Trustees of the Leland Stanford Junior University, SMM3 (Abridged).
Selected data have been disguised to protect the proprietary interests of the company. Financial support for development of this case was provided in part by the Strategic Management Program of the Graduate School of Business, Stanford University.

From 1962 to 1975 Signetics was owned by Corning Glass Works. In 1975 Signetics was purchased by the U.S. Philips Corporation, a subsidiary of N.V. Philips of the Netherlands. With worldwide sales in 1979 in excess of 33 billion guilders (approximately $16 billion 1979 U.S. dollars), N.V. Philips was a diversified manufacturing firm participating in industries ranging from lighting products to consumer electronics to scientific instruments and semiconductors.

Although operated independently of N.V. Philips, by 1980 Signetics' relationship with the Netherlands firm had become very important. Philips bought and sold products under the Signetics name and provided its subsidiary access to its worldwide research and development capability, advanced manufacturing process know-how, and technology.

MANUFACTURING INTEGRATED CIRCUITS

Producing ICs has been described as one of the most complex mass manufacturing processes in the industrial history of the world. The first stage, wafer manufacturing, was usually performed by large diversified chemical companies. Most wafer manufacturers were located in Japan, with Texas Instruments and IBM the only U.S. firms making wafers for in-house use, and Monsanto the only U.S. firm selling wafers. Wafer manufacturers grew silicon crystals of high purity, then "pulled" the crystals into ingots which were sliced into thin wafers. Finally, the wafers were polished and coated with a layer of silicon dioxide. Wafer sizes in 1980 were 3" to 5", but semiconductor manufacturers were in a race to increase that size: the larger the wafer, the more chips that could be produced during a manufacturing cycle.

The next step was for engineers to transfer an IC design to a set of masks to be used in lithography processes which imprinted the circuit patterns, layer by layer, onto a silicon wafer. This step was commonly referred to as *fabrication* (fab). The wafers had to be handled in a "clean room" because otherwise dust particles could contaminate the products. As semiconductor devices shrank in size, even the smallest particle of dust could ruin a chip. This became especially problematic as the line width between circuits was expected to be reduced to under one micron by the mid 1980s. To create a dust free environment, firms built clean rooms with special air ducts to filter out impurities in the air, provided special water supplies, and trained workers to wear special clean room attire. The sensitive nature of the process was expected to lead many IC manufacturers to automate their plants in the 1980s to further reduce the chances of human interference.

The next stage in production involved testing *(probe)* to find defects, then separating each chip from the wafer *(trim)*. Finally, the chips were packaged *(assembly)* so that their circuitry could be connected to external outlets. This labor-intensive assembly process was frequently done in low-wage countries. By 1980 almost all U.S. semiconductor firms and most Japanese firms had low-cost assembly operations in developing countries. The final stage of IC manufacture involved performing a battery of computerized tests *(final test)* to ensure reliability.

OPERATIONALIZING PPM PROBLEM SOLVING

During the preceding week, two problems with the ICs being shipped to the automotive customer had surfaced. After discussing them with a number of Signetics' product engineers and production engineers, as well as with the manufacturing manager, the product manager, and other members of the quality and reliability (Q&R) staff, it was now Endicott's responsibility to present Q&R's position regarding these problems. These two were particularly pressing and likely to recur. Thus, he thought it appropriate to summarize his views in such a way as to provide guidance in the future when similar problems arose.

The Wire Creep Problem

The automotive manufacturer had recently detected a low-level failure problem when ICs were tested during an accelerated environmental qualification program. Since the component failure might cause the malfunction of the entire computerized engine control system, this problem could have a significant impact on the final product's reliability and the customer's potential warranty claims. While so far the problem had occurred only under stresses that were not typical of the environment in which the IC component would be expected to operate, the customer had been concerned enough to add it to the list of problems that it felt Signetics should address.

The problem was not unique to Signetics' components; the whole IC industry had been aware of it for years. It involved the leads connecting the IC electrically to the package that housed it. The wire, made of pure gold, was only one-thousandth of an inch in diameter. Under certain stress conditions the leads would break close to where they were bonded to the IC. (**Exhibit 2** presents photographs of the wire creep or "grain growth" problem.) Although this problem was pervasive throughout the industry, it accounted for only a small fraction of the circuits that failed the 100% final test, and thus no company considered it important enough to solve. Moreover, although Signetics had observed such failures during its own accelerated testing, it was unaware of any failures occurring in customers' systems as a result of this problem. Thus, it too had chosen not to allocate resources to solving the problem.

After discussions with his colleagues, Endicott decided that at least three different courses of action (and implied levels of commitment) might be taken. The *first*, and perhaps the most limited level of commitment, would be to study the key variables that seemed to impact the bonding process and the subsequent possibility of wire breaks. Some of these variables had already been identified, and included:

- the manufacturing process used in preparing the gold wire
- the type of bonding capillary tip through which the wire passed
- the lead frame plating (where the gold wire bond was attached)
- bonding forces, dwell times, and temperatures during packaging
- package molding

Once the key variables were identified, Signetics would try to identify the acceptable limits for each variable which, when followed, would obviate the problem. Essentially, this approach did not really solve the problem but looked for a set of guidelines that would prevent the problem from occurring. It was engineering's estimate that perhaps an engineer-month of time might be required to conduct such an analysis, but that it would likely result in setting the key variables at levels that would lead to increased production costs.

A *second* level of commitment would be to not only identify the variables but determine how those variables could be controlled so that production costs would *not* increase significantly. This involved learning more about the production steps associated with those variables so that each step could be managed more effectively. Some of the division's engineering people estimated that such a study might take another two or three engineer-months of time, and the outcome could range from a 1% or 2% reduction in production costs to no reduction at all (i.e., maintaining the existing production costs level).

A *third* level of commitment would be required to go one step further and determine the root cause of the problem. Rather than simply seeking to control the key variables, this step would seek to determine the cause of the wire creep itself in order to eliminate it completely. This step would naturally follow the first two, but there was considerable uncertainty as to how much time and effort it would take to identify that root cause. While it might involve only three or four additional engineer-months, it might also involve considerably more. Also, it probably would tie up some fairly expensive and scarce lab equipment for several months.

As Endicott reflected on the advantages and disadvantages of each of these approaches, he was comforted by the fact that any of the three would satisfy the customer. The PPM contract required the solution of such problems, but even the lowest level of commitment would do so. Endicott's feeling from talking with customers was that they understood that the problem was both tough and industry-wide; thus, they were fairly tolerant. In fact, their tolerance— together with that of many other customers—might explain why the problem had never been solved.

Signetics' product manager did not feel this particular customer would get much payoff from any approach that would do more than simply solve its problem—even though the root cause remained. Even if Signetics discovered the cause, product marketing didn't think this would have much impact on Signetics' ability to obtain other contracts or the renewal of this one.

Engineering people had argued against committing a significant level of resources to the problem because, if Signetics solved the problem, it would be impossible to keep this knowledge secret for very long. Personal acquaintanceships, the movement of people among companies, and the diffusion of knowledge at professional associations all made it extremely difficult to prevent leaks. Thus, in solving the problem for this customer, Signetics would also solve it for all of its competitors.

Another issue that arose repeatedly during Endicott's discussions had to do with the trade-offs involved in assigning scarce resources. Since the same people who could work on this problem could also be assigned to solving several other problems, there was concern as to whether the wire creep problem was important enough to justify spending scarce resources at the second or third level of commitment. Worse, since the root cause had not been identified during the several years that people had been aware of the problem, this project would probably require some of the firm's best people, and they were in particularly tight supply.

Endicott's discussions also identified some concern as to how Signetics should organize to pursue the third level of commitment option that required maximum commitment. The first two options probably could be implemented with one engineer, but the third level was going to involve the Q&R labs, designers, process engineers, and manufacturing as well as other Q&R staff. There was concern about both the administration of and budget for such a cross-functional team. The departments that would probably be required to supply resources for this project didn't think they could cover it in their existing budgets, and wanted the Automotive Products Division to pick up the full tab. However, Automotive Products viewed it as a corporate commitment, and because the benefits would be shared by all Signetics products, didn't think they should get charged for the entire effort.

Manufacturing Process-Induced Functional Failures of the Basic Circuit

Two weeks earlier, one of the categories of IC components being shipped to the PPM customer had experienced a three-day hold on shipments because of what appeared to be a fairly significant manufacturing process problem. The situation had arisen when production of IC chips was shifted from a 3" to a 4" wafer, both to increase production volumes and to reduce costs. Because of the importance of this product, the usual immediate action was taken to notify the customer of the situation and then institute temporary screening tests to remove potentially defective material at the fabrication stage. This screen successfully removed the defective material (despite the large number of rejects) and it was possible to restart shipments after only a three-day interruption. But because such screening was extremely expensive and resulted in significant reduction in yield, it became necessary to resolve the problem in order to return the product to profitability.

The specific nature of the problem was soon identified. During the early stages of wafer fabrication, various layers of material were deposited on the wafer; parts of these layers were subsequently removed to form the complex circuitry of each IC. Sometimes, however, unwanted grains would form between layers of aluminum. Later, during stress testing, these grains would cause shorts in the circuit. Signetics' technical people had known about this problem for two or three years, but it had never been significant until this particular circuit made the transition to the 4" wafer (see **Exhibit 3**).

Signetics' people generally agreed that this was a much more significant problem than the wire creep problem, because of both its impact on Signetics' production costs and the probable difficulty of solving it. Preliminary discussions involving design, process, and product engineers as well as Q&R, marketing, and general management had identified three different options for consideration.

Option 1, which involved the lowest level of commitment, would take only a couple of man-weeks of intensive effort. Statistical data indicated that the problem was occurring largely in a single process step. With some investigation, that step could probably be replaced (albeit with perhaps a slightly more expensive process step), which would eliminate between 70% and 90% of the rejects. That would still leave at least 10% of the circuits subject to this potential problem and, while probably only 1% rejects or so would filter through to final testing, it clearly did not meet the philosophy of the PPM agreement. However, it was an important interim step and would allow Signetics to eliminate the expensive screening step now required.

Option 2 would require the circuit to be redesigned by the customer so that it would be less susceptible to this manufacturing problem. When combined with Option 1, this redesigned circuit would probably meet the PPM requirements, but Signetics was reluctant to make this request since it essentially avoided getting at the cause of the problem. Even if amortized over 12 to 18 months, the additional redesign costs (that Signetics would almost certainly be asked to pay) would reduce this product's profitability to almost zero.

Option 3 would be to make a major commitment to get at the root cause of the problem and eliminate it. Doing so might take anywhere from one to three engineer-years of effort and incur considerable lab and testing costs. Enough was known about the problem that Signetics engineers felt prolonged environmental stress testing (of up to 1,000 hours) would be required to collect sufficient statistical data to really identify the causes of the problem. In addition, large quantities of product (thousands of units) would need to be tested and those would not be reusable.

While Option 3 was extremely costly and would require some of Signetics' best people for several months, there was considerable uncertainty about how solvable the problem would be once its root causes were identified. However, this option was clearly consistent with the PPM philosophy. Understanding this type of interaction between the process steps in fabrication and subsequent circuit performance was at the heart of converting the production process from an art to a science. While some of the benefits of solving this problem were likely to be shared with the rest of the industry fairly quickly, the broad-based knowledge arising from such a solution was likely to improve significantly Signetics' overall understanding of IC manufacturing. Moreover, because of the fundamental importance of this problem, it was likely that getting at its source would also identify other problems that would be opportunities for ongoing future studies.

DECISION MAKING WITH REGARD TO PPM PROBLEM-SOLVING PROJECTS

While Endicott considered these two problems among the more significant Signetics had identified within the past few months, he felt the company was likely to identify one or two such problems as well as a number of smaller ones each year the contract was in existence. It was clear to him that Signetics could not afford to pursue all these problems at the third level of commitment as soon as they were identified. The company simply did not have sufficient people, technical equipment, or financial resources to do so, and while the PPM contract had been priced to cover a limited number of such pursuits, it could not support many of them at the most aggressive level. They could, however, all be pursued at the lowest (first) level of commitment and still be within the available resources.

Because of scarce resources, it also appeared infeasible to think about pursuing more than two-thirds of the opportunities identified at the highest level of commitment. Unfortunately, Endicott didn't know just what would be required in any particular situation, nor which problems (requiring which resources) were likely to arise in the future. While Signetics clearly wanted to fulfill the spirit of the PPM agreement, these management issues were making it extremely difficult to determine just what the most appropriate course of action would be on any given problem.

With these thoughts in mind, Endicott sat down to draft his recommendation for how the two major problems outlined above should be handled, and a more complete set of criteria and guidelines for addressing future problems as they arose.

Exhibit 1 Preliminary Estimated of PPM Requirements for Automotive Customer

A. Management Support Required

1. Reestablish priorities to resolve basic raw material issues.
2. Establish a liaison between fab and assembly.
3. Generate a constructive problem-solving atmosphere.
4. Reestablish priorities in wafer fab areas to resolve identified problems as they occur.

B. Signetics Resources Required

1. Additional Capacity

   Given the several million units we will ship to this customer each year, we will need to expand our wafer fab capacity at a cost of about $15 million. (This would be required to service this business even if there were no PPM program associated with it.) Our base prices for these ICs have been set up to provide the return on investment we will seek when building new capacity to service our customer.

2. Capital Investment Specific to the PPM Program

   We expect that additional burn-in and test equipment will be required, in addition to the standard test equipment, for this PPM program. We will request that the customer pay the full $2.4 million investment in this additional equipment.

3. Incremental Q&R Resources

   If this PPM program is undertaken, we will add 12 full-time exempt staff (equally split among Q&R professional, Sunnyvale engineering staff, and plant engineering staff) and 4 non-exempt staff. First-year salary and benefits will cost approximately $700,000. An additional $300,000 should be budgeted for expenses associated with the work to be done by these people. It is hoped that the customer will agree to pay a significant portion of these costs.

4. Additional Production Costs

   Given the more stringent production requirements under this PPM program, we estimate that unit production costs will be 10% to 15% higher than normal. About half of this increase will be direct fixed cost. We hope to pass this full amount through to the customer, but the degree that can be done will depend on prevailing competitive and market conditions.

C. Customer Support Required

In addition to the financial support outlined above, the customer will need to support PPM through the following activities:

1. In order to accelerate the learning curve for Signetics toward the PPM goal, it is requested that a technical interchange be set up to discuss the relationship of die layout rules and raw material specifications with respect to automatic assembly equipment.

2. The finely tuned correlation between Signetics' electrical test program and the customer's application can be attained only by open discussions of device characterization data, critical parameters, and the operating environment of the device in the customer's system. Only after working together in this manner will we attain PPM-level quality goals.

3. A second generation data gathering system for identification of line rejects and line reject rates needs to be developed within the customer's organization. This system must be agreed to by both companies to successfully achieve the 2090 PPM goal and to know when the goal has indeed been achieved.

Exhibit 1 Preliminary Estimated of PPM Requirements for Automotive Customer, concluded

D. Underlying Philosophy Required (Agreed to by Customer and Signetics)

1. General

   Signetics is creating this program in order to progress toward the 1982 customer's goal of 200 PPM. It is assumed that standard production cannot meet this goal and that additional in-line inspections/electrical testing will be needed until current processes/flows capabilities are known.

2. Quality Targets

   Signetics proposes that the initial quality goals at the customer's Incoming Inspection be based on a maximum percent defective; catastrophics to be 1,000 PPM and parametrics to be 2,500 PPM. Signetics proposes that the parametric category is further subdivided into major and minor categories with respect to application need. In order to maximize the use of our joint capacities, the electrical test program should be such that 100% screening is not necessary by both parties.

3. Feedback Loops

   An assembly module is being isolated in the Korean Plant for the manufacture of product for customers operating under the PPM concept.

4. Summary

   The preceding paragraphs represent a statement of intent that Signetics will work toward the 200 PPM 1982 quality goal. To achieve this goal, Signetics will set up a manufacturing line using the best knowledge currently available; it will be upgraded via feedback loops, corrective action programs, and automation. The corrective action programs must consider the tradeoffs between quality gains, costs incurred, and risks. Because of these complex interrelationships, the participation of the customer in the decision-making process will be a necessity.

Exhibit 2 Gold Wire Creep Problem[1]

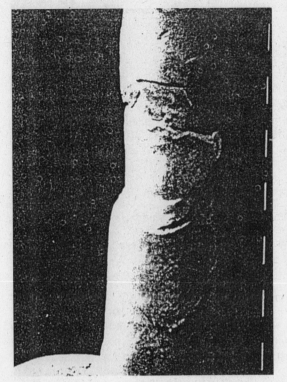

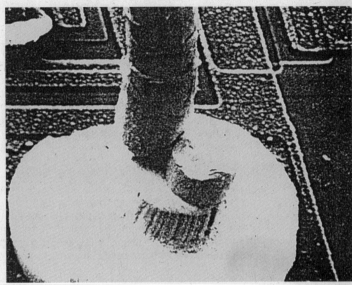

Typical example of advanced grain growth leading to complete failure

Typical grain growth, "wire creep" failure

---

[1] Technically referred to as "gold wire grain growth failure."

Exhibit 3 Wafer Fabrication Process-Induced Functional Failure Problem

A. Side View of Good Wafer

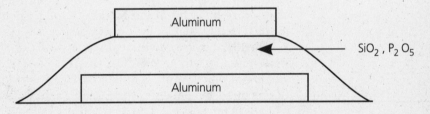

B. Side View of Bad Wafer

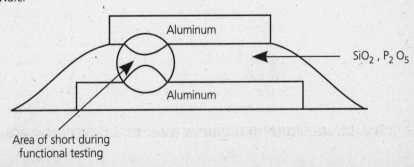

Area of short during functional testing

West Florida Regional Medical Center

Now that West Florida Regional Medical Center had successfully completed the Joint Commission on Accreditation of Healthcare Organizations (JCAHO) survey, John Kausch, its Administrator/CEO, felt that he and his management team should start 1992 by focusing on their Continuous Quality Improvement (CQI) process. There were a number of issues that he and the Quality Improvement Council could address, including: 1) performance reviews under CQI; 2) speeding up the work of the task forces; 3) focusing the process more on key competitive issues; and 4) deciding how much money to spend on it.

WEST FLORIDA REGIONAL MEDICAL CENTER

West Florida Regional Medical Center (WFRMC) is a Hospital Corporation of America (HCA)—owned and operated, for-profit hospital complex on the north side of Pensacola, Florida. Licensed for 547 beds, West Florida Regional operated approximately 325 beds in December 1991, plus the 89-bed psychiatric Pavilion, and the 58-bed Rehabilitation Institute of West Florida. The 11-story office building of the Medical Center Clinic, P.A., was attached to the hospital facility, and a new Cancer Center was under construction.

The 130 doctors practicing at the Medical Center Clinic and its satellite clinics admitted mostly to WFRMC, whereas most of the other doctors in this city of 150,000 practiced at both Sacred Heart and Baptist hospitals downtown. Competition for patients was intense, and in 1992 as much as 90%–95% of patients in the hospital would be admitted subject to discounted prices, mostly Medicare for the elderly, CHAMPUS for military dependents, and Blue Cross/Blue Shield of Florida for the employed and their dependents.

The continuous quality improvement (CQI) program had had some real successes during the last four years, especially in the areas where package prices for services were required. All of the management team had been trained in quality improvement techniques according to HCA's Deming-based approach and some 25 task forces were operating. The experiment with departmental self-assessments, using the Baldrige award criteria and an instrument developed by HCA headquarters, had spurred department heads to become

Source: Curtis P. McLaughlin, University of North Carolina at Chapel Hill.

further involved and begin to apply quality improvement techniques within their own work units.

Yet Kausch and his senior leadership sensed some loss of interest among some managers, while others who had not bought into the idea at first were now enthusiasts.

THE HCA CQI PROCESS

Kausch had been in the first group of HCA CEOs trained in CQI techniques in 1987 by Paul Batalden, M.D., corporate Vice-President for Medical Care. Kausch had become a member of the steering committee for HCA's overall quality effort. The HCA approach is dependent on the active and continued participation of top local management and on the Plan-Do-Check-Act (PDCA) cycle of Deming. **Exhibit 1** shows that process as presented to company employees. Dr. Batalden told the case writer that he does not work with a hospital administrator until he is convinced that that individual is fully committed to the concept and is ready to lead the process at his own institution, which includes being the one to teach the Quality 101 course on site to his own managers. Kausch also took members of his management team to visit other quality exemplars, such as Florida Power and Light and local plants of Westinghouse and Monsanto.

In 1991, Kausch became actively involved in the Total Quality Council of the Pensacola Area Chamber of Commerce (PATQC), when a group of Pensacola area leaders in business, government, military, education, and health care began meeting informally to share ideas in productivity and quality improvement. From this informal group emerged the PATQC under the sponsorship of the Chamber. The vision of PATQC was "helping the Pensacola area develop into a *total quality community* by promoting productivity and quality in all area organizations, public and private, and by promoting economic development through aiding existing business and attracting new business development." The primary employer in Pensacola, the U.S. Navy, was using TQM (total quality management) extensively and was quite satisfied with the results, and supported the Chamber program. In fact, the first 1992 one-day community-wide seminar presented by Mr. George F. Butts, consultant and retired Chrysler Vice President for Quality and Productivity, was to be held at the Naval Air Station's Mustin Beach Officer's Club. Celanese Corporation (a Monsanto division), the largest non-governmental employer in the area, also supported PATQC.

The CQI staffing at WFRMC was quite small, in keeping with HCA practice. The only program employee was Ms. Bette Gulsby, M.Ed., Director of Quality Improvement Resources, who serves as staff and "coach" to Kausch and as a member of the Quality Improvement Council. **Exhibits 2** and **3** show the organization of the Council and the staffing for Quality Improvement Program support. The "mentor" was provided by headquarters staff, and in the case of WFRMC was Dr. Batalden himself. The planning process had been careful and detailed. **Attachment A** shows excerpts from the planning processes used in the early years of the program.

WFRMC has been one of several HCA hospitals to work with a self-assessment tool for department heads. **Table 1** shows the cover letter sent to all department heads. **Table 2** shows the Scoring Matrix for Self-Assessment. **Exhibit 4** shows the Scoring Guidelines, and **Exhibit 5** displays the five assessment categories used.

FOUR EXAMPLES OF TEAMS

Intravenous Documentation

The Nursing Department originated the IV Documentation Team in September 1990 after receiving documentation from the Pharmacy Department that, over a 58-day period, there had been $16,800 in lost charges related to the administration of intravenous (IV) solutions. The Pharmacy attributed the loss to the nursing staff's record keeping. This was the first time that the Nursing Department was aware of a problem or that the Pharmacy Department had been tracking this variable. There were other lost charges not yet quantified, resulting from recording errors in the oral administration of pharmaceuticals as well.

The team formed to look at this problem found that there were some 15 possible reasons why the errors occurred, but that the primary one was that documentation of the administration of the IV solution was not entered into the Medication Administration Record (MAR). The MAR was kept at the patient bedside and, each time that a medication was administered, the nurse was to enter documentation into this record.

The team had to come to understand some terms as they went along. According to pharmacy bookkeeping, anything sent to the floors but not billed within 48–72 hours was considered a "lost charge." If an inquiry was sent to the floor about the material and what happened and a correction was made, the entry was classified as "Revenue Recovered." Thus the core issue was not so much one of lost revenue as one of unnecessary rework in the pharmacy and on the nursing floors.

The team developed Pareto charts showing the reasons for the documentation errors. The most common ones were procedural (e.g., patient moved to the Operating Room, or patient already discharged). Following the HCA model, these procedural problems were dealt with one at a time to get the accounting for the unused materials right. The next step in the usual procedures was to get a run chart developed to show what was happening over time to the Lost Charges on IVs. Here the team determined that the best quality indicator would be the ratio of "lost" charges to total charges issued. At this point the Pharmacy management realized that it lacked the denominator figure and that its lack of computerization led to the lack of that information.

Therefore, the task force had been inactive for three months, while the Pharmacy implemented a computer system that could provide the denominator.

Ms. Debbie Koenig, Assistant Director of Nursing, responsible for the team, said that the next step would be to look at situations where the MAR was not at the patient bedside, but perhaps up at the nursing station, so that a nurse could not make the entry at the appropriate time. This was an especially bothersome rework problem because of nurses working various shifts or agency nurses who were not available when the pharmacy asked for documentation for an IV dose of medication.

Universal Charting

There was evidence that a number of ancillary services results, "loose reports," were not getting into the patients' medical records in a timely fashion. This was irritating to physicians and could result in delays in the patient's discharge, which under Diagnosis-Related Groups (DRGs), which essentially fixed payment per case, meant higher costs without higher reimbursement. One employee filed a suggestion that a single system be developed to avoid running over other people on the floor doing the "charting." A CQI team under Ms. Debbie Wroten, Medical Records Director, was authorized. The 12-member team included supervisors and directors from the Laboratory, the Pulmonary Lab, the EKG Lab, Medical Records, Radiology, and Nursing. They developed the following "Opportunity Statement":

> *At present, six departments are utilizing nine full-time equivalents 92 hours per week for charting separate ancillary reports. Rework is created in the form of repulling inhouse patient records, creating an ever-increasing demand for chart accessibility. All parties affected by this process are frustrated because the current process increases the opportunity for lost documentation, chart unavailability, increased traffic on units creating congestion, and prolonged charting times, and provides for untimely availability of clinical reports for patient care. Therefore, an opportunity exists to improve the current charting practice for all departments involved to allow for the efficiency, timeliness, and accuracy of charting loose reports.*

The team met, assessed, and flow charted the current charting processes of the five departments involved. Key variables were defined as follows:

- Charting Timeliness—number of charting times per day, consistency of charting, and reports not charted per charting round
- Report Availability—number of telephone calls per department asking for reports not yet charted
- Chart Availability—chart accessibility at the nurses' station for charting without interruption
- Resource Utilization—labor hours and number of hours per day of charting

Each department was asked to use a common "charting log" track for several weeks to record the number of records charted, who did the charting, when it was done, the preparation time, the number of reports charted, the number of reports not charted (missed), and the personnel hours consumed in charting. The results were:

Department	Mean records per day	Range	Mean hours per day	Range	Comments
Medical Records	77.3	20–140	1.6	0.6–2.5	Daily
Pulmonary Lab	50.3	37–55	1.0	0.7–1.5	MWF
Clinical Lab	244.7	163–305	3.2	1.9–5.4	Daily
EKG Lab	40.2	35–48	0.8	0.1–1.0	Weekdays
Microbiology	106.9	3–197	1.4	0.1–2.2	Daily
Radiology	87.1	6–163	1.5	0.1–2.9	Daily

These data gave the team considerable insight into the nature of the problem. Not every department was picking up the materials every day. Two people could cover the whole hospital in three-quarters of an hour each or one person in 1.5 hours. The clinical chemistry laboratory, medical records, and radiology were making two trips per day, while other departments were only able to chart every other day and failed to chart over the weekends.

The processes used by all the groups were similar. The printed or typed response had to be sorted by floors and room numbers added if missing, then taken to the floors and inserted into patient charts. If the chart was not available, they had to be held until the next round. A further problem was identified in that, when the clerical person assigned to these rounds was not available, a technical person who was paid considerably more and was often in short supply had to be sent to do the job.

A smaller team of supervisors who actually knew and owned the charting efforts in the larger departments (medical records, radiology, and clinical chemistry) was set up to design and assess the pilot experiment. The overall team meetings were only used to brief the department heads to gain their feedback and support. A pilot experiment was run in which these three departments took turns doing the runs for each other. The results were favorable. The pilot increased timeliness and chart availability by charting four times per day on week days and three on weekends. Report availability was improved and there were fewer phone calls. Nursing staff, physicians, and participating departments specifically asked for the process to be continued. The hours of labor dropped from 92 weekly to less than 45, using less highly paid labor.

Therefore, the team decided that the issues were important enough that they should consider setting up a separate Universal Charting Team (UCT) to meet the needs of the entire hospital. "However, an unanticipated hospital census decline made impractical the possibility of requesting additional staffing, etc. Consequently, the group reevaluated the possibility of continuing the arrangement developed for the pilot using the charting hours of the smaller departments on a volume basis. It was discovered that this had the effect of freeing the professional staff of the smaller departments from charting activities and a very minimal allocation of hours floated to the larger departments. It also increased the availability of charters in the larger departments for other activities." The payroll department was then asked to develop a system for allocating the hours that floated from one department to another. That proved cumbersome, so the group decided to allocate charting hours on the basis of each department's volume. "In the event that one or more departments experience a significant increase/decrease in charting needs, the group will reconvene and the hourly allocation will be adjusted."

The resulting schedule has the lab making rounds at 6 a.m. and 9 a.m. and radiology at 4 p.m. and 9:30 p.m. Monday–Friday, while medical records does it at 6 a.m., 1 p.m., and 8 p.m. on Saturdays and Sundays. Continuing statistics are kept on the process, which is shown in **Attachment B**. The system continues to work effectively.

Labor, Delivery, Recovery, Postpartum (LDRP) Nursing

Competition for young families needing maternity services had become quite intense in Pensacola. WFRMC Obstetrical (OB) Services offered very traditional services in 1989 in three separate units—Labor & Delivery, Nursery, and Postpartum—and operated considerably below capacity.

A consultant was hired to evaluate the potential growth of obstetrical services, the value of current services offered by WFRMC, customers' desires, competitors' services, and opportunities for improvement. Focus group interviews with young couples (past and potential customers) indicated that they wanted safe medical care in a warm, homelike setting with the lowest possible number of rules. More mothers were in their 30s, planning small families with the possibility of only one child. Fathers wanted to be "actively involved" in the birth process. The message came back "We want to be actively involved in this experience and want to make decisions." The consultant challenged the staff to come up with their own vision for the department based on the focus group responses, customer feedback, and trends nationally.

It became clear that there was a demand for a system in which a family-centered birth experience could occur. The system needed to revolve around the customers rather than the customers following a rigid traditional routine. Customers wanted all aspects of a normal delivery to happen in the same room. The new service would allow the mother, father, and baby to remain together throughout the hospital stay, now as short as 24 hours. Friends and families would be allowed and encouraged to visit and participate as much as the new parents desired. The main goals were to be responsive to the customer's needs and provide safe, quality medical care.

The hospital administration and the six obstetricians practicing there were eager to see obstetrical services grow. They were open to trying and supporting the new concept. The pediatricians accepted the changes, but without great enthusiasm. The anesthesiologists were opposed to the change. The OB supervisor and two of the three head nurses were dead set against it. They wanted to continue operations in the traditional manner.

When the hospital decided to adopt the new LDRP concept, it was clear that patients and families liked it, but the nursing staff, especially nursing management, did not. The OB nursing supervisor retired; one head nurse resigned, one was terminated, and the third opted to move from her management position to a staff nurse role. Ms. Cynthia Ayres, R.N., Administrative Director, responsible for the psychiatric and cardiovascular services, was assigned to implement the LDRP transition until nursing management could be replaced.

One of the issues involved in the transition was clarification of the charge structure. Previously each unit charged separately for services and supplies. Now that the care was provided in a single central area, the old charge structure was unnecessarily complex. Duplication of charges was occurring and some charges were being missed because no one was assuming responsibility.

Ayres decided to use the CQI process to develop a new charge process and to evaluate the costs and resource consumption of the service. Ayres had not been a strong supporter of the CQI process when it was first introduced into the organization. She had felt that the process was too slow and rigid, and that data collection was difficult and cumbersome. Several teams were organized and assigned to look at specific areas of the LDRP process.

To reach a simplified charge process, as well as a competitive price, all aspects of the process had to be analyzed. Meetings were held with the nursing and medical staff. Management of the OB patient and physician preferences in terms of supplies and practices was analyzed. A number of consensus conferences were held to discuss observed variations. For example, each of the six obstetricians specified a different analgesic for pain control. Each drug appeared effective for pain control, but their cost per dose ranged from $10 to $75. The physicians agreed that the $10 product was acceptable, because the outcome was the same.

Another standard practice was sending placentas to the pathology laboratory for analysis after every normal delivery. This involved labor time, lab charges, and a pathologist's fee for review. The total procedure cost $196. When questioned about the practice, the current medical staff did not feel it was necessary medically nor the current practice nationally, but that they were just following the rules. Upon investigation, the team found that an incident involving a placenta had occurred 15 years ago which led the Service Chief (since retired) to order all placentas sent to the lab. The obstetricians developed criteria for when it was medically necessary for the lab review of a placenta. This new rule decreased the number of reviews by 95%, resulting in cost savings to the hospital and to patients.

The Charges Team reviewed all OB charges for a one-year period. They found that in 80% of normal deliveries, 14 items were consistently used. The other items were due to variations in physician preferences. The teams and the physicians met and agreed which items were the basic requirements for a normal delivery. These items became the basic charges for package pricing.

The Charges Team met weekly for at least one hour for over a year. Some meetings went as long as five hours. Initially, there was a great deal of resistance and defensiveness. Everyone wanted to focus on issues that did not affect themselves. The physicians objected that they were being forced to practice "cookbook medicine" and that the real problem was "the hospital's big markup." Hospital staff continued to provide data on actual hospital charges, resource consumption, and practice patterns. The hospital personnel continued to emphasize repeatedly that the physicians were responsible for determining care. The hospital's concern was to be consistent and decrease variation.

Another CQI Team, the Documentation Team, was responsible for reviewing forms utilized previously by the three separate units. The total number of forms used had been 30. The nursing staff were documenting vital signs an average of five times each time care was provided. Through review of policies, standards, documentation, and care standards, the number of forms was reduced to 20. Nurses were now required to enter each care item only once. The amount of time spent by nurses on documentation was reduced 50%, as was the cost of forms. Data entry errors were also reduced.

The excess costs that were removed were not all physician-related. Many had to do with administrative and nursing policies. Many were due to old, comfortable, traditional ways of doing things. When asked why a practice was followed, the typical response was, "I don't know; that's just the way we've always done it." The OB staff is now comfortable with the use of CQI. They recognize that although it requires time and effort, it does produce measurable results. The OB staff is continuing to review its practices and operations to identify opportunities to streamline services and decrease variation.

Pharmacy and Therapeutics Team

In late 1987, a CQI Team was formed jointly between the hospital's Pharmacy and Therapeutic's (P&T) Committee and the Pharmacy leadership. Their first topic of concern was the rapidly rising costs of inpatient drugs, especially antibiotics, which were then costing the hospital about $1.3 million per year. They decided to study the process by which antibiotics were selected and began by asking physicians how they selected antibiotics for treatment. They reported that most of the time they order a culture of the organism causing the infection from the Microbiology lab. A microbiology lab report would come back identifying the organism and the antibiotics to which it is sensitive and those to which it was resistant. Some physicians reported that they would look down the list until they came to an antibiotic to which the organism was sensitive and order that. That list was in alphabetical order. A study of antibiotic utilization showed a high correlation between use and alphabetical position, confirming the anecdotal reports. Therefore, the team recommended to the P&T Committee that the form be changed to list the antibiotics in order of increasing cost per average daily dose. The doses used would be based on current local prescribing patterns rather than recommended dosages. The P&T Committee, which included attending physicians, approved the change and reported it in their annual report to the medical staff. **Exhibit 6** shows what happened to the utilization of "expensive" antibiotics (more than $10 per dose) from 1988 to 1991. These costs were not adjusted at all for inflation in drug prices during this period. The estimated annual saving was $200,000.

Given this success, the team went on in 1989 to deal with the problem of the length of treatment with antibiotics. Inpatients do not get a prescription for ten days' supply. Their IM and IV antibiotics were continued until the physician stopped the order. If a physician went away for the weekend and the patient improved, colleagues were very reluctant to alter the medication until he or she returned. The team wrestled with how to encourage the appropriate ending of the course of treatment without hassling the physicians or risking undue legal liability. They settled on a sticker that went into the chart at the end of three days that said that the treatment had gone on for three days at that point and that an ending date should be specified, if possible. The hospital newsletter and the P&T Committee annual report noted that the physician could avoid this notice by specifying a termination date at the time of prescribing. This program seemed to be effective. Antibiotic costs again dropped, and there were no apparent quality problems introduced as measured by length of stay or by adverse events associated with these system changes.

In 1990, the team began an aggressive Drug Usage Evaluation (DUE) program, hiring an Assistant Director, Pharmacy Clinical Services, to administer it. The position had to be rigorously cost justified. DUE involved a review of cases to determine whether the selection and scheduling of powerful drugs matched the clinical picture presented. For example, if the physician prescribed one of three types of antibiotics known to represent a risk of kidney damage in 3%–5% of cases, the DUE administrator ordered lab tests to study serum creatinine levels and warn the physician if they rose, indicating kidney involvement. There was a sharp decline in the adverse effects caused by the use of these drugs. This program was expanded further to looking at other critical lab values and relating them to pharmacy activities beyond antibiotics; for example, use of IV solutions and potassium levels. By 1991, the unadjusted antibiotic costs for roughly the same number of admissions had dropped to less than $900,000.

LOOKING AHEAD

One of the things that had concerned Kausch during 1991 had been the fact that implementation had varied from department to department. Although he had written in his annual CQI report that the variation had certainly been within the range of acceptability, he was still concerned about how much variation in implementation was appropriate. If maintaining enthusiasm was a concern, forcing people to conform too tightly might become a demotivator for some staff. This issue and the four mentioned in the introductory paragraph should all be addressed in the coming year.

ATTACHMENT A: PLANNING CHRONOLOGY FOR CQI

Initiation Plan: 3 Months, Starting May 25,1988

May 25:   Develop initial working definition of quality for WFRMC.

May 25:   Define the purpose of the Quality Improvement Council and set schedule for 2 p.m.–4 p.m. every Tuesday and Thursday.

May 25:   Integrate HQT into continuous improvement cycle and hold initial review.

June 2: Start several multifunctional teams with their core from those completing the Leadership Workshop, with topics selected by the Quality Improvement Council using surveys, experience, and group techniques.

June 2: Department Heads complete "CEO assessment" to identify customers and expectations, determine training needs, identify department opportunities. To be discussed with assistant administrators on June 15.

June 16: Present to QIC the Task Force report on elements and recommendations on organizational elements to guide and monitor QIP.

June 20: Hold division meetings to gain consensus on department plans and set priorities. QIC reviews and consolidates on June 21. Final assignments to Department Heads on June 22.

June 27: Draft initial Statement of Purpose for WFRMC and present to QIC.

June 29–July 1: Conduct first Facilitators' Training Workshop for 16.

July 1: Task Force reports on additional QIP education and training requirements for:
Team training and team-members handbook
Head nurses
Employee orientation (new and current)
Integration of community resources (colleges and industry)
Use of HCA network resources for Medical Staff, Board of Trustees

July 19: Task Force reports on communications program to support awareness, education, and feedback from employees, vendors, medical staff, local business, colleges and universities, and HCA.

August 1: Complete the organization of the Quality Improvement Council.

Quality Improvement Implementation Plan to June 30, 1989

Fall: Pilot and evaluate "Patient Comment Card System."

Oct. 21: Obtain QIC input to draft policies/guidelines regarding: forming teams, quality responsibility, and guidelines for multifunctional teams. Brainstorm at October 27 meeting, have revisions for November 10 meeting, and distribute to employees by November 15.

Oct. 27: Review proposals for communicating QIP to employees to heighten awareness and understanding, communicate on HCA and WFRMC commitments; key definitions, policies, guidelines, HQT; QIP; teams and improvements to date; responsibility and opportunities for individual employees; initiate ASAP.

Nov. 15: Prepare statements on "On further consideration of HCA's Quality Guideline"; discuss with department heads, hospital staff; conduct employee orientation; use to identify barriers to QI and opportunities for QI. Develop specific action plan and discuss with QIC.

Dec. 1: Identify and evaluate community sources for QI assistance—statistical and operational—including colleges, companies, and the Navy. Make recommendations.

Early Dec.:	Conduct Quality 102 course for remaining department heads. Conduct Quality 101 course for head nurses and several new department heads.
Jan. 1, 1989:	Develop and implement a suggestion program consistent with our HCA Quality Guidelines, providing quick and easy way to become involved in making suggestions/identifying situations needing improvement; providing quick feedback and recognition; and interfacing with identifying opportunities for QIP.

QIP Implementation Plan, July 1989–June 1990

Aug. 1:	Survey department heads to identify priorities for additional education and training.
Sept. 14–15:	Conduct a management workshop to sharpen and practice QI methods; to include practice methods; to increase management/staff confidence, comfort; to develop a model for departmental implementation; to develop process assement/ QIP implementation tool; to start Quality Team Review.
September:	Develop a standardized team orientation program to cover QI tools and group process rules.
Fall:	Expand use of HQTs and integrate into HQIP—improve communication of results and integration of quality improvement action plans. Psychiatric Pavilion to evaluate and implement HQT recommendations from "Patient Comment Card System" —evaluate and pilot.
October:	Incorporate QIP implementation into existing management/ communication structure. Establish division "steering committee functions" to guide and facilitate departmental implementation. Identify QI project for each department head/ assistant administrator. Establish regular Quality Reviews in department manager meetings.
December:	Evaluate effectiveness of existing policies, guidelines, and practices for sanctioning, supporting, and guiding QI teams. Include Opportunity Form/Cross Functional Team Sanctioning; Team Leader and Facilitator responsibilities; Team progress monitoring/guiding; standardized team presentation format (storyboard). Demonstrate measurable improvement through Baxter QI team.
Monthly:	Monitor and improve the suggestion program.
January:	Pilot the Clinical Process Improvement methodology.
All Year:	In all communications, written and verbal, maintain constant message regarding WFRMC commitment to HQIP; report successes of teams and suggestions; and continue to educate about principles and practices of HQIP strategy.
January:	Successfully demonstrate measurable improvement from focused QIP in one department (Medical Records).
Spring:	Expand use of HQTs and integrate into HQIP. Pilot HQT in Rehab Center. Evaluate and implement Physicians' HQT. Pilot Ambulatory Care HQT.
Summer:	Expand use of HQTs and integrate into HQIP. Human Resources—Pilot HQT Payers—Pilot HQT

ATTACHMENT B: UNIVERSAL CHARTING TEAM FOCUS-PDCA OUTLINE

F   Opportunity Statement:

At present, six departments are utilizing nine full-time equivalents 92 hours a week for charting separate ancillary reports. Rework is created in the form of repulling inhouse patient records, creating an ever-increasing demand for chart accessibility. All parties affected by this process are frustrated because the current process increases the opportunity for lost documentation, chart unavailability, increased traffic on units creating congestion, prolonged charting times, and provides for untimely availability of clinical reports for patient care.

Therefore an opportunity exists to improve the current charting practice for all departments involved to allow for efficiency, timeliness, and accuracy of charting loose reports.

O   Team members include:

Debbie Wroten, Medical Records Director—Leader
Bernie Grappe, Marketing Director—Facilitator
Joan Simmons, Laboratory Director
Mary Gunter, Laboratory Patient Services Coordinator
Al Clarke, Pulmonary Services Director
Carol Riley, Pulmonary Services Assistant Director
Marlene Rodrigues, EKG Supervisor
Patti Travis, EKG
Debra Wright, Medical Records Transcription Supervisor
Mike West, Radiology Director
Lori Mikesell, Radiology Transcription Supervisor
Debbie Fernandez, Head Nurse

C   Assessed and flow charted current charting practices of departments. Clarified and defined key quality characteristics of the charting process:

- **Charting Timeliness**—number of charting times per day, consistency of charting, and reports not charted per charting round
- **Report Availability**—number of telephone calls per department asking for reports not yet charted
- **Chart Availability**—chart accessibility at the nurses' station for charter without interruption
- **Resource Utilization**—laborhours and number of hours per day of charting

U   Gathered data on departments' charting volumes and time spent charting.

S   Data gained through the pilot indicated that significant gains were available through the effort to justify proceeding with the development of a Universal Charting Team.

Date	Charting tech vs. clk	Prep time	# Reports charted	# Reports not charted	Charting time (amt)	Hour of day	Comment

P   The team developed a flow chart of the charting process using a universal charting team rather than previous methods. In order to pilot the improvement, the group decided to set up a UCT using current charters from the three major charting departments—medical records, laboratory and radiology. The team also developed written instructions for both the charters and participating departments. A subgroup of the team actually conducted a one-day pilot before beginning extensive education to ensure that the UCT would work as planned and to be sure that the charters from each of the large departments were well versed on possible situations that might occur during the pilot.

D   Piloted proposed Universal Charting Team using current charting personnel from radiology, laboratory, and medical records to chart for all departments.

C   Pilot results were positive and indicated the UCT concept offered significant advantages over the previous charting arrangements. Results were:

- **Timeliness/chart availability**—Pilot reduced daily charting to four scheduled charting times daily for all departments. Smaller departments did not chart daily prior to pilot. The charting team also reduced the number of occasions that charters from different departments were on the nursing unit needing the same chart.
- **Report availability**—Telephone calls were reduced and nursing staff, physicians, and participating departments specifically asked for UCT following the pilot.
- **Resource utilization**—Number of manhours spent charting and preparing to chart was reduced from 92 hours weekly to less than 45 hours. The improvement also allowed the use of less expensive staff for charting.

A   The group reached consensus that the easiest configuration for the UCT would be to set up a separate UCT that would serve the needs of the entire hospital.

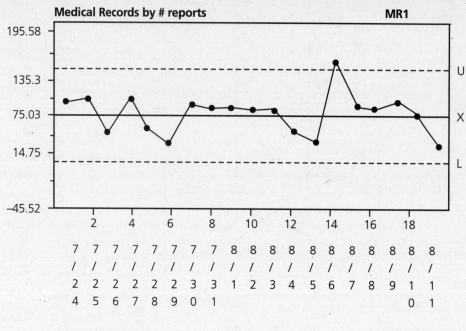

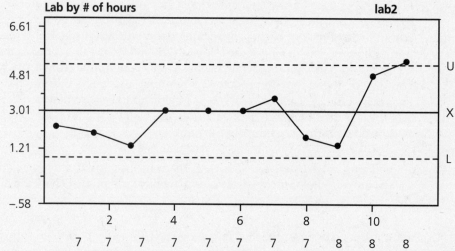

- This was to be proposed to administration by the team as the conclusion of their efforts. However, an unanticipated hospital census decline made impractical the possibility of requesting additional staffing, and so forth. Consequently, the group reevaluated the possibility of continuing the arrangement developed for the pilot using the charting hours to the smaller departments on a volume basis. It was discovered that this had the effect of freeing the professional staff in the smaller departments from charting responsibilities for a very minimal allocation of hours floated to the larger departments, and it increased the availability of charters in the larger departments for other activities. The payroll department was then involved in order to develop the proper mechanism and procedure for floating hours.

- This modification of the previous pilot was piloted for a month with continued good results. Streamlining of the hours floating process may be necessary to place less burden on the payroll department.
- Because no major changes were required following the pilot, the group has elected to adopt the piloted UTC format. Allocation of charting hours is based on a monthly review of charting volumes for each department. In the event that one or more departments experiences a significant increase/decrease in charting needs, the group will reconvene and the hourly allocation will be adjusted.

LESSONS LEARNED

Because of the size and the makeup of the team, which included a number of department heads, it was found helpful to set up a smaller team of three supervisors who actually knew and owned the charting efforts in the major departments. This group designed and assessed the initial pilot and actually piloted the pilot before bringing departmental charters into the process. As a result, overall team meetings were primarily used to brief department heads and gain their feedback and consensus.

Exhibit 1 The FOCUS-PDCA Problem-Solving Approach (©1988, 1989 Hospital Corporation of America, Nashville, TN)

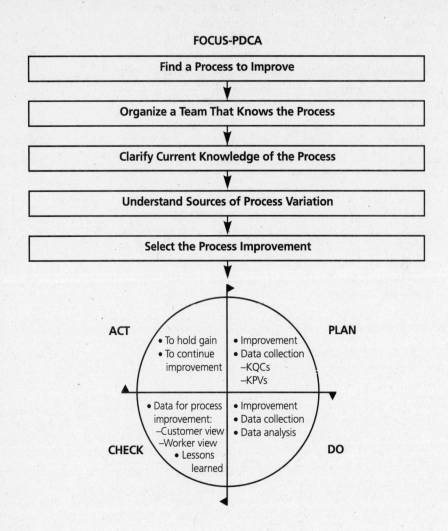

Exhibit 2 Organization Chart with Quality Improvement Council (shaded box)

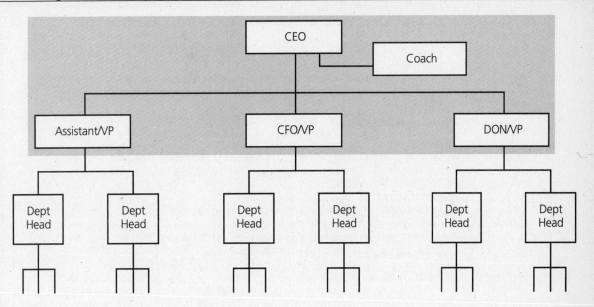

Exhibit 3 Organization Chart with CEO QIP Support (shaded box)

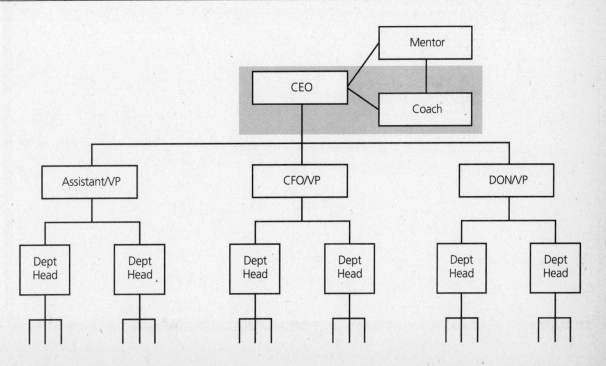

Table 1 Departmental Quality Improvement Assessment

In an effort to continue to monitor and implement elements of improvement and innovation within our organization, it will become more and more necessary to find methods that will describe our level of QI implementation.

The assessment or review of a quality initiative is only as good as the thought processes that have been triggered during the actual assessment. Last year (1990), the Quality Improvement Council prepared for and participated in a quality review. This exercise was extremely beneficial to the overall understanding of what was being done and the results that have been accomplished utilizing various quality techniques and tools.

The Departmental Implementation of QI has been somewhat varied throughout the organization and, although the variation is certainly within the range of acceptability, it is the intent of the QIC to understand better each department's implementation road map and, furthermore, to provide advice/coaching on the next steps for each department.

Attached please find a scoring matrix of self-assessment. This matrix is followed by five category ratings (to be completed by each department head). The use of this type of tool reinforces the self-evaluation that is consistent with continuous improvement and meeting the vision of West Florida Regional Medical Center.

Please read and review the attachment describing the scoring instructions and then score your department category standings relative to the approach, deployment, and effects. This information will be forwarded to Bette Gulsby by April 19, 1991, and, following a preliminary assessment by the QIC, an appointment will be scheduled for your departmental review.

The review will be conducted by John Kausch and Bette Gulsby, along with your administrative director. Please take the time to review the attachments and begin your self-assessment scoring. You will be notified of the data and time of your review.

This information will be utilized for preparing for the next Department Head retreat, scheduled for May 29 and 30, 1991, at the Perdido Beach Hilton.

Table 2 A Scoring Matrix for Self-Assessment

APPROACH	DEPLOYMENT	EFFECTS (Results)
• HQIP design includes all eight dimensions* • Integration across dimensions of HQIP & areas of operation	• Breadth of implementation (areas or functions) • Depth of implementation (Awareness, knowledge, understanding and application)	• Quality of measurable results
100%		
• World-class approach: sound; systematic; effective; HQIP based; continuously evaluated, refined, and improved • Total integration across all functions • Repeated cycles of innovation/improvement	• Fully in all areas and functions • Ingrained in the culture	• Exceptional, world-class, superior to all competition; in all areas • Sustained (3–5 years), clearly caused by the approach
80%		
• Well-developed and tested, HQIP based • Excellent integration	• In almost all areas and functions • Evident in the culture of all groups	• Excellent, sustained in all areas with improving competitive advantage • Much evidence that they are caused by the approach
60%		
• Well-planned, documented, sound, systematic, HQIP based: all aspects addressed • Fair integration	• In most areas and functions • Evident in the culture of most groups	• Solid, with positive trends in most areas • Some evidence that they are caused by the approach
40%		
• Beginning of sound, systematic, HQIP based; not all aspects addressed • Fair integration	• Begun in many areas and functions • Evident in the culture of some groups	• Some success in major areas • Not much evidence that they are caused by the approach
20%		
• Beginning of HQIP awareness • No integration across functions	• Beginning in some areas and functions • Not part of the culture	• Few or no results • Little or no evidence that any results are caused by the approach
0%		

* The eight dimensions of HQIP are: leadership constancy, employee-mindedness, customer-mindedness, process focused, statistical thinking, PDCA-driven, innovativeness, and regulatory proactiveness.

Exhibit 4 Department QI Assessment Scoring Guidelines

In order to determine your department's score in each of the five categories, please review the scoring matrix for self-assessment. The operational definitions for Approach, Deployment, and Effects are listed in the small boxes on the top of the scoring matrix. Each criterion is divided into percent of progress/implementation (i.e., 0%–100%). For example, you may determine that your departmental score on category 3.0 (QI Practice) is:

APPROACH	DEPLOYMENT	EFFECTS
20%	20%	20%

This means that your departmental approach has fair integration of QIP practice, your departmental deployment is evident in the culture of some of your groups, and it is not actually evident that your departmental effects are caused by the approach.

Please remember that this is a *self-assessment* and only *you* know your departmental progress. This assessment is not a tool to generate documentation. However, if you would like to bring any particular document(s) to your review, please do so. This is only meant to provide a forum for you to showcase your progress and receive recognition and feedback on such.

Remember, review each of the self-assessment criteria of approach, deployment, and effects and become familiar with the levels or percentages described. You have three scores for each Departmental QI Assessment Category (categories 1.0–5.0).

Exhibit 5 Departmental QI Assessment Categories

1.0 DEPARTMENTAL QI FRAMEWORK DEVELOPMENT

The QI Framework Development category examines how the departmental quality values have been developed, and how they are projected in a consistent manner, and how adoption of the values throughout the department is assessed and reinforced.

Examples of areas to address:

- Department mission
- Departmental quality definition
- Departmental employee performance feedback review
- Department QI plan
- QI methods

APPROACH	DEPLOYMENT	EFFECTS
____%	____%	____%

2.0 CUSTOMER KNOWLEDGE DEVELOPMENT

The Customer Knowledge Development category examines how the departmental leadership has involved and utilized various facets of customer-mindedness to guide the quality effort.

Examples of areas to address:

- HQT family of measures (patient, employee, etc.)
- Departmental customer identification
- Identification of customer needs and expectations
- Customer feedback/data review

APPROACH	DEPLOYMENT	EFFECTS
____%	____%	____%

3.0 QUALITY IMPROVEMENT PRACTICE

The Quality Improvement Practice category examines the effectiveness of the department's efforts to develop and realize the full potential of the work force, including management, and the methods to maintain an environment conducive to full participation, quality leadership, and personal and organizational growth.

Examples of areas to address:

- Process improvement practice
- Meeting skills
- QI storyboards
- QI in daily work life (individual use of QI tools, i.e., flowchart, run chart, Pareto chart)
- Practice quality management guidelines
- Departmental data review
- Plans to incorporate QI in daily clinical operations
- Identification of key physician leaders

APPROACH	DEPLOYMENT	EFFECTS
____%	____%	____%

Exhibit 5 Departmental QI Assessment Categories, concluded

4.0 QUALITY AWARENESS BUILDING

The Quality Awareness Building category examines how the department decides what quality education and training is needed by employees and how it utilizes the knowledge and skills acquired. It also examines what has been done to communicate QI to the department and how QI is addressed in departmental staff meetings.

Examples of areas to address:

- JIT training
- Employee orientation
- Creating employee awareness
- Communication of QI results

APPROACH	DEPLOYMENT	EFFECTS
____%	____%	____%

5.0 QA/QI LINKAGE

The QA/QI Linkage category examines how the department has connected QA data and information to the QI process improvement strategy. Also examined is the utilization of QI data-gathering and decision-making tools to document and analyze data (how the department relates the ongoing QA activities to QI process improvement activities).

Examples of areas to address:

- QA process identification
- FOCUS-PDCA process improvement
- Regulatory/accreditation connection (JCAHO)

APPROACH	DEPLOYMENT	EFFECTS
____%	____%	____%

Exhibit 6 Anabolic Utilization Ratio*

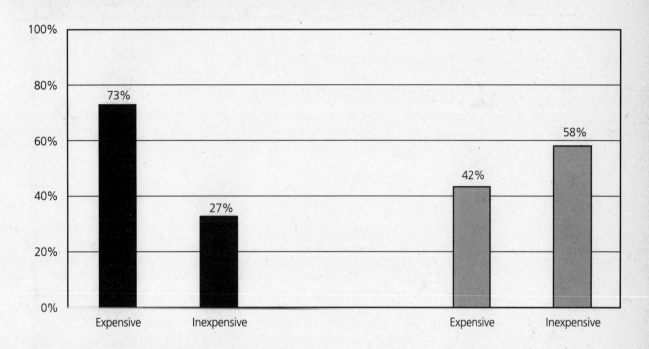

*   Expensive and inexpensive doses dispensed (expensive antibiotics are those costing more than $10 per dose).
     ■, 1988 data; ▨, 1991 data.

Holston Valley Hospital and Medical Center

After five years of training and team projects, Mr. Paul Bishop, Administrator of Holston Valley Hospital and Medical Center (HVHMC) was seeing the positive results of his Quality Management program in many ways in administrative areas, but he was still concerned about how to make more headway with the clinical use of resources.

Quality improvement had become a community-wide effort in Kingsport, a thriving industrial town of 36,365 in northeastern Tennessee. Quality management was a community-wide concern, involving employers, the Chamber of Commerce, the school system, the community college, and both hospitals in town. Most people agree that this concern began in 1982 with Eastman Chemical Company (ECC), a subsidiary of Eastman Kodak, employing over 11,000 at their Kingsport plants. Faced with stiff foreign competition in its markets, ECC adopted a program which included a customer focus, employee empowerment, statistical methods, performance management, continuous improvement, education, and training management leadership. This program received an all-out push in 1985 and in 1988 Eastman was one of the nine finalists for the Malcolm Baldrige National Quality Award. **Exhibit 1** outlines the sequence of quality events at the hospital and in the community.

QUALITY FIRST

In 1986 Eastman executives were instrumental in having the Chamber of Commerce sponsor a QUALITY FIRST training session for community leaders at Northeast State Community College (then called Tri-Cities Community College). Mr. Bishop and a team of Holston Valley Hospital executives attended it. The program was taught by two professors from Jackson Community College in Michigan where the QUALITY FIRST program was developed with assistance from the Ford Motor Company. QUALITY FIRST is a 16-week, project-focused program for teams of four or more from a firm. This program emphasizes data collection and analysis, control charting, and prevention of error methods, all generally based on the precepts of W. Edwards Deming. Mr. Bishop, trained as a hospital administrator, was impressed with the approach and eventually sent more than 20 teams with approximately 90 participants.

Source: Curtis P. McLaughlin and Kit N. Simpson, University of North Carolina at Chapel Hill.

Documented savings at HVHMC from these team efforts included $72,000 in lower costs of linens, reductions in nurse turnover (costing $10,000–$20,000 per nurse) of 6%, and reductions of medication delivery lead time from the pharmacy to the nursing floors from 3 to 1¼ hours.

The executives on that first team in August 1986 had had trouble translating Deming concepts like a "single supplier" into the hospital context. Since they did not directly supervise service delivery, they took as their project the development of a patient satisfaction survey. Yet they sent four more teams that year, mostly on the basis of the reported successes of the industrial teams. Then they began to see results like:

- Admitting wait and processing times were reduced from 30 minutes to 5.6 minutes
- Preadmission lab testing went from 30% to 75%
- Length of stay dropped one day, mostly due to the efforts of the discharge planning team

In some ways the QUALITY FIRST program was ideal for the hospital. People were gone only one day every other week for 16 weeks. The course was project-oriented, so people could see the effects in the workplace.

PARTNERSHIPS FOR EXCELLENCE

Seven major projects were completed by the end of 1988, but Mr. Bishop wanted to speed up the process. So did the city manager of Kingsport. He went to Eastman Chemical, which agreed to donate the services of Mr. David J. McClaskey, a Quality Management Coordinator, to help adapt and use his "Managing for Excellence" training course to allow HVHMC to bring quality training "in-house." David McClaskey was an Examiner for the Malcolm Baldrige National Quality Award and helped develop the Examiner preparation course. One assistant administrator at HVHMC, Mr. Dale Richardson, received more than 100 hours of training. Then the management team and two potential in-house facilitators—a nurse and a business manager—went through the initial 80 hours of training over about seven months. During this initial run the participants found that about 30% of the material required modification to replace industrial illustrations with health situations. With Mr. McClaskey's cooperation they modified the material which they now call "Partnerships for Excellence." By June 1991 the hospital was staffed with six full-time facilitators. The hospital had some 23 "natural teams" which included direct reporting relationships from the administrator through assistant administrators to department directors and to their supervisors. By June 1991 80% of the natural teams had completed the "Partnerships for Excellence" process with the remainder scheduled to complete the process within eight months.

The TQM program consisted of four training modules. The first 80-hour module was for natural teams (groups with common supervision). It was an introduction to Deming's 14 points, Peter's "A Passion for Customers," the Red Bead experiment, team-building exercises, listening skills, managing customer expectations, developing process measures, flow- charting, statistical thinking, and the whole QUALITY FIRST process. This was followed by an exercise in developing a performance management plan for the unit and planning the rollout of Quality Improvement in the department. There were also two modules on Process Teams and one on quality improvement projects averaging 40 hours each. Process and Project Teams were both responsible for multifunctional issues with the Process Teams intending to maintain their oversight of a process, while the Project Teams had more of an ad hoc nature.

An example of a quality improvement project was the one concerned with nursing turnover, which had been averaging 25% annually. The initial task had been to define turnover, measure it and then set a goal of reducing the rate. The target for reduction was set at 6% with the new target at 19%. **Exhibit 2** illustrates the run chart developed by the team before and after its efforts started in August 1990 with hour meetings every other week. The project team decided not to deal with nursing recruitment, with anyone working fewer than 32 hours per month, with issues of absenteeism, nor with non-nursing employee turnover. Turnover was defined as the number of full and part-time FTEs transferred/terminated/resigned monthly divided by the budgeted number of full and part-time RN, LPN, nonlicensed and clerical personnel FTEs. There was always a tension over whether to focus on total employee turnover or RN turnover only. There was a felt need to benchmark HVMC against other comparable hospitals to test the target that some had presented of a 6% annual turnover. The costs of recruiting and training a new RN-level nurse had been estimated at $10,000–$20,000.

Because the program can be modularized, some groups, especially the process teams, did not receive the full 80 hour course. A Process Team works together for an extended period of time to study an important patient care process; for example, the "heart process" involving open heart and cardiac cath patients. Process Teams were started most recently, require a well-trained facilitator, and generate the most conflict. Mr. Bishop noted "We are still developing the Process Team framework. It is very hard for managers to stay out of the business of the Process Team long enough for them to produce results—we have found that we have had to limit participation of managers unless they are specifically assigned to the team." **Exhibits 3** and **4** show how the roles of the Natural Teams and Process Teams have been defined to deal with the ownership role, which is called the process steward at HVHMC.

When a team completes the program, its members receive certificates, called licenses (implying the need for renewal), at a celebration ceremony in front of all the managers, including first-line supervisors. Often a figure from the community and/or the hospital board is asked to hand out the certificates.

HVHMC has also adopted the "Service Excellence" modules developed by the Einstein group of Philadelphia. Fifteen hundred of the hospital's 1,800 employees have received this training, with the rest slated to receive it by the end of 1991.

COMMUNITY COMPETITION

The Tri-Cities area involving Johnson City, TN; Kingsport, TN; Bristol, TN and Bristol, VA, represents the nation's 82nd largest Metropolitan Statistical Area (MSA), with a 1990 population of 436,047. It ranked 31st out of the 281 MSAs in manufacturing earnings as a percent of total earnings in 1988. During the first quarter of 1991, when the national unemployment rate was 7.1%, Kingsport's rate was 3.8%, Johnson City's 5.6%, and Bristol TN-VA's 5.4%. It is heavily doctored. There are four substantial hospitals, two in Kingsport, and a medical school as part of East Tennessee State University in Johnson City. By mid-1991, Kingsport had 18 obstetrician-gynecologists with two more coming soon. Hospital lengths of stay, despite managed care, were above the national average. Advertising for hospitals and doctors abounded in the press, on billboards and in local business periodicals.

Both HVHMC and Indian Path Medical Center, owned by Hospital Corporation of America (HCA), operated well below their licensed bed level. HVHMC was licensed for 540 beds, after giving up 50 beds to help bring in a for-profit rehab hospital, but operated 350–375 beds, having converted its wards and semi-private rooms to all-private room status. Most community-based physicians practiced at both hospitals. Most of the physicians in the town belonged to the Kingsport Independent Practitioners' Association (IPA) which contracted to deliver services to Heritage National Healthplan (an HMO established and owned by John Deere, initially founded to service its own employees). Sixty-two percent of Eastman Chemical Company's employees were covered under contracts with Heritage. The rest were covered by Blue Cross-Blue Shield of Tennessee under a contract which covered a wide range of services, including some preventive care. **Exhibit 5** provides a financial and statistical statement of operations for fiscal years ending June 30, 1988 to 1992.

HVHMC was structured with a parent holding company, Holston Valley Health Care, Inc. (HVHC). The hospital was one of three separate divisions, together with a foundation for endowment, and the for-profit HVS Company, which managed a home-health agency, respiratory therapy services, weight loss programs, psychiatric counseling, laundry and other services to physicians' offices, and a number of joint ventures, which included diagnostic imaging. HVHMC included a trauma center, a neonatal intensive care unit, an open-heart surgery team, and a cancer center. It was one of the larger servers of the medically indigent in the state.

The Indian Path Medical Center administrative team had also participated in the same initial QUALITY FIRST training program. They also had gone through HCA's Deming-based quality management training in 1989. One project there had reduced outpatient registration wait time from 35 minutes to 5 minutes.

COMMUNITY COOPERATION

Despite the intense competition, Kingsport also became involved in a cooperative effort to improve the community's health. In 1988 the Midwest Business Group on Health, after studying health purchasing and quality assessment tools, received funding from the John A. Hartford Foundation of New York to develop three demonstration sites for community cooperation to stress teamwork and reduce variations in health. Kingsport became the first demonstration site. Someone at HCA, which itself invests heavily in Deming-based quality management programs, suggested Kingsport and the request was finally brought to the attention of Mr. Rob Johnson, Manager, Benefits Coordination at Eastman. He coordinated the development of the Kingsport Area Health Improvement Project (KAHIP) which involved representatives of the Kingsport Area Business Council on Health Care (KABACH), HVHMC, Indian Path Medical Center, Indian Path Pavilion (psychiatric), the IPA and Heritage.

After going through an intensive quality training session, the KAHIP members' representatives reviewed the health problems affecting Kingsport's population and finally selected the area of respiratory diseases as its focus. Four improvement projects were undertaken:

- reducing the number of readmissions for chronically ill respiratory patients, whom the group dubbed "frequent flyers"

- developing a more effective process for transitioning respiratory patients to nursing homes
- developing a process to encourage youth to quit/not start smoking
- determining the most appropriate means of conducting third party utilization review

Three of the teams attended the QUALITY FIRST program with their tuition paid for by the Midwest Business Group on Health and the four worked with an individual facilitator.

In retrospect, Rob Johnson noted that this process has been frustrating. "We didn't do a good job of using our project selection criteria. The projects we selected were difficult to deal with. They were too broad or aimed at a system instead of a process. Our data system wasn't effective enough to narrow the projects down to processes. Ownership was also a problem in this type of organization. Everybody has ownership or nobody has ownership. Because KAHIP is a community-oriented project, no one organization could claim ownership." Three of the four teams have continued to meet and the superintendent of schools is trying to reorganize the Youth and Smoking Team. The team working with nursing home placements has had some concrete successes and the other teams continue to collect and interpret data.

The Heritage National HMO has also started its own quality management program in Kingsport and at its Illinois headquarters assisted by facilitators from Eastman and HVHMC. Under the leadership of the doctors in the IPA, a team from the IPA, the HMO and the hospitals studied the resources used for post-surgical care of gall bladder removals. They found that there were about as many processes as there were physicians and developed a standard process. The net result has been to reduce the average length of stay for this procedure by two days. Dean Anderson, operations manager of Heritage, says "Ultimately we hope to have improvement teams in doctors' offices. Potential improvement areas we've identified include pediatric office scheduling, lab work, and billing processes. We want to spread the quality virus and get all physicians involved. Physicians develop different practices, but through quality we hope to combine the various procedures into one formalized process."

Dr. Paul Pearlman, president of the IPA, comments, "As physicians, we have to be interested in promoting health care. Physicians have varied backgrounds, so everyone manages problems differently. What we're trying to do through KAHIP is find out why there are variations and how we can reduce them to make our processes better. It shouldn't make a difference which emergency room a person goes to. What's important is that they get quality care wherever they go." One fact that encouraged Rob Johnson was the physicians' choice of low-cost California managed care group practices as their cost and length-of-stay benchmark for their gall bladder study.

KAHIP has also become the task force on health for the Kingsport Tomorrow project, a community-wide program to envision Kingsport in the 21st century. Rob Johnson observed that "We're reassessing teams, poring over new data systems and targeting physicians' offices for facilitators. If we can't zero in on the problems with our present projects, then we'll discontinue them. There are a lot of resources yet to be tapped. We feel we haven't accomplished a great deal, but others looking at Kingsport and KAHIP from the outside see what we're doing here and are amazed. While it's natural for us in Kingsport to cooperate, it is not in other communities."

Community cooperation was the style in Kingsport. Eastman and the other employers wanted a happy, attractive community to attract skilled personnel to their expanding businesses. On the other hand, if health care costs had to be cut they could and would act unilaterally. Eastman had made a study of medical admissions for low back pain and had severely restricted payments for that service. The number of admissions and their length dropped sharply, especially the admissions by primary care physicians. Eastman was aware that it could achieve the lowest health care costs by selecting a subset of physicians in the town and forming a closed-panel HMO, but Rob Johnson did not want anything that confrontational yet. "That just is not Eastman's style." Besides he felt that it was best to work with the total system rather than minimizing Eastman's share, since cost shifting one way or another ended up saddling employers with the costs of uncompensated care throughout the community.

NATIONAL CENTER FOR QUALITY

Another cooperative venture of the quality management community in the Tri-Cities area, building on the QUALITY FIRST program, is the National Center for Quality. This is a non-profit corporation formed by the three chambers of commerce in 1988 that is dedicated to promoting a national interest in quality and productivity improvement. It has established a core set of courses for organizations to call on. **Exhibit 6** shows the board membership as of January 1990. In June of 1989, Jim Wallin, community programs coordinator for Eastman, was loaned to the center as its interim director. In January 1990 the board approved handing over the operation to Northeast State Technical Institute, and Al Thomas, director of the QUALITY FIRST program, was asked to serve as part-time executive director of the center.

The center offers a number of courses:

- Seizing the Quality Initiative
- Leading the Quality Transformation
- Survey Techniques
- Quality & Performance Management for Educators
- Malcolm Baldrige National Quality Award
- Managing for Excellence in Healthcare

It currently has under development programs on Quality for Small Business and Quality Consultant Training. On August 5–6, 1991 the center, in cooperation with the four area hospitals, offered "A Competitive Healthcare and Quality Management Conference." The conference coordinator was Ms. Esther Luster, an assistant administrator at HVHMC. Paul Bishop observed, "Our psychological contract with the supporters of quality management includes our making a special effort to disseminate our story."

The Second Conference was held April 23–24, 1992 and included such well-known presenters as Dr. Paul Batalden, Vice President of Medical Affairs, HCA, and Dr. James Roberts of the Joint Commission on Accreditation of Healthcare Organizations.

ACTIVITIES AT HVHMC

Paul Bishop was genuinely pleased with the hospital and the community efforts which were attracting national recognition. For example, he had been asked to prepare and give a presentation at the 1991 Business Week Symposium of Health Care CEOs, Rockefeller Center, New York City, June 20–21, 1991, which he entitled "Innovation as A Team Sport: Solutions Through Partnership." Yet when asked about issues to be worked on, he replied, "There are hundreds of them. In health care the average time that people are satisfied with an improved service is half-an-hour. They immediately internalize the new achievement as the new standard and complain about how poor the service is." Over time, however, he felt that people were beginning to realize that the quality of care genuinely has improved.

His major concerns beyond day-to-day implementation were 1) how fast to change the organizational structure and the human resource infrastructure to adjust to quality management and performance management, 2) how to increase the emphasis on quality management in clinical decision making, and 3) how to get his vision of the future of this change process across to people. Early on the quality assurance (QA) effort was merged with and made subordinate to the Quality Management program. The existing QA staff, two medical records specialists who had been doing physician utilization review, were assigned to the new head of quality management, a former nursing supervisor. They then received quality management training. The quality management department grew rapidly with the addition of the six quality management facilitators, who had the title of Quality Management Consultant. Their backgrounds included nursing supervision, clinical laboratory support, financial office support, quality management with the telephone company, undergraduate training in statistics, and medical records experience. Dale Richardson, the assistant administrator responsible for quality management, had worked as a consultant with SunHealth, a hospital consulting firm in Charlotte, North Carolina, before coming to Kingsport and still took occasional quality management assignments with them.

The performance appraisal system had been modified some to include contributions to quality management and so had the job descriptions. Yet Paul Bishop was still concerned about how fast to move away from the periodic appraisal system and move toward performance management. Some senior managers who had been successful under the old style of management and believed that "The cream rises to the top" would probably resist such a move. This didn't mean that institutionalization of the concepts of quality management wasn't pretty far along. People had internalized the concepts and terms throughout the organization. A number of physicians were quite interested in some of the projects. Some people who had complained about their supervisors' passiveness were actually saying that they saw positive changes in management, while others sometimes complained about too much time spent in meetings.

The original "Heart Process" Team had not been terribly successful, because the individuals responsible for spearheading the process review had come from outside it. "We went to school on that one," one of the internal consultants said. "Since then the process stewards have all come from within the process. That cuts down on barriers and defensiveness." During the past year, a consulting company from New York (APM, which specializes in service line development) and the team have made great strides with the heart process. The key has been in getting commitment from the physicians for improvement of the process, including cost control.

The Linen Management System

The eighth group sent to Tri-Cities Tech, for example, was a team made of four nursing staff, the director of linen and laundry services, and a hospital buyer. The project assigned to them by the administrative staff was the frequent set of complaints from the nursing units about the shortage or excess of laundry delivered by the in-house laundry to the floors. The laundry department had tried to project the daily nursing usage on each unit, but there was little communication or coordination between the Laundry and the Nursing Units. The existing system provided no linen accountability or control and poor utilization of personnel.

When the team first met, there was little agreement on the perceived cause of this lack of coordination. Through the use of brainstorming sessions, the group reached a consensus on improving the linen distribution system. They developed the system flow chart shown in **Exhibit 7**. The team identified all the units involved in the process which involved the purchase of linen and its processing by the laundry, and its distribution over two miles of hospital corridors to 22 nursing unit linen closets. They then prepared the cause-and-effect (fishbone) diagram relating to inadequate linen distribution shown in **Exhibit 8**.

The group realized that they were still dealing with rather broad generalities and knew little about the specifics of linen utilization. With the cooperation of the 22 nursing units, a linen inventory was conducted. On February 8, 1989 the nursing staff arrived at work to find that their first task was to count each clean piece of linen in patient rooms and linen closets. Then for the next two days all soiled linen was sent to the laundry in bags color coded by the unit of origin, so that the laundry could do a usage count. These counts are shown as **Exhibits 9** and **10**. A tour of the hospital left team members agreeing that there were adequate supplies of linens, but they were distributed poorly with too many wash cloths on some units and too few on others. Crowded storage spaces did not allow enough room for storing enough pillows on most units, also leading to linen falling on the floor and needing to be reprocessed. If a unit could not store enough pillows in the linen closet, housekeeping then arranged to store some in the closets of the patient rooms.

The team then decided to conduct a pilot test of linen control on the Neuro-Orthopedics unit. Control charts were developed based on data on usage over a 16-day period. Linen closets were rearranged and shelves labeled and marked with red tape to meet planned levels. **Exhibit 11** contains an example of these control charts. Target inventory levels were set at the upper control limits on these C-charts. Since each day the closets were stocked neatly up to the specified amount, there were few shortages necessitating trips to the laundry and no excesses. The team calculated that the savings in inventory investment on the pilot floor was more than 50%. Extrapolated to the whole hospital, the reduction in investment was estimated at $72,000.

An unexpected benefit resulted from the fact that the pilot unit was going to be renovated and the new plans called for inadequate linen storage space. The team went to the architect and the hospital administration and arranged to have the storage space increased.

The team reported that there were additional savings in personnel time and energy that were difficult to quantify. They suggested that the amount of linen stored could be reduced even further, if the laundry had more storage space, if laundry equipment reliability was improved, or if "mysterious disappearance of linen inventory" could be countered.

The Linen Team decided to stay intact to expand the approach to all nursing and ancillary departments, to expand the system to additional items such as scrub suits, and to monitor and adjust the system to changing requirements.

Radiology Transport Team

The Radiology Process Team attended the Quality First Project training a little after the Linen Team. The Radiology Process Team met with the Administrative

Management Team to discuss Major Improvement Opportunities (MIOs) and selected 1) Financial Viability, 2) High Touch, and 3) Decreased Length of Stay.

Various subgroups were asked to develop a priority listing for improvements. The one developed by the radiology technologists is shown as **Exhibit 12**. Their priorities were representative, so the team went to work on processes used to transport in-patients. Patients were constantly complaining that it took too long to get back to their rooms after an exam; in some cases waits of up to two hours were noted. Staff members complained of delays in sending for patients. A patient sent for at 10 a.m., might not arrive until 2 or 3 p.m. Then work flow was disrupted, schedules were delayed, and referring physicians were upset with the total wait time. These delays could hold up other tests and procedures and have a negative impact on the Length of Stay MIO.

The team decided to focus on patient delays in radiology and the wait time after a procedure was completed on an inpatient. The first piece of data collection was to determine the amount of time it would take an able-bodied transporter (orderly) to walk from the farthest point in the hospital to the radiology department. The Transporter Team member reported 15 minutes. Therefore, the team set its standard for a wait for transportation as 15 to 30 minutes. A Technologist Team member asked each patient over a period of several days what he or she felt was a reasonable wait after a procedure. Patients appeared to consider under ten minutes a reasonable time and 20 minutes to be the maximum. Given a focused definition of the problem, the team then decided to find the root cause. They started with a flow diagram (**Exhibit 13**). With the aid of their facilitator, the team then developed a cause and effect diagram (**Exhibit 14**). Based on this understanding of the process, the team conducted a survey of the transporters about the causes of the delays they encountered. They confirmed the importance of a lack of wheelchairs and stretchers, the subject of another team's analysis which was already underway.

An initial survey showed that the system was meeting the target less than 50% of the time. However, there were some questions about the times reported under the "honor system," so a new study was conducted using a Simplex clocking device on which the technologist clocked in when the patient was sent for and the transporter clocked in when he received the card and when he left the radiology department. With the new data system, the figures improved, but still were unsatisfactory 32% of the time.

Further study identified the fact that seven radiology transporters all worked various areas of the Imaging Section. Furthermore, they reported not to a radiology manager, but to Dispatch Services, a source of territorial battles and attitudinal problems. The head of Dispatch Service was asked to join the team. The other team members suggested that the radiology transporters should be pooled.

At the transporters' suggestion each transporter kept a detailed log of how time was spent, accounting for transport travel time (T.P.T.), travel to and from the patient (T.T.), and dead time (D.T.). Over half of the time was dead time, raising questions about the need for more transporters (**Exhibit 15**).

Given the low utilization of the transporters, the team suggested to management that the seven transporters be assigned to Radiology for supervision, solving the issue of "Who is my boss?" and be retrained and upgraded to a Radiology Assistant so that they could perform duties such as developing film and obtaining reports. This would help solve the attitude problems, since it would expand the job and increase the pay.

During the implementation phase a radio base was purchased, an area set up for the transporters, and the six months of retraining commenced. At the time of the team presentation, Nursing Administration was putting pressure on Dispatch Services to cover weekend shifts without overtime costs. Radiology and Administration worked this out in Radiology by adding one person to be a dispatcher. The team report noted that:

> In all there will be cost in a radio base, carpentry work, raise in pay, and one full-time employee. Sounds like a lot of money and not very financially viable.
>
> The original seven covered shifts from 6:00 a.m. to 8 p.m., Monday through Friday, and on overtime shifts from 7:00 a.m. to 4 p.m. on Saturday only. Upon implementation, the shifts covered will be 5:30 a.m. to 11:00 p.m., Monday through Friday and 7:00 a.m. to 11:00 p.m., Saturday and Sunday. At the addition of one employee, 53 additional hours will be added to the transportation schedule. Overtime has been reduced, the overall utilization of transportation has been increased, and we are projecting this to be at no cost. Now that is financial viability that even Sam Walton would be interested in.

MOVING ON TO CLINICAL QUALITY

The hospital had recently received its initial set of SysteMetrics/McGraw-Hill IMPAQ III reports, one of the first sets sent out, providing internal resource utilization, mortality, and complications by diagnosis, by payer, and by physician. Paul Bishop saw two major issues immediately 1) how to adjust them for patient risk, and 2) how to transmit the information to the physicians in a way that would maintain the spirit of cooperation that existed, but still motivate review and action. HVHMC looked good on mortality and not as good on resource utilization. **Exhibits 16** and **17** show some sample statistics from that report which, except for the mortality data and average DRG weights were based entirely on internal comparisons. The same data was available by individual physician. The variable "payer mix index" was based on the amount that the hospital was actually paid after contractual discounts and allowances, claims denials, and bad debts. Other definitions are shown in **Exhibit 18**.

In some situations Paul Bishop was not sure whether the discrepancies were due to coding errors or biases or were rooted in physician behaviors. He wanted to use this new information in a way that would enhance HVHMCs effectiveness and financial viability. The hospital was currently operating in the black and he wanted it to stay that way. On the other hand he had been careful so far to have the quality program avoid issues that might upset physicians enough to take more of their cases to competing hospitals.

Rob Johnson had suggested sharing the data with the IPA and letting them take ownership for the quality improvement process. "Our experiences with medical backs and gall bladders show that changes in physician practice patterns show up immediately in both hospitals. Why should Paul pay all the costs of the change when Indian Path will get just as much benefit?"

Exhibit 1 Quality Events Time Line

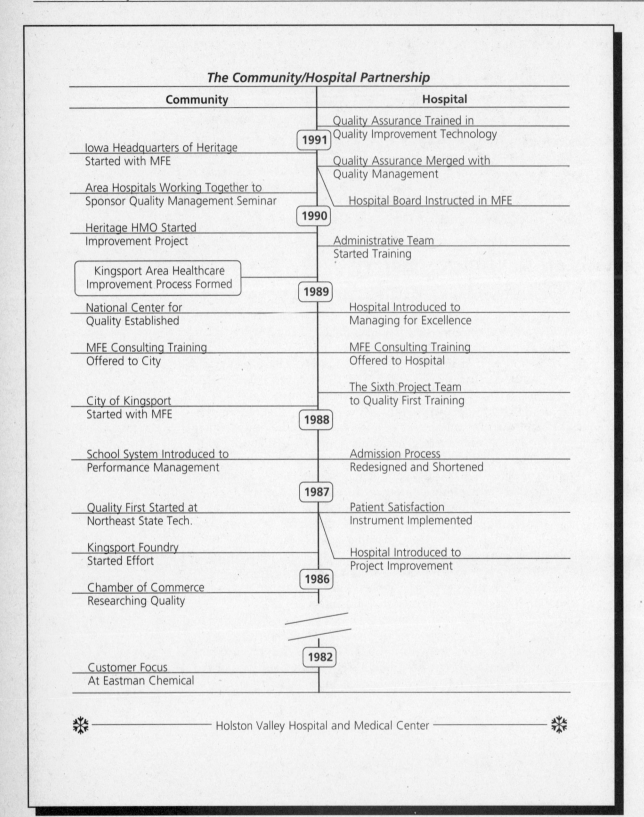

The Community/Hospital Partnership

Community	Hospital
	Quality Assurance Trained in Quality Improvement Technology
1991	
Iowa Headquarters of Heritage Started with MFE	Quality Assurance Merged with Quality Management
Area Hospitals Working Together to Sponsor Quality Management Seminar	Hospital Board Instructed in MFE
1990	
Heritage HMO Started Improvement Project	Administrative Team Started Training
Kingsport Area Healthcare Improvement Process Formed	
1989	
National Center for Quality Established	Hospital Introduced to Managing for Excellence
MFE Consulting Training Offered to City	MFE Consulting Training Offered to Hospital
City of Kingsport Started with MFE	The Sixth Project Team to Quality First Training
1988	
School System Introduced to Performance Management	Admission Process Redesigned and Shortened
1987	
Quality First Started at Northeast State Tech.	Patient Satisfaction Instrument Implemented
Kingsport Foundry Started Effort	Hospital Introduced to Project Improvement
1986	
Chamber of Commerce Researching Quality	
1982	
Customer Focus At Eastman Chemical	

Holston Valley Hospital and Medical Center

Exhibit 2 Run Chart of Nursing Turnover

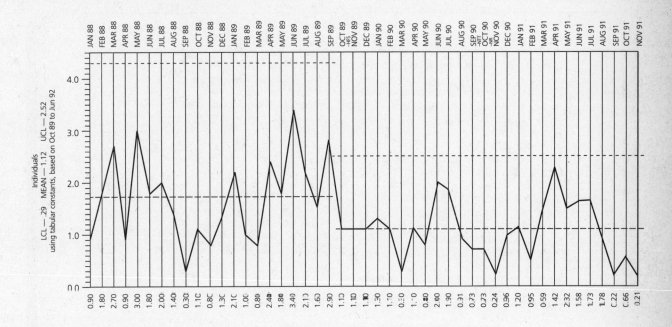

Exhibit 3 Relationship of Process Teams and Natural Management Teams (Owners)

- Process Teams regularly report progress/accomplishments to Natural Team.

- Owner & the Process Team member communicate to all departmental employees information regarding changes to the process.

- Priorities of what to work on are discussed and negotiated with Departmental Natural Team.

- In determining what to work on, Process Team considers input from:

  customers of process
  team members
  "Owner's Team"

- Major decisions and changes to process should be discussed with Departmental Natural Team.

 ———————————— Holston Valley Hospital and Medical Center ————————————

Exhibit 4 Responsibilities of Process Teams*

1. Understand customer needs and define customer requirements.

2. Determine where the process stands in relation to customer requirements.

3. Study/analyze process:

   a. Flowcharts
   b. Discussions with people involved with process
   c. Analysis of data
   d. Benchmarks

4. Determine measures of process:

   a. Results/output measures
   b. In-process

5. Determine and list areas for improvement.

6. Feedback to Natural Unit Management Team.

7. Work on improvement projects agreed on by Natural Unit Management Team.

8. Routinely manage the overall process by:

   a. Routinely monitoring process measures.
   b. Detecting and appropriately responding to process upsets that cannot be handled routinely within the process.
   c. Receiving and listing ideas to improve the process.

---

* When appropriate, the "team" can be just the process steward.

 ———— Holston Valley Hospital and Medical Center ———— ❄

Exhibit 5 Comparative Statement of Operations

	Year Ended 6–30–88	Year Ended 6–30–89	Year Ended 6–30–90	Year Ended 6–30–91	Estimated Year Ended 6–30–92
Patient Serv. Revenue ($000)	100,184	118,130	137,970	164,926	193,738
Revenue Deductions	24,992	30,551	41,629	51,562	68,195
Other Operating Rev.	2,438	2,457	4,672	5,781	5,407
Net Revenue	77,630	90,036	101,013	119,145	130,950
Operating Expenses	74,857	86,849	97,935	113,356	129,470
Non-Operating Rev.	963	768	1,922	1,867	3,271
Non-Operating Exp.	512	601	130	39	58
Net Non-Operating Income	451	167	1,792	1,828	3,214
Net Gain (Loss)	3,224	3,354	4,870	7,617	4,693

STATISTICS

	Year Ended 6–30–88	Year Ended 6–30–89	Year Ended 6–30–90	Year Ended 6–30–91	Estimated Year Ended 6–30–92
Adult Admissions	15,202	15,804	15,718	15,432	14,970
Adult Patient Days	111,803	110,459	105,498	106,304	103,368
Newborn Days	4,982	4,594	4,444	4,889	4,657
Open Heart Cases	469	498	496	556	547
Surgical Procedures	7,949	8,266	8,872	9,657	10,291
Same Day Service Visits	5,637	5,563	5,344	6,961	7,931
Emergency Room Visits	52,943	55,725	56,294	57,086	58,324
Radiological Procedures	75,959	77,797	78,963	81,318	84,662
CT Scan Procedures	6,784	7,098	7,523	8,263	8,941
Lab Procedures	824,391	903,724	978,338	1,020,393	1,108,309
Cath Lab Procedures	2,416	2,010	2,103	2,224	2,428
MRI Procedures	1,742	2,839	3,889	4,113	3,968
Length of Stay	7.3	7.0	6.7	6.9	6.9
Average FTE's	1,578	1,707	1,666	1,820	2,323
FTEs/Ave. Occup. Bed	4.3	4.7	4.7	5.0	5.3

Exhibit 6 National Center for Quality

Members of the Board

R.C. Hart
Eastman Chemical Company
(Chairman of the Board)

Curtis Burnette
Aerojet Ordinance Tennessee
(President)

Will Hutsell
Eastman Chemical Company
(Vice President)

Dr. R. Wade Powers
Northeast State Technical
Community College
(Treasurer)

D. Lynn Johnson
Eastman Chemical Company
(Secretary)

Al Thomas
National Center for Quality
(Executive Director)

Vic Dingus
Eastman Chemical Company

James R. White
Eastman Chemical Company

Paul Bishop
Holston Valley Hospital & Med. Ctr.

John Andersen
First American National Bank

Bill Ring
Kingsport Foundry & Manuf. Corp.

Don Royston
Kingsport Chamber of Commerce

Dennis Wagner
United Telephone System

Marie Williams
Greater Bristol Area Chamber
of Commerce

Jerry Moeller
Bristol Regional Med. Ctr.

Tim Jones
Johnson City Chamber
of Commerce

Ed. Fennell
City of Johnson City

Dr. James Hales
East Tenn. State University

Ann Peace
Kingsport, TN

Reneau Dubberly
Johnson City, TN

Jim Wallin
Eastman Chemical Company

Dick Wetherell
Texas Instruments

Dr. Allan Spritzer
College of Business, E.T.S.U.

❄ ——————————— Holston Valley Hospital and Medical Center ——————— ❄

Exhibit 7 Flow Chart for Linen Distribution

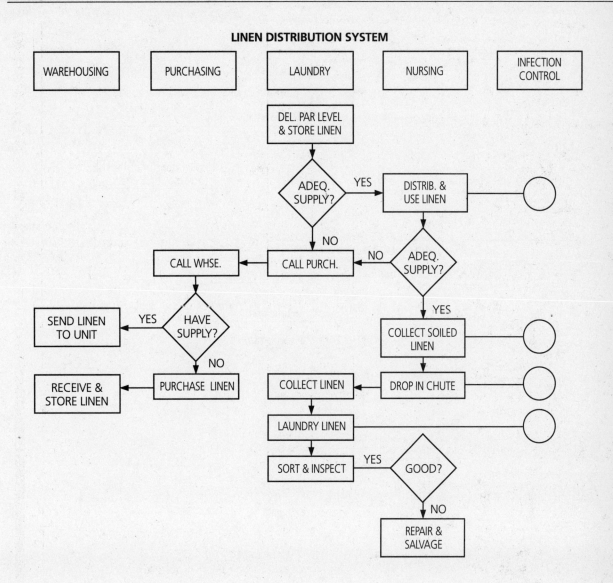

Exhibit 8 Cause-and-Effect Diagram for Linen Distribution

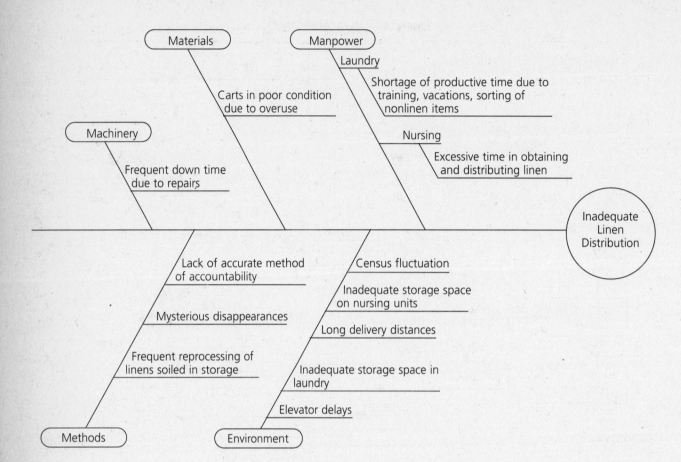

Exhibit 9 Sample Clean Linen Inventory Report

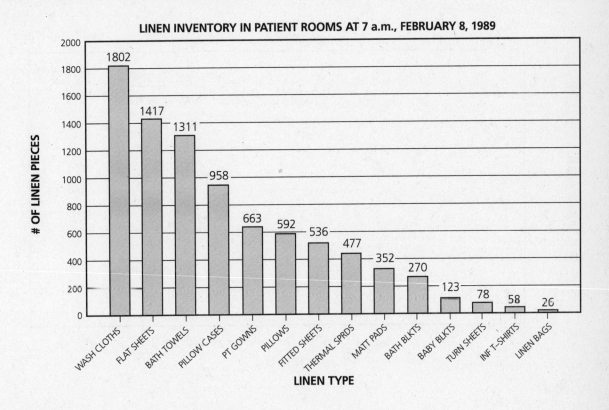

Exhibit 10 Sample Soiled Linen Usage Report

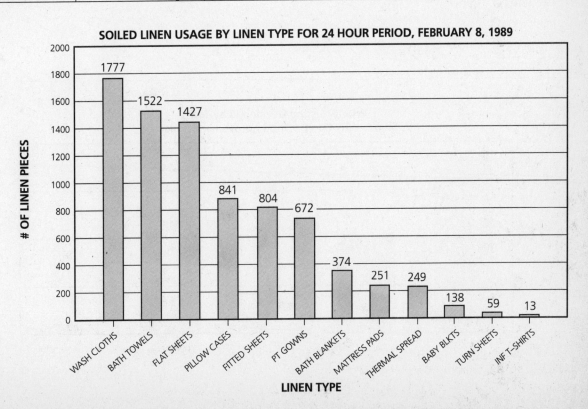

Exhibit 11 C-Control Chart

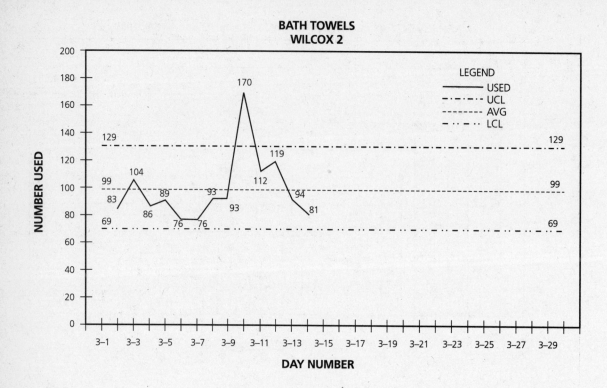

**BATH TOWELS
WILCOX 2**

Exhibit 12 Radiology Improvement Projects

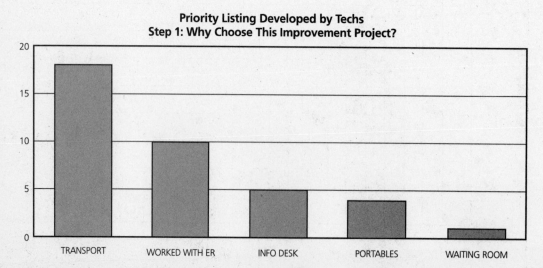

**Priority Listing Developed by Techs
Step 1: Why Choose This Improvement Project?**

Developed During February 1990 Meeting

Exhibit 13 Radiology Transport Process

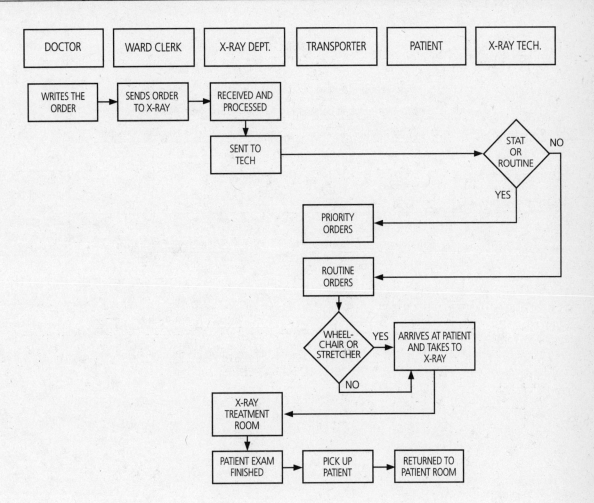

Exhibit 14 Cause-and-Effect Diagram on What Causes the Delays

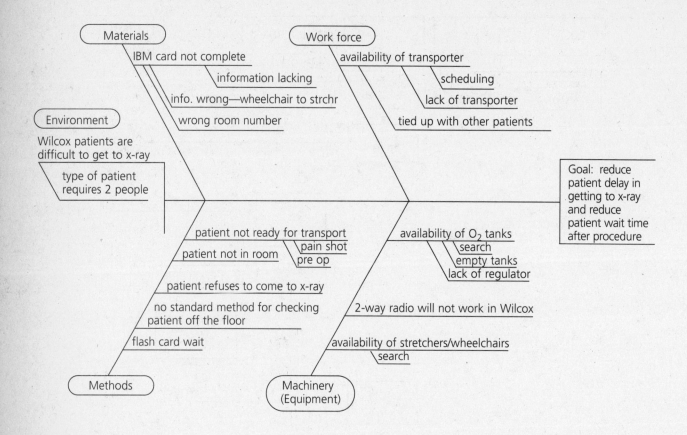

Exhibit 15 Radiology Transporter Time Breakdown

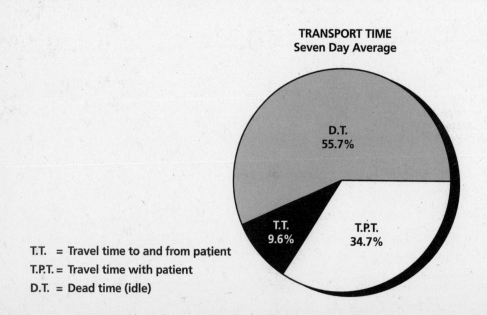

TRANSPORT TIME
Seven Day Average

D.T.
55.7%

T.T.
9.6%

T.P.T.
34.7%

T.T. = Travel time to and from patient
T.P.T. = Travel time with patient
D.T. = Dead time (idle)

Exhibit 16 Resource Demand Information by Payer (October–December 1990)

	Cases	% Cases	Mortality Ratio	Days Exceeding Expectation	Charges Exceeding Expectation
All Cases	4,197	100		0	
Medicare		47.8	1.263	2,347	616,185
Medicaid		10.3	1.444	–1,185	–146,910
Commercial		19.1	1.091	– 471	–281,633
Blue Cross		9.5	0.667	–273	–132,976
HMO		3.8	3.0	–297	–185,562
Self Pay		6.7	0.667	–35	212,526
Worker's Comp		2.8	0.5	– 86	– 85,944

Exhibit 17 Resource Demand Information by Product Line (October–December 1990)

	Cases	Efficiency Ratio	LOS Ratio	Ave. DRG Scale	HVHMC Resource Demand Index	Payer Mix Index
Cardiac–Medicine	651	84.9	1.2	1.0752	0.853	66
Cardiac–Surgery	162	93.5	1.1	1.0799	4.670	69
Cancer–Medicine	158	112.3	1.2	1.0677	0.891	64
Cancer–Surgery	45	89.2	1.1	1.0044	1.125	66
Neuro–Medicine	222	76.8	1.0	0.9673	0.730	70
Neuro–Surgery	110	96.2	1.1	0.8965	1.894	73
Renal/Urology–Medicine	98	102.6	1.1	0.9996	0.639	65
Renal/Urology–Surgery	61	82.0	0.9	0.9169	0.673	69
Women's Health	573	111.3	0.4	0.9665	0.397	67
Orthopedics	238	94.1	1.2	0.9580	1.229	67
Respiratory	310	82.3	1.1	1.0569	1.276	64
Medicine	530	99.2	1.3	1.0055	0.623	66
General Surgery	255	101.0	1.0	0.9895	1.310	69
Other Surgery	265	97.5	1.2	1.1616	1.521	68
Newborn	341	153.0	0.8	1.0696	0.302	65
Psychiatry	80	70.1	1.0	1.0484	0.900	66
Ophthalmics	7	89.2	0.8	0.8457	0.622	70
Trauma–Medicine	69	120.6	1.2	0.9907	0.535	61
Trauma–Surgery	9	126.1	1.1	1.2811	1.224	62
Dental	2	84.1	0.6	1.0000	0.422	64
Substance Abuse	11	73.7	0.9	1.0436	0.826	59
All Cases	4,197			1.0261	1.00	66

Exhibit 18 Definitions of Terms from SysteMetrics Report

The product line efficiency ratio measures the extent consumption exceeds demand. The higher the ratio, the greater the inefficiency. . . . Demand is set by the clinical criteria of patients, consumption is determined by charges which constitute cost to the buyer or payer. . . . Because the efficiency calculation is specific to each patient, and because the efficiency norm is derived from typical practice patterns of physicians utilizing services in your hospital, the ratio is a reasonable estimate of how average overall product line performance compares to average overall performance in the hospital. . . . In other words, to the extent average clinically adjusted charges in a product line exceed average clinically adjusted charges in the hospital, to that extent charges are inefficient either due to payer mix pricing strategy, a greater use of ancillary charges, longer lengths of stay, or some combination of these. . . .

LOS Efficiency Ratio recognizes aggregate variation from legitimate demand for resources. It answers the question, from the buyer's point of view; that is to say, with all things considered—price, use of ancillaries, length of stay—how efficient is the hospital in a particular Product Line, DRG, payer, or at the physician level? . . . (It) is a unique, discrete analysis of how favorably your actual length of stay compares with the LOS you should expect, given patient clinical condition and discharge habits at your hospital compared to those in the national database.

For example, a ratio of 1.15 means that actual LOS exceeds expected LOS by 15%. More specially, it means that discharge policy and procedures affecting the PL, coupled with physician disposition practices, result in a 15% longer length of stay in the Product Line than would be expected given overall hospital policy, procedures and practice patterns and their comparison to national norms specific to identical disease categories.

* * * * *

Once senior management has drawn conclusions about Product Line utilization and efficiency, and their effect on limited, acute resources, the next logical place to turn is to the possible improvement of net patient revenue across payers. . . . As with product lines, this analysis begins with an assessment of legitimate payer resource demand relative to total hospital acute demand. Number of cases is often a poor proxy for estimating resource allocation across payers. The legitimate need is not only dependent upon volume, but also in illness severity, and ultimately dependent upon resource efficiencies which would increase or lower the allocation requirement.

Mortality—a special "mortality scale" has been developed to predict mortality based on risk of death associated with the stage or progression of disease, and the effect of the interaction of comorbid conditions upon that risk. Ratios greater than 1.0 indicate the extent (percent) actual deaths exceed the national norm for the specific clinical conditions exhibited across the payer population.

The Saturn Project

In June, 1982, General Motors (GM) assigned its Advanced Product and Design Team to answer the question, "Can GM build a world-class-quality small car in the U.S. that can compete successfully with the imports?" This effort grew into what GM called the Saturn Project. The team used a "clean-sheet" approach—unbound by traditional thinking and industry practices—to set up the small car project. This approach afforded the opportunity to design the manufacturing process in parallel with the product and to adopt lean projection philosophies and techniques. The Saturn Project's challenge in designing the process, product, and manufacturing facility was to eliminate the $2,000 per unit cost advantage that Japanese auto makers held over U.S. manufacturers.

With the Saturn Project under way, another GM group gathered to study ways to improve management-labor relations. This "Group of 99," composed of GM managers and staff personnel from 17 GM divisions and United Auto Workers (UAW) members from 140 regions, revealed the willingness of these two factions to work together as partners to accomplish business objectives. In 1985 the Saturn Project merged with the Group of 99 to become the Saturn Corporation. With a 5 billion commitment, GM established Saturn as a wholly owned subsidiary. A "Gang of Six" was appointed, which included a president and vice presidents for planning, engineering, manufacturing, sales, and finance.

The newly assembled group immediately separated into Research Teams to study intricate aspects of what Saturn could be. During a two-month period, members of the new team visited 49 GM plants and 60 benchmark companies worldwide to gather ideas in preparation for setting up the new system. According to Jay Wetzel, vice president for engineering, "We had the benefit of being able to start everything new, where other (GM) platforms had to work off their heritage and their existing facilities. We had the opportunity to take some risks in high technology that other units of General Motors may not have pursued."[1] GM planned to export successful processes

---

1   Charles J. Murray, "Engineer on a Mission," *Design News*, Engineering Quality Award Issue.

Source: Jeanne Busemeyer, adapted from Martin Starr, *Operations Management: A Systems Approach*, 1996, Boyd and Fraser (now South-Western College Publishing).

and operations developed at Saturn to improve efficiency and competitiveness at all its manufacturing facilities.

In July, 1985, the selection of Spring Hill, Tennessee, as the site for the new manufacturing facility was finalized. Five years later the first Saturn rolled off the assembly line. Saturn manufactured its one millionth car in early summer, 1995. The company sold 267,450 units of its 1994 models, up from 228,833 of the 1993 models. Saturn's share of the total U.S. new-car market is more than 3%. In defining Saturn's mission and philosophy, team members established Saturn's commitment to protect and preserve the environment (see **Exhibits 1** and **2**). Saturn designed and built the mile-long, 4.5-million-square-foot manufacturing facility in Spring Hill around this commitment to protect the environment and to maintain the aesthetic value of the land.

The Spring Hill plant is a "fully integrated" auto factory. This means all major parts for Saturn's coupes, sedans, and wagons are manufactured at one facility. The integrated nature of the plant facilitates interaction between business units and perpetuates quality-mindedness and information exchange throughout the system.

Saturn manufactures approximately 1,150 cars per day. In a 20-hour day of two 10-hour shifts, that's roughly one car per minute. In 1995, the average price of a Saturn was $14,950; Saturn team members know that the company loses about $14,950 every minute the production line is down. As of spring 1995, approximately 8,000 team members work at the Spring Hill facility.

The three major "business units" at Saturn are Powertrain (engine and transmission), Body Systems, and Vehicle Systems (general assembly and interior systems). Components manufactured in Powertrain, Body Systems and Interior Systems are conveyed overhead into the Vehicle Systems assembly area. **Exhibit 3** illustrates the basic layout of the Saturn manufacturing and assembly complex.

PRODUCTION ACTIVITIES

Following is a brief summary of the production activities within the business units:

Powertrain

- **Die cast operation:** Molten metal casting of parts including transmission cases, transmission parts, and engine covers.
- **Lost foam casting:** Casting technology using polystyrene beads as patterns for molten metal casting. Parts produced here include engine blocks, engine heads, crankshafts, and differential housing.
- **Transmission assembly:** Manual and automatic transmissions built on the same line. Flexibility to build up to 75% of either transmission to meet market demand.
- **Engine machining line:** Flexible machining allows for one machining line instead of the traditional two.
- **Final engine assembly:** Assembles both high-performance and standard engines on the same line.

Body Systems

- **Steel body (or spaceframe) components:** Rolled steel is cut to size on large transfer presses. These presses allow for a finished part to be manufactured using one press instead of the traditional five or six. Quick die changes are an integral part of Saturn's stamping plans. Saturn team members have achieved die changes of less than ten minutes.

- **Body panels:** Utilizing three different types of polymer pellets, composite panels are prepared in a 24 hour-a-day injection molding operation.
- **Body fabrication:** Various components of the spaceframe, including the body side, motor compartment, rear compartment and floor pan are welded. The central point in body fabrication is the body framing and respot welding line.
- **Paint:** Various components for Saturn vehicles are run through a phosphate and ELPO system which applies the rust-resistant undercoating, a robotic and manual sealer process, and a base coat/clear coat paint system. A completely automated panel storage and retrieval system has the capacity to store up to 900 complete sets of exterior panels.

Vehicle Systems

- **Skillet application:** Spaceframes and associates move along the assembly line via a unique ergonomic means that emulates a stationary work station. Associates step on the moving wooden skillet platform, move with the car to perform work, then step off when they're finished.
- **Cockpit operation:** All components are installed and tested for electrical functionality prior to installation in vehicles. Cockpit installation is traditionally a cumbersome procedure involving technicians getting down on their backs to do the necessary wiring on the instrument panel. At Saturn the cockpit is built outside the car so people don't have to assume the awkward positions.
- **Trim installation:** Employing the skillet system, all interior and exterior trim is installed.
- **Towveyor operation:** A conveyor tows the completed Powertrain, then installs it in spaceframe.
- **Exterior (body) panels scissor lift:** Scissor lifts are used to elevate a car for ease of panel installation by team members.
- **Interior Systems:** Injection molding and trim fabrication for interior.

QUALITY AND TEAMWORK

Quality is paramount to success in the small car market. Meeting and exceeding customer requirements and expectations on a consistent basis is one of Saturn's key strategies for success. Quality at Saturn starts at the shop-floor level with the teams. (Saturn refers to teams on the shop floor as "work units.") Teams are responsible for day-to-day car building and product-quality monitoring.

All Saturn employees are called "team members." Everyone at Saturn is associated with a team. All shop-floor UAW members are on a team. Each business unit (Powertrain, Vehicle Systems, and Body Systems) has about 217 work units (or teams) for a total of 651. Business units are divided into modules which are subdivided into teams (or work units). (As an example, the "Door Finesse" Team is in the "Front-end" module of the Vehicle Systems business unit.) Each team has from 8 to 15 members.

Within each team one person is responsible for gathering and analyzing information on quality issues. This person shares all quality information with team members. Module quality advisors look at outgoing (or between team) quality. The advisors provide a communication bridge between the teams so each team knows what its internal customers upstream and downstream in the process require to make a quality, world-class vehicle. A series of Quality Councils, composed of team members and management meet on a periodic basis to set quality goals and provide general direction in terms of quality elements.

When problems arise, the team identifies the cause. The team may solicit help from engineering and operations (whose work areas also are located in the factory) in deciding what actions to take to solve the problem. A Total Quality Action Team (TQAT) may be formed to work on a specific problem. Saturn team members are not told by management how to perform work or solve problems. They are made aware of what needs to be done, then the teams decide how to proceed. This includes who performs the jobs and whether a job is best done by a robot or a person. All decisions are made by consensus with the goal of promoting quality.

Quality is considered from the very beginning of a project in ascertaining what Saturn's target customers are looking for in a vehicle. Other quality inputs are obtained through warranty information and outside surveys done by organizations such as J.D. Power and Associates, which generates customer satisfaction comparisons. (In 1995, Saturn ranked #1 in J.D. Power's Customer Satisfaction Survey. In 1994, it was the only domestic nameplate within the top five.) All customer-related quality information gathered is analyzed and formatted to be understood by the teams. This helps team members understand what piece of the information they can affect to improve the product from the customer's perspective. In other words, customer feedback in this format is the means through which product quality is improved at Saturn.

DISCUSSION QUESTIONS

1. Discuss the role of TQM in the Saturn Project.
2. What was the importance and symbolism of the Group of 99 and Gang of 6 to the "clean-sheet approach?" Discuss.
3. Explain how the Saturn Project in effect "reengineered" the automobile manufacture process?
4. If each business unit has 217 work units, and each work unit has 8 to 15 members, how many Saturn employees are "associated with" teams rather than "members" of teams? What kinds of functions do you think these Saturn employees perform?
5. How do and how should the Saturn teams impact TQM?
6. How is quality ensured at Saturn? Discuss the role of Quality Councils and the TQAT.

Exhibit 1 Saturn's Mission

MISSION

Market vehicles developed
and manufactured in
the United States that are
world leaders in quality,
cost and customer
satisfaction through
the integration of
people, technology and
business systems and
to transfer knowledge,
technology and
experience throughout
General Motors.

Exhibit 2 The Saturn Philosophy

PHILOSOPHY

We, the Saturn Team, in concert with the UAW and General Motors, believe that meeting the needs of Customers, Saturn Members, Suppliers, Dealers and Neighbors is fundamental to fulfilling our mission

To meet our customers' needs:
- Our products and services must be world leaders in value and satisfaction.

To meet our members' needs:
- We will create a sense of belonging in an environment of mutual trust, respect and dignity.
- We believe that all people want to be involved in decisions that affect them, care about their jobs and each other, take pride in themselves and in their contributions and want to share in the success of their efforts.
- We will develop the tools, training and education for each member, recognizing individual skills and knowledge.
- We believe that creative, motivated, responsible team members who understand that change is critical to success are Saturn's most important asset.

To meet our suppliers and dealers' needs:
- We will strive to create real partnerships with them.
- We will be open and fair in our dealings, reflecting trust, respect and their importance to Saturn.
- We want dealers and suppliers to feel ownership in Saturn's mission and philosophy as their own.

To meet the needs of our neighbors, the communities in which we live and operate:
- We will be good citizens, protect the environment and conserve natural resources.
- We will seek to cooperate with government at all levels and strive to be sensitive, open and candid in all our public statements.

By continuously operating according to this philosophy, we will fulfill our mission.

Exhibit 3 The Saturn Manufacturing and Assembly Complex

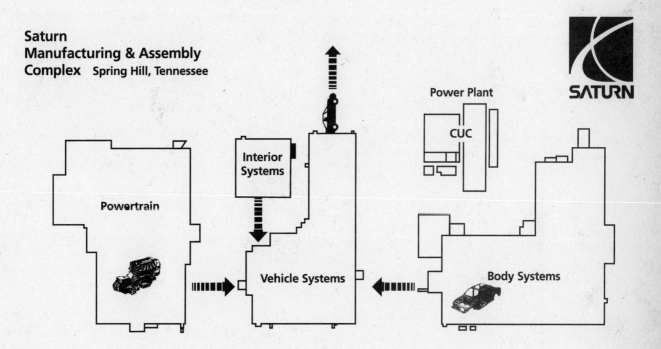

Saturn
Manufacturing & Assembly
Complex   Spring Hill, Tennessee

Power Plant

CUC

Interior
Systems

Powertrain

Vehicle Systems

Body Systems

SATURN

PART II

Building

TQM

Culture and

Management

Systems

Learning Quality Techniques at Target Stamping

Target Stamping is an American company founded in 1937 as a high precision die company, but transformed into a stamping company in the 1960s. While the company's growth plateaued in the mid 1980s, since 1988, when the company started to work for Japanese auto industry "transplants," it has shown impressive growth.

Its annual sales went from $10 million in 1987 to $23 million in 1992. Since 1988, the company has won on-going business from about 15 Japanese transplant accounts. Presently, about 80 percent of jobs come from Japanese-owned companies with production facilities in the United States. The company manufactures various types of metal stampings and stamped assemblies. The key products are parts for the steering system, interior support structure, and air-conditioner and heater systems. The company employs 160 permanent and 40 temporary employees. Virtually all of its sales (90 percent) are to the automotive market.

Prior to working for the Japanese transplant companies. Target had tried to implement quality management techniques on its shop floor, primarily at the request of GM. At the time, 65% of its total sales came from GM and GM suppliers. "GM demanded that we implement SPC." In l982, a few managers went to a local university for SPC training. In 1984, a consultant was hired by Target to lead the implementation of SPC. For the next three years, the consultant worked as a facilitator of SPC and installed a computer system for SPC. Everybody in the company was eventually trained in SPC. However, the shop floor workers "never really worked with SPC data," and "it seemed data was collected just to make GM happy" and not for the improvement of quality. According to the management, this effort was focused largely on gaining the Spear 1 status with GM. GM had suggested that, with this status, the company would be given a privilege to bid on all new jobs. In 1987, Target finally obtained the Spear 1 status from GM. However, GM added no new jobs and began to withdraw existing jobs. It was, therefore, ironic that this status led to getting more jobs from Japanese companies than from GM. "When GM withdrew jobs from us (due to some internal reasons) after giving us the Spear 1

Source: Thomas Y. Choi, College of Business Administration, Bowling Green State University, Bowling Green, Ohio. This case is based on an actual company based on data obtained via interviews with six managers and nine workers. The name of the company has been changed to ensure anonymity. This case is written based on a study funded by the U.S. Air Force Office of Scientific Research and the Japan Technology Management at the University of Michigan.

status, Honda became interested in us because of this status." This new relationship with Honda has been credited with eventually leading to more transplant accounts. "The accounts from the transplants just snowballed."

Honda started to visit Target in early 1987. What surprised the managers of Target the most was Honda's request to see the books and other financial records that were considered confidential with no promise of future jobs. Honda "saw all our dirty laundry." At the end of many visits and long conversations with Target's managers and engineers, Honda finally submitted a "target price" in early 1988 and asked the company to accept it. The target price allowed for a very tight profit margin, but the company obliged. Target subsequently made its first shipment to Honda at the end of that year.

In 1989, Target began to get more inquiries from other first-tier Japanese suppliers to Honda. In 1990, as more and more transplant supplier accounts were gained, "they gave us more stringent requirements (even compared to Honda), and we had to do more FMEA and QFD. Everybody's got their own requirements and their own forms to fill out. We must go through a learning curve for each new customer." Honda sent a representative "to help with our quality program." He talked with everybody and told us about the ideology of continuous improvement, performance quality, elimination of waste, and associate involvement. He also told us about building quality into products and foolproofing the work processes." In this way, Honda made a profound impact on this company's learning of quality management techniques. Both managers and workers acknowledged that this representative played a major role in teaching the concepts of various quality techniques. Honda also offered seminars and opened its plants for visits.

According to the managers at Target, Honda understood that with its target pricing practices, the only way to increase profit margin was to reduce wasteful practices on the shop floor. Further, the managers have approached the problem of reducing overhead on several strategic accounts. For instance, by working with the vendors, the raw material inventory has been reduced from 14% of the total sales five years ago to 1.6% of the total sales. The use of temporary workers has become more extensive using an indigenously developed screening process, which has contributed $100,000 annual savings. A company-wide freeze has been placed on hiring workers for non-value added work, and on production.

DISCUSSION QUESTIONS

1. What was GM's approach to get its supplier to implement quality techniques? What was Honda's approach? Any similarities or differences?
2. How long did it take Honda to award the first job to Target from the time of its first plant visit? Why do you think it took as long as it did?
3. What was the primary difference between GM's approach to pricing and Honda's approach to pricing?
4. With the tight target pricing, what did Target's management do to increase the profit margin?
5. We saw some evidence of Honda's effort to develop its suppliers. What are the possible reasons for investing in supplier development?
6. A subsequent survey at Target revealed that SPC, although it had been in existence the longest compared to other quality techniques, was one of least effective techniques. Why do you think this is the case?

Office of Personnel:
The Incident

The mail notice read:

> *A faculty ID card must be shown to withdraw books from the library, to use the faculty dining facilities, and to obtain the faculty discount at the University bookstore. To schedule an appointment for an ID photo, call the Personnel Office at 555-5858.*

Ann Mills had been a full-time instructor at the University for a year, but had not yet obtained a faculty ID card. Last year she had been informed that ID photos would be taken only on Mondays, Wednesdays, and Fridays at 3:30—all times when she was teaching classes. When the August notice came around, Ann placed a call to Personnel.

Male voice:	Personnel
Ann:	Hi. I need to schedule an appointment to get a faculty ID.
Male voice:	Okay. How would Friday afternoon work?
Ann:	This Friday is bad. Do you have any times next week?
Male voice:	I could give you next Wednesday at 3 o'clock.
Ann:	That would be fine.
Male voice:	How do you spell your name?
Ann:	ANN MILLS
Male voice:	And your ID number?
Ann:	210-58-5858
Male voice:	And what department are you in?
Ann:	SMG—Operations Management
Male voice:	Okay, you're all set.
Ann:	Thanks.

Source: Janelle Heineke, Boston University.

On Wednesday Ann arrived 30 minutes early at the Personnel office, hoping the picture could be taken and she could leave. She waited in line for a few minutes behind two men who were completing application forms. When she arrived at the head of the line, Ann informed the woman behind the desk that she was early for a 3 o'clock appointment for a faculty ID card.

Woman at desk:	The appointment wouldn't be for 3 o'clock. Faculty ID pictures are taken at 3:30.
Ann (politely):	The man I spoke to told me 3 o'clock.
Woman at desk:	Man? I see your name here but, we only take pictures at 3:30. I don't know who would have told you that.
Ann:	I didn't ask for his name, but he did say 3 o'clock.

At this point a tall young man walked over and rather sheepishly said,

I guess that would be me. I said 3 o'clock.

Ann (to young man):	Well, good for you for speaking up!
Woman at desk (to Ann):	Do you have your letter?
Ann:	Letter?
Woman at desk:	We need a letter to verify that you are really faculty.
Ann:	I'm sorry, but no one told me about a letter.
Woman at desk:	Well, we'll need a letter. (Looking around) You can wait or come back.
Ann:	Come back when?
Woman at desk:	At 3:30.

Ann returned at 3:30. She waited five minutes behind two men who were instructed regarding verification of information and signing their faculty ID cards, then was handed hers. Her name and ID number were correct and she signed the card and completed an information sheet as instructed. The woman at the desk reminded Ann that she needed to have a letter verifying her faculty status sent to the Personnel office and gave her an addressed envelope to use. The woman moved from behind the desk to a small room about six feet away and took pictures of the two faculty and two other new employees. Ann waited 20 minutes to have her picture taken while the others were completed, then another ten minutes for her picture to be affixed to the card, laminated, and handed to her. She left the Personnel office frustrated and angry about the interaction.

DISCUSSION QUESTIONS

1. Is the Personnel Office a service department? Who are its customers?
2. What could the people in the Personnel Office have done to make Ann's encounter more positive? Could the procedure have been changed? Was changing the procedure necessary?
3. How could some of the confusion in this situation been avoided?
4. As an employee of the same organization, what is Ann's responsibility for improving quality?
5. If you were the woman's supervisor in Personnel and overheard the interaction above, what action would you take?

Office of Personnel:
Improving Customer Satisfaction

Joe and Mary walked down Commonwealth Avenue to the Boston University Office of Personnel after their first Quality Lunch, and neither had much to say. They had been enthusiastic when they asked Mike, Bill, and Ann, all professors in the Operations Management (OM) department, to meet with them to discuss starting a Quality Improvement Program in the Office of Personnel, but the discussion had taken an unexpected turn.

The meeting had started out well enough with a lot of general enthusiasm about quality management concepts all around the table, but during dessert, Bill turned to Ann and asked, "Did you show Joe and Mary the case you wrote?" Ann looked a little uncomfortable, but began her story about her recent visit to the Office of Personnel.

> *This is my first year here and I'd already been through the new faculty orientation, but I still needed to get a BU ID card to be able to use the library and to get a computer account. So I called your office and made an appointment for 3:00 one afternoon. When I got there I was rather rudely told that I could not have the ID made until 3:30—and the receptionist informed me that no one would have told me that 3:00 would be possible. Finally a work-study student stepped up and admitted that he had scheduled the appointment. He hadn't told me about needing a letter from my department chairman, either, but they told me they would make the card for me anyway. I had to either wait or come back later, so I left and came back and then had to wait for another half-hour behind two other faculty members. Making the ID couldn't have taken two minutes! I was really frustrated and upset when I left—so I wrote a case about it to use in my Quality Management course.*

Ann had been matter-of-fact in her description of the incident, but Mary, the Director of the Office of Personnel, was embarrassed. "The first few weeks of a new semester are always really hectic and we're very short staffed. We don't have the resources to deal with the peaks in demand. We only have one receptionist and she's responsible for answering phones, greeting people, making IDs, scheduling . . ."

Source: Janelle Heineke, Boston University.

Mike interrupted. "Mary, that's not a quality answer. You know that there are busy times and they're pretty predictable. If you really want to serve your customers better, you'll be prepared."

There was awkward silence around the table for a few seconds, then Mary said, "Ann, can I have a copy of your case?"

"Sure," Ann replied. "The real point of the case is that no one is to blame, but the system needs to be fixed to serve customers better."

Talk had turned to more general quality topics and the rest of the lunch was uneventful. As Mary and Joe approached their offices, though, they agreed that it was time to pay some attention to the Personnel Reception Area. They knew, from Ann's story and from other complaints, that customer satisfaction was generally not very high and they had done enough general quality training in the department to form a Quality Improvement Team.

The Work of the QIT

One month later, the Office of Personnel's first Quality Improvement Team had been formed to address issues of effectiveness and customer satisfaction in the reception area. There were four team members: Paul, Amy, Adam, and Susan, the receptionist. Four managers agreed to function as a steering committee, offering help and resources when necessary.

During the first team meeting the group agreed to collect data on the kinds of tasks the receptionist performed. They all felt that a written questionnaire to get customer feedback would be a good idea and that developing the questionnaire together would be their first joint task. Each of them would take on another task, too.

- Susan would keep a checklist that identified the number of phone calls received each day by the receptionist.
- Paul and Amy agreed to observe the reception area for one hour each week to see how customers moved through the physical setting and how they acted.
- Adam agreed to identify the steps for scheduling and producing a faculty ID card.

The group met for one hour each week for a month. By the end of that time, the questionnaire (**Exhibit 1**) had been developed—and reviewed by Ann in the OM department—and data on the phones had been tabulated (**Table 1**).

Adam presented the steps he had identified for producing a faculty ID. First, a mail notice was sent by the Office of Personnel to all faculty, reminding them that IDs were made on Monday and Wednesday afternoons and that appointments were necessary. Then, when a faculty member called, whoever answered the phones would check the schedule, offer a time, and write the appointment on the calendar. The faculty members were informed that a letter verifying faculty status was required to make an initial or replacement ID.

When faculty members arrived at the Office of Personnel, the receptionist (or work-study student) would greet them and ask them to fill out a form with name, social security number, title, and signature. The receptionist would then ask for their letters of verification of faculty status and, if the letters could be produced, ask them to wait until all ID customers arrived so that picture taking could be done in a "batch." If a member of the faculty did not have an employment verification letter, the receptionist would call the faculty member's department to verbally verify employment. Once pictures were taken, faculty members waited again for the photos to develop and for the cards to be laminated.

This procedure was not written down, but was the way Susan had been told to do faculty IDs. Because work-study students often helped staff the reception desk, however, the procedure was not always followed because they were not certain of the steps involved.

Susan began to administer the questionnaires to "customers" of the reception area one week after it was completed. During the first week, seven faculty members, 20 staff members, and 34 job applicants completed surveys. The questionnaire asked customers to evaluate the promptness, courteousness, and overall impression of their service at the reception desk on a five point scale where 1 indicated poor service and 5 indicated very good service. The first 11 people to complete the survey responded as shown in the **Table 2**.

Most customers indicated that they were satisfied with their experiences, but 43 customers wrote comments that indicated that they were displeased with the service they received. Their comments were categorized by the Quality Improvement Team as related to information, attitude, process, decor, and other (**Table 3**).

DISCUSSION QUESTIONS

1. State the quality improvement theme for the Office of Personnel.
2. Using the data provided in Table 1, produce a run chart of calls received in the Personnel reception area for the data collection period.
3. Draw a process flow diagram of the procedure for processing faculty ID cards.
4. Produce a bar chart which shows the types of respondents to the Office of Personnel Survey using the information provided in the case.
5. Using the data in Table 2, produce scatter plots that show (1) the relationship between survey respondents' satisfaction with promptness and overall satisfaction and (2) the relationship between survey respondents' satisfaction with courteousness and overall satisfaction.
6. Using the data in Table 3, develop a Pareto diagram that shows the categories of survey comments.
7. Using the data in Table 3, produce a fishbone diagram, including the "effect" statement. For each cause brainstorm items that might contribute to each cause (ask the 5 "WHYs").

Exhibit 1 Office of Personnel Customer Satisfaction Survey

Date: _____

1. Is this your first visit to Boston University?   ❏ Yes   ❏ No

2. Is this your first visit to the Boston University   ❏ Yes   ❏ No
    Office of Personnel?

3. Did you have a scheduled appointment?   ❏ Yes   ❏ No

4. How often do you conduct business in the Office of Personnel?

    ❏ Daily   ❏ Weekly   ❏ Monthly   ❏ Once a year or less

5. Are you: ❏ Faculty   ❏ Staff   ❏ Other _____

    ❏ Job applicant (not employed by Boston University)

6. What was the purpose of your visit?

    ❏ Job Application/View Job Posting   ❏ Orientation

    ❏ Promotion & Transfer Application   ❏ Training

    ❏ Identification Card   ❏ Benefits Information

    ❏ Meeting with Personnel Staff member.   With whom? (optional)

    ❏ Meeting with a member of the Administrative Service Staff.   With whom? (optional)

    ❏ Other

	POOR	SATISFACTORY		VERY GOOD	
	1	2	3	4	5
7. Evaluate the PROMPTNESS of the service you received in the front lobby.	❏	❏	❏	❏	❏
8. Evaluate the COURTEOUSNESS of the service you received in the front lobby.	❏	❏	❏	❏	❏
9. What was your overall impression of the service you received at Personnel's front office?	❏	❏	❏	❏	❏

10. Was the information you requested provided?   ❏ Yes   ❏ No

    (If yes, was it helpful: Please explain. If not, please explain why it did not meet your needs.)

    _____

11. Do you have recommendations or suggestions to help us better serve you? (Please explain below.)
    ●

PLEASE USE THE SPACE BELOW TO EXPLAIN ANY OF YOUR ANSWERS OR TO MAKE OTHER COMMENTS.
(Please feel free to use the back of this survey to write additional comments.)

_____

_____

If you would like to discuss your experience further, please leave your name and phone number and a staff
member will call you. _____

THANK YOU FOR TAKING THE TIME TO COMPLETE THIS SURVEY.

Please drop this form in the sealed box by the exit. All information will be kept confidential and will be used solely
for the purpose of improving the services delivered by the Office of Personnel.

TABLE 1 Phone Calls Received in the Reception Area (by day of week)

Week	Day	Number of Calls
1	Monday	164
	Tuesday	122
	Wednesday	124
	Thursday	126
	Friday	106
2	Monday	159
	Tuesday	118
	Wednesday	122
	Thursday	120
	Friday	109
3	Monday	155
	Tuesday	124
	Wednesday	119
	Thursday	130
	Friday	102
4	Monday	161
	Tuesday	120
	Wednesday	128
	Thursday	118
	Friday	99

TABLE 2 Individual Responses to Survey Questions on Satisfaction

Person	Satisfaction with Promptness	Satisfaction with Courteousness	Satisfaction Overall
1	3	1	1
2	3	2	2
3	2	3	2
4	2	1	3
5	3	2	3
6	4	3	3
7	5	4	3
8	3	4	4
9	4	5	4
10	5	4	5
11	4	5	5

TABLE 3 Categories of Survey Comments

Category	Comment	Number
Information	No follow-up sent	2
	No copies of job postings	6
	No information provided by phone	2
	Jobs posted slowly	3
	Information not provided	3
Attitude	Receptionist rude	11
	Receptionist pre-occupied	2
Process	ID hours poor	1
	Phones too busy	3
	No customization of service	1
	4 job limit	1
	Too much work for one person	3
Decor	Lobby not cheerful	3
Other	No water fountain	2

Selma Instruments Company

The Selma Instruments Company was the successful bidder on a contract, offered by the prime contractor, for a component of an intercontinental missile. Two important items for this component had to be purchased from outside suppliers. These were 5,000 instrument housings and 100,000 transistors. In bidding on this contract the company had cut its quotation approximately to cost. As a result, after the award, instructions were sent to all departments to increase their efficiency in every respect in order to meet the price commitment.

The purchasing manager discovered that the contract provided large progress payments during its two-year term. Therefore, the financing of inventories, one of the usual considerations in setting inventory levels, could be disregarded. Under these circumstances the company could place orders for immediate delivery of its entire requirements rather than spacing shipments over the two-year period.

Competition to supply the transistor and the instrument housings was keen, and the Selma Company was able to negotiate considerably lower prices than those originally estimated. The transistor order was given to a single supplier, and the housing order was split between two suppliers with whom the company had had a long and satisfactory relationship.

The transistors were purchased subject to the manufacturer's standard warranty. The packages stated plainly that replacement would be made for any transistor found to be defective within one year of the date of delivery. The Selma Company inspection department followed a different inspection practice depending on the product. When transportation costs were high, inspection was conducted at the supplier's plant. Statistical sampling techniques were used for high-volume technical items with close tolerance levels. When an item was procured that carried a guarantee (mostly shelf-stock items), a visual identity inspection by the receiving department was deemed sufficient.

After a period of 16 months, it was discovered that there had been an undue proportion of defective transistors. By this time about 30% of the transistors had gone into production.

Because the Selma Company had realized that all its departments would be working at or beyond their capacity, its contract with one of the housing

Source: Gary J. Zenz with George H. Thompson, *Purchasing and the Management of Materials.* John Wiley & Sons, Inc., New York, Seventh Edition, 1994, pp. 668–670.

suppliers had specified that inspection would be done at the supplier's plant by a Selma Company inspector. In this way the pressure on the Selma Company's inspection facilities would be reduced. Each housing required 45 minutes for inspection because of the close tolerances specified. The purchase from the second supplier of housings was governed by the standard clause of the Selma Company's purchase order, which stated, "Material is subject to inspection for a period of 75 days after delivery."

As source-inspected material was received from the supplier, it was moved directly to the production line. Housings from the other supplier were stored for later use. This procedure was followed by the inspection department because of the many activities it had to perform during the initial stages of the contract. Delivery by both housing suppliers was completed within four months. It was not until after seven months that housings from the second supplier moved onto the production line. The first 10 housings inspected were immediately rejected because holes had been drilled in the wrong places.

The supplier was called in at once but refused to take responsibility for replacement. It was pointed out that the Selma Company had had adequate time to inspect the housings and that if they had inspected them within the prescribed period, the error could have been corrected before the order was completed. Since the supplier had already been paid, it was assumed that the shipments had been satisfactory. The supplier agreed that the holes were slightly misplaced but pointed out that the Selma Company had dealt with the supplier company for years and had frequently specified closer tolerances than necessary and had not previously rejected goods that had exceeded tolerances. The supplier felt that he should have been warned if this contract was to be subject to different standards of acceptance.

DISCUSSION QUESTIONS

1. What courses of action are open to the purchasing manager of the Selma Company in these two cases?
2. Could this situation have been avoided?
3. Should shelf-stock items be inspected as received if they are procured in such quantities that they will not be used before the guarantee period has passed?

Fielding Industrial Plastics

Al Fielding, Sr. founded Fielding Industrial Plastics in Havelock, North Carolina, as a supplier of specific parts for the coal mining industry. In 1977, he moved the company to his hometown of Wilson, Texas. With high expectations for the sale of chutes used in coal washing, it appeared that a superior product could offset his company's remote location. With a starting capital of $30,000, Al felt confident his business could survive. However, it soon became obvious that the coal mining industry was not coming to Texas for Fielding's product.

Al Fielding, Jr., a graduate of Georgia Tech in mechanical engineering had begun an excellent career in Atlanta when it became evident that his father's company needed help. With a one-year guarantee for half of his present salary, Al, Jr. returned to Texas. However, even with Al, Jr. the company floundered without a steady cash flow and Al, Jr. reentered the job market as a sales-manager to supplement his parents' income.

In 1980, knowledge and luck produced the strike needed for success. Al, Jr. fielded an inquiry by a North Carolina firm concerning the manufacture of a vacuum seal for paper machines. Called a suction roll strip, the product was to provide a seal allowing air to be sucked through wet paper sheets to shape and dry them. Not familiar with the industry, but confident in their abilities, the Fieldings began researching the product. The inquiring company provided machine support to establish the plant and the Fieldings entered the suction roll seal business. To secure the support, they agreed to make the other corporation the sole distributor and drop ship under their name.

The first product was a polyester product utilizing Dacron fibers. Its initial reception was startling as sales volume jumped 600% in the first year. It seemed that everything was working smoothly when reports of product failure began filtering down to the company. Al, Jr. requested an on-site inspection to discern the problem, but the distributor preferred that "outsiders" did not meet with the customer. Intensive product investigation revealed a serious flaw: The original specifications called for an operating temperature of 180 degrees. Unfortunately, in temperatures above this level, thermal expansion caused the seals to wear unevenly, operating temperatures to further increase,

Source: Elizabeth Schubert and Lawrence A. Ward, Louisiana Tech University and Robert Orwig, Northeast Louisiana University.

and eventual product deterioration. Research and development returned to the drawing boards to correct these deficiencies.

One day, in passing conversation, a supplier suggested that Al, Jr. try Kevlar. Using Kevlar, he found that he could combine felt and long fibers to reduce the thermal expansion, increase strength, and provide prolonged longevity. This K-2 material became the mainstay of Fielding Plastics developments.

During this time, the distributor continually asked Fielding to reproduce a lesser quality product, similar to that of its competitors. By chance, Al, Jr. obtained a product sample from the market. The distributor was marketing it as Fielding's K-2, but obviously it was not. Litigation led to a settlement whereby Fielding Industrial Plastics purchased the remaining equity on the equipment and was released from its contractual obligations. The next day Al, Jr. closed a deal with a customer that realized the true "K-2" it had been purchasing from the distributor was Fielding's product.

Although maintaining a low volume of production, Fielding Plastics proceeded to grow and the S-corporation provided a satisfactory income to the six shareholders. Al, Sr. was content to enjoy the fruits of his labors without aggressively seeking expansion. His attitude was justifiable in many respects when viewing the financial figures:

Year	Sales	Purchases
93	$854,904.50	$186,662.66
92	$765,741.85	$218,833.35
91	$858,971.61	$220,392.41
90	$792,701.30	$207,868.02
89	$632,723.39	$198,380.92

In 1991, following a transition period in which Al, Jr. took on more responsibility, Al, Sr. retired and passed control to his son. Al, Jr. knew that consistent expansion would be necessary to support the six shareholders. Two choices were available: competing domestically with established products, or penetrating the European market where his superior product was not well-known. The latter option turned his attention toward the Scandinavian market. He decided to hire a marketing sales manager, enroll his workforce in Total Quality Management courses, and work with a local university to develop a responsible expansion program.

PRODUCTS

Fielding Industrial Plastics produces two main products: the suction roll seal strip and the spreader bar. The Polytron K-2, the suction roll seal strip, is the primary product. It combines Kevlar and Teflon in a product which Fielding describes as "too good" because of its longevity. A Teflon strip provides a seal which wears smoothly and provides a depth gauge to assist in customer evaluation. Because customers employ various machines with rigid specifications, Fielding records measurements and order frequency for each customer. The second primary product, the spreader bar, maintains constant tension on the paper as it rolls out, thus ensuring it does not shift or fold. Like the suction roll seal strip, it is of extremely high quality. Fielding holds patents on the K-2 material in both the U.S. and Canada and is prepared to vigorously defend them.

Fielding also sells the raw K-2 product, which is a steady "cash cow." However, the only use for this product is to manufacture products competing with Fielding's finished lines. Al, Jr. views the raw material sales as necessary since many customers are content to purchase the raw material and employ subcontractors to produce their end product. Al feels that if he restricts his customers to purchasing only the finished product, they may turn to a lower quality item to maintain control.

While Fielding's plant could produce additional products, development has not been pursued. Research falls under Al, Sr. who maintains a small, but well-equipped shop that allows him to respond to potential problems. Little interest is directed toward the potential recycling of trimmings from the primary products. Trimmings consisting of dust, shavings, and small slivers could be recombined with polymer to produce smaller, less structurally critical products.

PLANT LAYOUT

The layout of the plant is illustrated in **Exhibit 1**.

Production flow proceeds from the rear of the shop to the lay-up table and then unidirectionally across the various operation tables. Each section of the shop is self-sufficient and performs its function either in sequence with the other tables or from base stock maintained on the racks. Capacity is limited primarily by the lay-up table which accommodates only one layout per day. Al, Jr. is working to develop a lay-up box assembly that would free up the lay-up table and allow multiple pourings per day.

PROCESS

Developing Polytron is not mechanically intricate, but chemically rather complicated. As with all chemical processes, temperature is critical and must be strictly controlled. Chemicals are carefully measured and blended in the mixing room with specificity and patience. Once mixed, a thin sheet of Mylar film is laid on the table and the resin-based combination is poured out on the lay-out table much like spreading syrup. Once the layer is spread, felt and fiber Kevlar fabrics are immersed in the mixture in specific sequences. The procedure is repeated to achieve desired thickness; then a Mylar sheet is placed over the mixture. Both temperature and humidity are critical to the process so a log is kept daily to monitor the chemical reactions in case of raw material inconsistencies.

Once cured, the sheet is moved to the planer and planed to tolerance, then to the ripper table for edge trimming and lengthwise cuts to order. At this point the product is completed for the stock rack or a material order. Specific machined orders may be continued to the machining stations and the finishing table where angles, contours, and grooves are machined to the established tolerance. The finishing table also addresses final sanding, waxing, and installation of Teflon inserts.

STAFFING

Exhibit 2 illustrates Fielding Plastics' organizational chart. Al, Jr. readily admits that the "one-man" direction will eventually have to be relinquished, but he does not look forward to it.

MARKETING EFFORTS

Initially, marketing was handled by the distributor; later, sales representatives were handled through the front office. Shortly after Al, Jr. incorporated his own style of management, it became obvious that a full-time sales manager was needed to facilitate expansion. Al, Jr.'s wife, Sandra, had extensive experience in sales and was a natural choice for the family company. She was hired to coordinate sales efforts and serve as a liaison between the company, representatives, and customers. **Exhibit 3** illustrates the sales territories and customer locations.

Sandra immediately added six representatives to blanket the lucrative North East market. The decision facing Fielding's staff is the best approach to the European Market if and when the move is finally made. Al, Jr. is currently busy in two Scandinavian countries showing the product as viable to their needs. Sandra is trying to determine the best manner of providing the product: direct order, distributorships, or licensed manufacturing.

Al, Jr. sees the evolution into Europe as one which entails the direct sale of product to distributors. In time he envisions developing a warehousing hub with individual subcontractors licensed to machine the K-2 seal strip in the individual market zones. This would preclude direct involvement in the personnel, marketing, and quality assurance concerns.

ISO 9000

While examining the prospects for business in Europe, Al, Jr. was introduced to ISO 9000, a series of five international standards that establish requirements for the quality systems of organizations. Al learned that as Europe has become more economically unified, ISO 9000 has become a tool to ensure cross-border quality. The European Community (EC) currently requires regulated products to be registered to ISO 9000 standards and encourages other producers to register their products. Registered companies display the EC mark as a seal of approval and ISO 9000 is becoming a de facto market requirement for companies desiring to do business with the EC, and increasingly with other areas of the world.

Due to the great emphasis on ISO 9000 quality standards, Al, Jr. realizes that he must pursue certification if he intends for Fielding Plastics to gain and hold a competitive position in Europe. Looking over several articles and a book loaned to him from the local university, Al, Jr. began to see the enormity of changes he would need to incorporate. Some of the quality system elements covered by ISO 9000 include: management responsibility; quality system; document control; process control; design control; control of non-conforming product; corrective action; handling, storage, packaging, and delivery; and quality records, quality audits, training and servicing. Al, Jr. noticed that many of the requirements focus upon control systems and documentation, which Fielding has not concentrated on in the past.

ADMINISTRATION

Originating as a two-man show, the Fieldings saw little need for extensive documentation. Through the rapid expansion Al, Jr. felt no need to change that philosophy and still operates from his financial data. Looking at the documentation required for ISO 9000 Al, Jr. just cannot understand why he needs production or raw material documentation. Regarding quality control, no paperwork has ever been kept since a responsible man checks the output. Grudgingly, Al, Jr. is beginning to realize that international operations may require him to modify his procedures. His present habit of operating on monthly financial figures is comfortable to him, but will not meet long-term needs.

DISCUSSION QUESTIONS

Current questions facing Fielding Plastics include:

1. Would complying with ISO 9000 require drastic changes within the company and large expenses associated with the certification process?
2. Could transformations to meet the requirements be accomplished by the time Fielding wants to begin European entry? Al has to decide quickly whether to pursue the ISO 9000 certification; if pursued, what time frame to assign to the transformations; and, whether to launch an expansion into Europe before or after the ISO 9000 certification is obtained.

Exhibit 1 Plant Layout

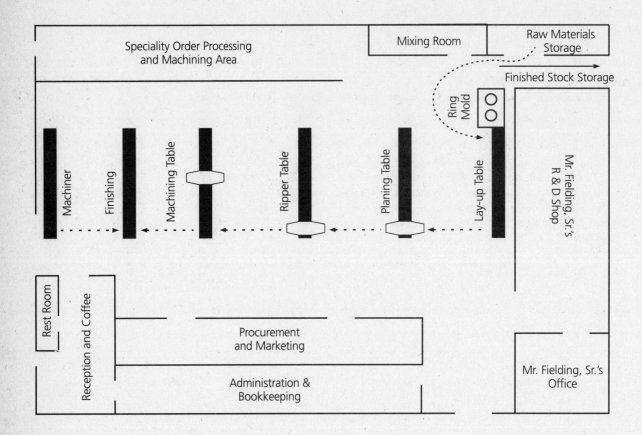

Exhibit 2 Fielding Staffing

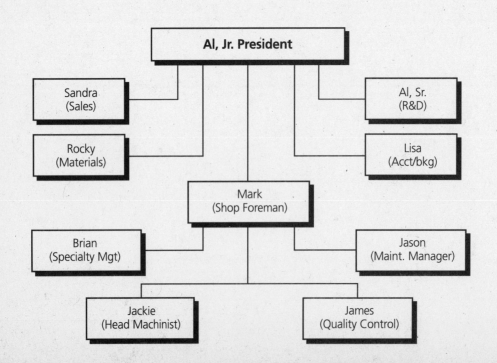

Exhibit 3 Fieldings Plastics Domestic Market

★ CURRENT CUSTOMERS

● POTENTIAL CUSTOMERS

Note: Numbers in northeast states indicate potential customers.

TQM and Mobil Chemical's Washington, N.J. Facility

Total Quality Management (TQM) is a management philosophy that strives to involve the entire organization in efforts to satisfy customers. This can take the form of customer surveys, products/processes designed for quality, statistical process control, preventive maintenance, greater involvement with suppliers and distributors, and extensive employee training programs. TQM involves employee empowerment and the use of team problem solving. An important component of TQM is continuous improvement (CI), which seeks gradual, continuous improvements of products and processes as opposed to dramatic steps in improvement. One way for companies to do this is through competitive benchmarking. This entails identifying firms known for "excellence in manufacturing" (world-class leaders), and by visiting these plants in order to analyze the disparities between world-class plants and one's own firm.

Many organizations including Mobil Chemical are looking to TQM as one mechanism for becoming more competitive in a global marketplace. At the Mobil Chemical's Washington, N.J. plant, efforts in this direction began in 1991.

MOBIL CHEMICAL AND ITS WASHINGTON, N.J. FACILITY

Mobil Chemical is a wholly-owned subsidiary of the Mobil Corporation and is an integrated manufacturer of petrochemicals, polypropylene packaging films, additives and synthetics, and fabricated plastics products for institutional and consumer markets. Figures for 1992 show that Mobil Chemical employs over 14,000 employees with a total sales revenue more than $4 billion. It operates 27 domestic facilities and six international sites. If Mobil Chemical were an independent company separate from Mobil Corporation, it would be a Fortune 200 company in its own right. Mobil Chemical's four major divisions are Chemical Products, Petrochemicals, Plastics, and Films.

Built in 1972, Mobil Chemical's Washington facility is one of 11 plants in Mobil Chemical's Plastics division. The plant, located on 75 acres in Washington, New Jersey, has 225,000 square feet with 80,000 square feet for

Source: Harold Dyck and Sue Greenfeld, School of Business and Public Administration, California State University, San Bernardino.

production and the balance for warehousing and storage. There are 9,000 skids located on-site and 32,000 skids at an off-site location. The primary products are plastic trash bags of the Hefty line including "Twist-Tie," and "CinchSak." The "Twist-Tie" can run six lines capable of producing 46 million pounds per year. The "CinchSak," started in 1988, can run four lines with a yearly capacity of 27 million pounds. The reclaim department has two lines capable of 18 million pounds per year, for internally generated scrap and outside purchased scrap. The plant, with 143 people, has three shifts and runs seven days a week, 24 hours per day (8 a.m.–4 p.m., 4 p.m.–midnight, midnight–8 a.m.). The plant layout is presented in **Exhibit 1**.

Plant manager Win Clemmons indicated that the Washington facility became OSHA Star certified for the first time in 1986 and recertified in 1989 and 1992. This certification is part of OSHA's Voluntary Protection Program (VPP). This program was initiated in 1982 to establish a cooperative relationship in the workplace between management, labor, and government, and to recognize and promote effective safety and health management.

THE PRODUCTION PROCESS

The production process begins when polyethylene resin is unloaded from rail-cars located behind the plant facilities. It is then stored in silos that hold up to 120,000 pounds (equivalent to one railcar). The resin is piped into blending systems by the use of blowers, and controls and power are designed to minimize noise, dust, and employee exposure to risk of fire or explosion. A dust collector keeps dust from entering the atmosphere. Refer to **Exhibit 2** for a picture of the extrusion flow diagram.

The resin pellets are fed into the extruders through a hopper. There are six extruders for "Twist-Tie" and two extruders for "CinchSak." The extruders heat (300°) the resin pellets to a liquid form. Coloring takes place with a dye which has been shipped by large trucks and unloaded at the loading docks. An operator monitors the extrusion process through a system of controls, alarms and warning devices.

Once melted, the resin is forced out through a circular device called a die. Almost like a large cyclone, a bubble of continuous plastic is pulled upward, inflated and cooled as it extends to four stories in height. Some of the cooled extruded material will go directly into bag making machines in the "Twist-Tie" lines while other material will be placed on large rolls for "CinchSak" lines. "Twist-Tie" is a continuous process while "CinchSak" is a two-step process. One advantage of the latter process is the flexibility that rolls provide. They can be moved around to different lines, or placed in storage. However, the just-in-time manufacturing philosophy may not see this as an advantage. Throughout the process, statistical quality control charts are used to insure uniformity of the product.

The collapsed bubble of plastic forms one long double-layered sheet that is cut and sealed into bags (e.g., "Hefty" kitchen and trash bags, etc.). The bags are folded, counted, and packed into predetermined box-sizes (e.g., 18, 24, 30 counts). After the product is boxed, finished product is placed on wooden pallets where they are wrapped with stretch material before being either stored or shipped. Scrap material is returned to the two reclaim lines to be eventually turned into new bags.

Until 1992, the packaging was labor intensive, but "now, no one touches the bags anymore, except for quality checking," says Donna Murling, Safety/Training Facilitator at the Washington, N.J. facility. Previously, people worked eight hours a day slapping coupons on a stack of bags going by on a conveyer belt. Back injuries, carpal tunnel syndrome and other ergonomic problems were eliminated through automation. Equipment is run by programmable logic controllers (PLCs).

Safety and quality are two distinct aspects related to the automation of a manufacturing system. All machinery in the Washington, N.J. plant has protective Plexiglas guards to prevent unauthorized access. Conveyer belts over walkways and aisles have yellow safety netting underneath them. Throughout the plant, railings and other guarded areas are painted bright yellow. When maintenance is performed on any machine, the machine is completely turned off and secured with a safety lock, preventing it from being turned on accidentally during the maintenance procedure. Quality is also affected by automation through standardization. Variation in process time and other variables are minimized.

TQM AND CONTINUOUS PRODUCT IMPROVEMENT EFFORTS

Prior to 1991, there was a Quality Leadership Team (QLT) composed of the plant manager and staff who met monthly to discuss strategic issues. The QLT did not include hourly workers close to the process. Following a consultant's recommendation, the QT was expanded to 20 individuals (including ten hourly and ten salaried workers) who participated in a "High Involvement Seminar." The focus of the QLT meetings changed from informative to participative, and the team was challenged to look at where the plant needed the most help. One issue was: How could they translate information from these monthly meetings into meaningful implementation? Some questions from those early meetings included: Should they create an organizational design team? Should they call in another consultant? Should they visit other facilities? Which management practices could they adopt? Also it became apparent that there was some frustration from hourly personnel who did not have a means to channel their suggestions. The QLT wanted to address this frustration.

In 1991, as a means for resolving some of these issues, the plant created its own internal 5-point Star Quality Program. This 5-point Star Quality Program is divided along five functional areas: Quality & Productivity, Safety, Planning, Learning & Development, and Personnel. A quality and productivity facilitator was also hired to help launch the new program. These plant initiatives complemented divisional activities, such as the implementation of Juran's philosophy, and statistical process control. **Exhibit 3** shows the purpose and the vision of The Star Model.

To help them address some of their concerns, the QLT wanted to see how other organizations used teams. Specifically, in April of 1991, Mark Geuss, Manager of Employee Relations, and Production Manager Jeff Phillips, visited a Du Pont plant in Pennsylvania. This visit was prompted by a *Fortune* magazine article in which Du Pont's team-based organizations were referenced. A second visit with the entire QLT group to Du Pont's plant followed in May, 1991. Du Pont has been engaged in implementing ISO 9000 which is a certification process for those companies desiring to trade with the European Community (EC). International Organization for Standardization's (ISO) Quality Management and Quality Assurance Committees created the ISO 9000 standards to "force the establishment of quality management procedures on firms doing business in the EC. . . . The standards may achieve worldwide acceptance."[1]

They also visited Stanley Vidmar, part of Stanley Works of Connecticut. These visits proved invaluable given them working example of how to organize natural work teams. According to Mark Geuss, "it really does pay to get the people closest to the process involved in the decision making. You can't pay lip service. If anything will shoot you in the foot faster, it is trying to implement high involvement, but retaining control. They see through that like you wouldn't believe. It is difficult for some of our managers to grasp."

The Quality and Productivity Point of the 5-Point Star

"Quality and productivity" is one point on the 5-Point Star with a leadership committee of 14 employees including management and hourly employees. The overall mission statement for this point is to "develop and facilitate the process of improvement in the plant by providing guidance for the [Process Improvement Teams] PITs." Individual mission statements have been developed for CinchSak, Twist-Tie, Recycle, Warehouse, Maintenance, QC and Downgauging. **Exhibit 4** presents the Quality & Productivity Subcommittee mission statements.

To improve the quality of the "Hefty" bags, statistical process improvement (SPI) charts track several variables at various points of the production process. **Exhibit 5** shows an example of a SPI x-bar and r chart for the variable "width" on line 776A. Notice that on the 14th subsample action was taken to increase the width when the range became large. Also notice the out-of-control point on the 37th subsample.

In terms of improving the scheduling process, scheduler Sam Rafalko receives a monthly rough cut of the production requirements for each line from Mobil Chemical Plastics headquarters in Rochester, N.Y., where two- to three-month forecasts for product demand takes place. Headquarters gives case quantities for each line. After the weekly production meeting with the plant manager and personnel from production, engineering and maintenance, Sam puts a ten-day schedule for the operating lines onto a magnetic wall board. For example, there may be 1,600 cases of "Twist-Ties" that will run on line 703 from the eleventh until the twentieth of the month. The schedule assumes 100% line utilization, but he modifies the schedule as the plant runs ahead or behind its production goals. He updates the schedule as changes come in.

The schedule shows the item number, the case quantity, the day Rochester wants the line to start, and specifics about the item itself (i.e., count, gauge, nonpoly part numbers, ship dimension, corrugate dimension and approximately the number of cases to be produced daily). From that, Sam orders the "nonpoly" corrugated cardboard, glue, tape, drawstrings, coupons and any other items in the right quantities so that delivery will be in time for each production run. Warehousing time is minimal. For example, "nonpoly" and other items used to arrive two weeks prior to their scheduled use; but now, warehousing runs around three days. This has decreased warehousing costs and has minimized problems associated with the "nonpoly" becoming damaged or dirty.

Purchase orders for some items are sent to Rochester, N.Y. where they are bought in large quantities. The Washington, N.J. plant has its own suppliers for

---

1 Barry Render and Jay Heizer, *Principles of Operations Management: Building and Managing World-Class Operations*, Boston, MA, Prentice-Hall, 1995, p. 93.

such items as corrugate, draw strings, and glue. Currently, there are two cor-rugate suppliers, but Mobil Chemical may be moving to one supplier in the near future.

Inventories of finished goods (i.e., "CinchSaks" and "Twist-Ties") have also decreased over time as these goods are shipped as they are made on a regular basis. This has helped to reduce obsolescence of finished goods, and minimize the need for repackaging. A distribution information system keeps track of the locations and status of all items in transit.

Planned preventive maintenance occurs continually, but a complete plant shutdown for a total maintenance servicing occurs twice a year. These times are two weeks in the summer and the period between Christmas and New Year's Day.

The Safety Point of the 5-Point Star

Safety is another point on the 5-point Star. A structured weekly meeting occurs that includes about 34 people (or 26% of the total plant); of these 34 people about 28 are hourly employees. A typical meeting involves introducing guests, reviewing first aid/near miss/recordable injuries, reviewing the injury inci-dence rates,[2] giving reports, discussing OSHA regulations, VPP business, and other agenda items. Currently, a "CinchSak" operator, Bob Keating, is the Chair (or Strategic Leader) of the Safety Leadership Committee.

As an example of the preventive role it plays, the committee reviewed a Safety Improvement Opportunity Form (IOF) which noted a potential problem close to a doorway inside the plant where three- to four-foot heavy metal bins had been stacked three high. The danger existed of a fork-lift knocking these bins over, possibly injuring a worker. As a result of an investigation, foot traf-fic was re-routed, and a guardrail was erected, creating a buffer zone. Bins were required to be stacked no more than two high along the buffer zone, thus averting an unsafe incident. A potentially dangerous situation had been cor-rected before an accident had occurred.

To heighten safety awareness in the plant, past committee projects have included a "safety passport" and a yearly calendar. The "safety passport" is an incentive plan that awards $50 gift certificates for those who perform 12 safety actions (three per quarter) over a year. Safety actions include becom-ing CPR certified, submitting a safety suggestion, attending safety circle meetings and nine other types of activities. The design of the yearly plant cal-endar is also used to promote safety. A safety contest is conducted where employees' children and grandchildren submit illustrated safety posters, with slogans such as "Stay away from buzzing bees. If you bother them, they will sting," or "Don't jump on the bed, you might fall and hit your head." An outside panel of judges select the 12 or so pictures to be included. Although the calendar is expensive to produce, it has been very popular with the employees.

The implementation of the internal Star program has caused a number of issues to surface. These include peer appraisal, employee assistance programs, policy and procedures, and recreation. For example, should doctors come and give annual hearing tests, blood tests, or prescribe smoking cessation patches?

---

[2]   Injury incidence rates are calculated as $(N/EH) \times 200,000$ where:
       N = number of recordable injuries in one year
       EH = total number of hours worked by all employees in one year
       200,000 = equivalent of 100 full-time workers working 40 hour weeks for 50 weeks per year

What would be the cost of these benefits? How well would these be received? Could there be possible problems of privacy?

In terms of safety, the net result has been impressive. One measure of the plant's success has included a 1991 President's Cup award to the facility as the plant with lowest incidence rate among the 11 plants in the Plastics Division. Their incidence rate in 1991 was 1.35.

THE DEBATE OVER WORKER-MANAGEMENT TEAMS

Worker-management teams, such as the QLT, have not been without controversy. According to a *Wall Street Journal* (WSJ) article, a major ruling by the National Labor Relations Board (NLRB) in June of 1993 ordered Du Pont to "disband seven such panels and to deal instead with the company's chemical workers union."[3] The Board maintained that Du Pont circumvented the union because decisions made by these management-labor teams were actually subject to management approval. Unions assert that the company cannot bypass the union as the bargaining agent.

However, U.S. Department of Labor Secretary Robert B. Reich is a supporter of worker-management teams, and views them as a mechanism to solve problems in the workplace. At the state level, some states are already *requiring* worker-management teams for workplace safety issues. In Connecticut, "companies must begin establishing worker-management teams to investigate accidents, evaluate prevention programs, and determine possible safety fixes."[4] Others states following suit include Alaska, Minnesota, Nebraska, North Carolina, Oregon, Tennessee, Washington, and West Virginia. As a nonunionized plant, the Washington, N.J. facility is somewhat removed from the legal debate surrounding worker-management teams.

DISCUSSION QUESTIONS

As Mobil Chemical's Washington, N.J. facility looks towards meeting its customers needs, plant personnel wonder:

1. Will they be able to establish a solid base of operation whereby every member is involved in continual improvement?
2. Will they be able build a cohesive, informed workforce capable of performing quality workmanship with cost reduction and technology improvement?
3. Will they be able to work together as a team, and how does teamwork lead to individual promotion and compensation?
4. Will direct employee involvement in safety improve plant safety performance, and long-run cost savings?

---

3   Kevin Salwen, "Du Pont Is Told It Must Disband Nonunion Panels," *The Wall Street Journal*, June 7, 1993, A2.
4   Jyoti Thottam and Kevin G. Salwen, "As U.S. Mulls Worker-Safety Mandate, Some States Require Company Action," *The Wall Street Journal*, June 22, 1993, A2, A4.

Exhibit 1 The Plant Layout

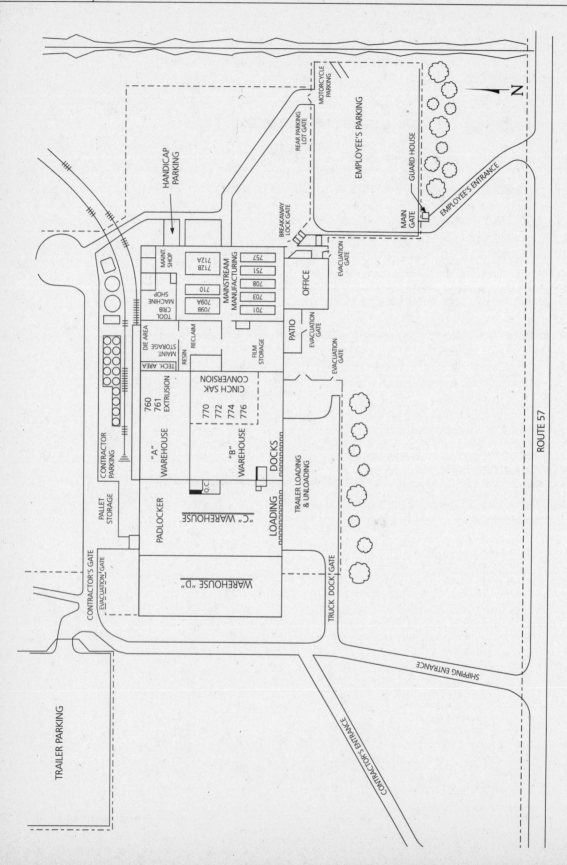

Exhibit 2 Extrusion Flow Diagram

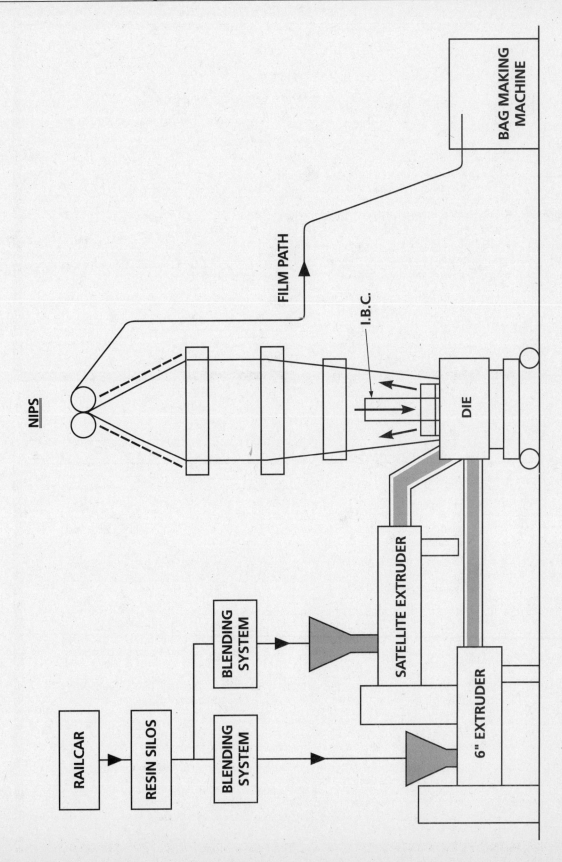

Exhibit 3 The Star Model

WHY: To improve the way we operate the Washington plant

PURPOSE: To produce higher quality products by maximizing individual contribution

HOW: A five-point organization structure (STAR) focusing personal involvement on the most important activity areas in the plant

WHAT: The STAR model will:

- Enhance competitiveness through maximizing teamwork
- Increase individual involvement and contributions (more as a stakeholder)
- Provide the framework for the plant's CQI effort
- Enable more pride, satisfaction, and motivation
- Increase leadership and team skills at all levels

VISION: Our goal is total commitment to the Continuous Quality Improvement process. Our standard of performance will be to constantly strive to safely provide cost competitive products and services that fully satisfy the requirements of our customers.

          We will develop responsibility and accountability at all levels of the organization so that everyone's efforts will make a difference.

Exhibit 4 Quality and Productivity Subcommittee Mission Statements

CinchSak PIT   Work toward developing a manufacturing environment that is dedicated to meeting our customers' needs, expectations, and desires, improving quality and reducing costs.

Twist-Tie PIT   Improve Twist-Tie operations in all areas. We will do this by getting ideas from suggestion forms, people on the floor, fellow team members, and any other available source.

Recycle PIT   Strive to safely produce and distribute cost effective reprocessed materials that consistently meet our customers' expectations. We will establish a solid base of operations involving every member of the department in the process of continual improvement of both existing processes and in the implementation of new technology.

Warehouse PIT   To continually improve the distribution function. This will be accomplished through teamwork and the implementation of warehouse improvement projects.

Maintenance PIT   To have a cohesive, well informed, knowledgeable maintenance department, capable of performing quality workmanship to the satisfaction of all with a commitment to continually improve through progressive concepts.

QC PIT   To work together as a team to educate and guide the plant in the manufacturing of quality products.

Downgauging   To implement the division request for reduced caliper production in the Twist-Tie area without any incremental increase in reclaim or downtime.

Exhibit 5 Statistical Process Improvement $\overline{X}$ and R Chart

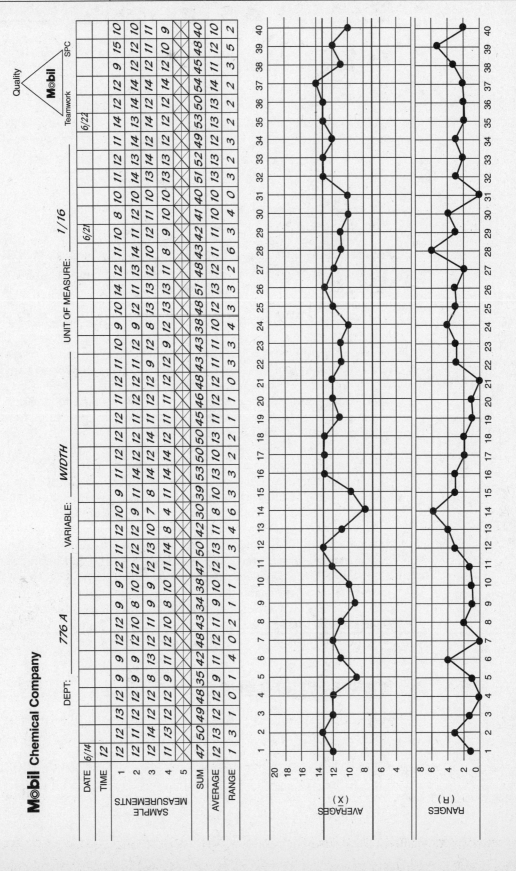

Microsoft Ireland

In November 1990, Microsoft U.K. was moving its headquarters to a new location in Winnersh, in the southeast of England, five miles away from their previous site in Reading. At this time, Jeremy Butler, Vice President of International Operations, felt it opportune to evaluate the implications of future warehousing requirements for distribution channel structure in the U.K. In particular he was concerned that the phenomenal growth rates being experienced in the industry could lead to customer service problems and have significant cost implications for the company. This problem was compounded by the fact that there was a lack of suitable warehousing space at the new headquarters. In consequence, the decision had been taken to separate the warehousing function from the marketing and technical support functions currently being performed by Microsoft U.K.

At about the same time Microsoft Europe (the European headquarters of the organisation located in Paris) had requested Brian Reynolds, the General Manager of Microsoft Ireland, to draw up a detailed distribution study with particular regard to the organisation's warehousing and channel strategy.

Having recently revamped manufacturing operations at his own plant with the objective of producing customer demand on a daily basis, Brian Reynolds was fully aware of the need to consider the direct implications of this radical change in manufacturing philosophy for the marketing operations of Microsoft U.K., and in particular the impact it could have on channel relationships with distributors and dealers. As Reynolds entered his office at 8.00 a.m. on November 7th 1990, he was aware that a decision on the future of the U.K. warehouse was to be made in Paris the following January. With this in mind, he set about drawing up the report requested by Microsoft Europe.

MICROSOFT IRELAND

Microsoft Ireland is the European manufacturing base of the U.S. multinational, Microsoft Corporation. Located in Dublin since 1985 in a 80,000 square foot facility, the company employs 350 people at this manufacturing site.

From this facility, the company supplies software packages to all major European markets, with Britain, Germany and France accounting for in excess

Source: Brian Fynes, London Business School and Sean Ennis, University of Strathclyde.

of 60% of all sales. A further 350 individuals (100 of whom are non-nationals) are employed at a 56,000 square foot facility for software development and localisation (customizing software for different countries). This was as a result of a £10 million expansion in 1990. Microsoft Ireland spent 85% of their £100 million annual raw materials budget in Ireland. In general, the overseas software sector in Ireland has established strong linkages with a number of indigenous sectors. For instance, the computer manual printing industry grew from £6 million per annum to £90 million between 1987 and 1992. As a result an estimated 1,400 jobs have been created in this sector and over a dozen indigenous printing companies are as technologically advanced and internationally competitive as any in Europe. In addition, the software industry in Ireland turns over some £1.74 billion annually (**Exhibit 1**). It is one of the top five exporting sectors in the economy, accounting for 10% of all exports. It is estimated that Ireland accounts for over 30% of total European PC software sales.

MICROSOFT CORPORATION

With its headquarters located at Redmond, Washington in the USA, Microsoft grew exponentially in the 1980s to become the world's leading software company with a market value of $21 billion, even greater than that of General Motors. Between 1988 and 1992 worldwide net revenues increased from $591 million to $2,759 million, net income from $124 million to $708 million and net income per share from $0.49 to $2.41 (see **Exhibits 2** and **3**). Founded by chairman Bill Gates in 1975, Microsoft emerged in the 1990s, according to *Business Week*, "as clearly the most important single force in the entire computer industry."

While other software manufacturers were announcing sinking market share, losses or layoffs in 1992, Microsoft added $975 million in annual revenues, accounting for more than 90% of all the revenue growth in the personal computer software industry. Dataquest, an industry analyst, estimated that the company's share of the world desktop PC software market reached 44% in 1992. In addition, they held in excess of 60% of the market for programs that work with Windows, the high growth graphical user interface (GUI) segment. Analysts predicted that if sales were to rise by 36% to $3,750 million in 1993 that Microsoft would have more revenues than its seven closest independent rivals combined and, at nearly $1,000 million, have more than twice their income.

Global Organisational Structure

The company, which employed 5,600 people worldwide in 1989, now has in excess of 14,000 people on its payroll in 27 countries. The extremely flat management organization with few layers between the lowest worker and the chairman is a typical feature of world-class organisations. A "shared resource model" is used by the corporation to ensure a common direction in finance, human resource management and information systems. Interestingly enough, the marketing function is not governed by this model. Instead each country manager exercises a lot of autonomy in most marketing decisions such as promotion and channel management. The company is divided into three main groups; the Products Group, the Sales Support Group, and the Operations Group.

The *Products Group*, which is responsible for new product development and innovation, accounted for the majority of the $352 million spent on research and development in 1992 and introduced 48 new products, including well over 100 international versions. Most phenomenal of all was the introduction of

Microsoft Windows 3.1. Now running on more than 12 million systems world-wide, Windows has become the fastest-selling graphical user interface ever. In the two years since its introduction these figures represent a new customer every 10 seconds. Other leading software products include Microsoft Word, Excel, Powerpoint, and Project.

The *Sales and Support Group* is responsible for providing software support for Microsoft's different types of customers; i.e., distributors, hardware manufacturers, software vendors, major resellers, and users in business, government, education, law and home settings. Over 2,000 people are employed in this group and in 1992 and they answered 4.6 million phone calls. Seventy per cent of all callers received help in less than 60 seconds in 1992. This group also includes Microsoft Consulting Services (MCS) for helping customers develop sophisticated business solutions, and Microsoft University (MSU) which provides the technical education and training needed by corporate information systems managers, developers, and support professionals using Microsoft software.

The *Operations Group* is responsible for finance, operations, human resource management, MIS, facilities, and the assembly of software packages. This group is broken down on a geographical basis. Manufacturing facilities are located at Bothell in the United States (serving North America and the rest of the world), Dublin (serving the European market) and Hunacao in Puerto Rico (serving North and South America).

The Competitive Environment

Throughout the 1980s Microsoft collaborated closely with IBM on the development of MS-DOS, the standard operating system software for IBM compatible personal computers. The phenomenal early growth of Microsoft can be largely attributed to this alliance. However as both companies began working on a new operating system, OS/2, the relationship began to degenerate. In September 1990 they agreed to compete openly, with Microsoft concentrating on Windows and IBM on OS/2. Both companies introduced new versions in 1992 (Windows 3.1 and OS/2 Version 2.0), with IBM targeting the corporate sector in particular. Industry estimates predicted sales of 12 million units of Windows and 2 to 4 million units of OS/2 for 1992.

When Apple Computers introduced Macintosh in January 1984, Microsoft was the first major software company to develop a line of supporting applications. Apple's competitive edge was traditionally based on graphical user interfaces. As with IBM, however, the relationship with Microsoft soured with the launch of Windows. In 1988 Apple launched a $4.4 billion copyright infringement lawsuit against Microsoft. In April 1992, Judge Vaugh Walker dismissed most of Apple's case. Only months prior to the decision Apple and IBM formed an alliance to develop and market an object-oriented, hardware-independent operating environment. Many industry analysts commented cynically on the future of such an alliance.

The main independent publicly traded competitors of Microsoft are Novell, Lotus, Borland, WordPerfect, Adobe, Symantec, and Software Publishing. The first three of these dominate the 56% of the market that is not controlled by Microsoft.

Novell Inc., the $933 million U.S. developer of networking software has been the biggest player to successfully fend off Microsoft to date. Holding 70% of this lucrative market with their Netware product, Novell are nonetheless very conscious of Microsoft's intention of incorporating network features on Windows NT, a new product scheduled for release in 1993. A feature of their overall marketing strategy has been to extensively use independent third parties to handle many aspects of their marketing operations, e.g., customer and product support.

Lotus Development, the major player in spreadsheets with Lotus 1-2-3 in the MS-DOS world, had its first ever layoffs in 1992. During the 1980s it held 75% of this market but this dropped to 55% by 1991. In 1991 the first version of Lotus 1-2-3 for Windows was launched but encountered many technical problems. As a result, Lotus now holds just 20% of the $756 million Windows spreadsheet market as against the 73% claimed by Microsoft's Excel. It is now beginning to concentrate its resources in programs such as Notes, which helps groups of workers to collaborate. The 1992 budget for R&D amounted to $35 million

Borland International is the $500 million player that holds an estimated 50% to 60% of the $1 billion database software with its d-Base package. Borland laid off 15% of its 2,200 workers in December 1992, having reported a $61.3 million loss for the last quarter and postponing a word processing package that had been two years in development. Expenditure on R&D at Borland amounted to $50 million in 1992. This is in stark contrast to Microsoft's new database program, Access, developed at a cost of $60 million and offered at an introductory price of only $99, less than one third the retail price for similar packages. The impact was of this offer was immediate—700,000 copies were sold in just three months in an annual market of just 1.2 million units. In addition, in March 1992, Microsoft acquired Fox Software Inc., a leading competitor of Borland for $175 million. Analysts predicted that Microsoft would garner 25% of this market within a year. The price of Borland stock fell by $7 when the deal was announced.

WordPerfect Inc., whose revenues had doubled every year since 1980, managed to move from a 35% share of the market for word processing packages in 1987 to in excess of 60% by 1989. Sales in 1991 amounted to $532.5 million, but as with other software companies, WordPerfect was caught napping with the launch of Microsoft's Word for Windows, which made significant inroads into their market share. At the end of 1992, WordPerfect, Microsoft and Lotus dominated this sector of software development.

The Issue of Market Dominance

Phillipe Kahn, chairman of Borland, blamed Microsoft's forays into the database market for his company's problems, commenting that "Microsoft is the IBM of the '90s and uses exactly the same marketing tactics IBM used to." This is hardly accurate, however, as IBM's market dominance was company-driven while Microsoft's is customer-driven. Microsoft's dominant position has been criticised as quasi-monopolistic by competitors and commentators alike. As a result the Federal Trade Commission launched an investigation into the company in 1991 which proved inconclusive. In the aftermath of the investigation, *Forbes* a leading U.S. business magazine, suggested that the proceedings were stalled because "the next generation of computers will leave Microsoft with nothing like its historic dominance in operating systems."

Manufacturing Operations in Microsoft Ireland, 1985–1988

When initially established in Ireland, the plant was allocated direct responsibility for manufacturing and shipping to U.K. and European destinations. Marketing, sales and technical support were provided by each national sales subsidiary (of which there were ten in Europe).

In the early days, Microsoft had operated like most other manufacturers—long production runs, large inventories, lengthy set-up times, quality control problems and multiple suppliers. In the late 1980s the manufacturing process was based on traditional mass production principles. From a total product range of 280 products, high volume lines such as Word would be produced in batches of 10,000 units once a week, and lower volume lines once a month. This traditional approach was based on the primary objective of minimising costs associated with long set-up times. Such a process necessitated bulk deliveries of raw materials from their suppliers and required a warehouse of 40,000 square feet housing eight weeks of inventory with associated storage costs. At the end of a production run, the finished goods were moved back to the finished goods warehouse where they awaited shipment.

In terms of order cycle periods, orders were received on the tenth day of each month and were processed through the MRP (materials requirements planning) system. This took roughly five days. When this was completed, production would begin and delivery to customers resulted at the end of the month. This approach lent itself to stockouts as production capacity was locked into a given line for considerable periods of time.

With two shifts per day, the manufacturing process at Microsoft was (and still essentially is) a two-stage one. The first stage was the duplication of software packages from master disks. The second stage of the process was the assembly of the finished software package. The assembly process was labour intensive and consisted of placing the duplicated disks, manuals, licence agreement and packing material in the appropriate carton. These were then shrink-wrapped to await shipment.

Turnaround: the Road to Becoming a World Class Manufacturer, 1988–1990

In 1988, Brian Reynolds attended a conference where the keynote contributor was Richard Schonberger. With top-selling management books such as *Japanese Manufacturing Techniques: Nine Hidden Lessons in Simplicity*, *World Class Manufacturing*, and *Building a Chain of Customers*, Schonberger had espoused the need to reform the traditional practices of western mass production and introduce the leaner customer-driven manufacturing operations that had been important in the emergence of Japan as a major economic power. Emphasising the contribution of just-in-time (JIT) techniques, total quality management (TQM) strategies and employee involvement (EI), he was acknowledged as being one of the most influential proponents of the argument that western industry urgently needed to confront the issues of simplifying manufacturing, managing the supply chain and ensuring that operations should be customer-driven.

Reynolds, an MBA graduate of University College Dublin, was impressed with what he heard. Confronted with problems of working capital tied up in inventory, quality and product availability, he decided to apply the approaches suggested by Schonberger in his plant. He commissioned a consultancy study which highlighted that on average, Microsoft's process lead-time was 151 days—60 days in raw material, 1 day in work-in progress and 90 days in finished goods. On the other hand the product received value for only 4 minutes (the time it took the package to be assembled on the line) during a normal production run. Faced with a value-added to non value-added ratio of 4 minutes: 151 days, his response was immediate. He transferred his Materials Manager, Tom Doyle, to the role of project manager with responsibility for implementing world-class manufacturing on the factory floor. Emphasising throughput, a policy decision was taken to manufacture smaller lots more frequently. The objective was to receive supplies daily and build (assemble) daily. The company identified four critical dimensions in the implementation process.

Suppler Reduction. For Microsoft, too many suppliers meant poor communication and higher transaction costs. The company's supplier base included indigenous printing companies (manuals), packaging manufacturers, disk manufacturers and freight forwarders. By reducing the supplier base, Microsoft initiated a process of selecting strategic partners. In return for providing their suppliers with a long term commitment, standardisation of product design and rolling sales forecasts, Microsoft received assurances with regard to mutual cost reduction and daily deliveries. These commitments were not based on legally binding contractual agreements but rather on the basis of "gentlemen's agreements" with quarterly reviews. The result of cutting its supplier base by 70% led to a significant reduction in transaction and communication costs. In addition the enhancement of supplier capability that resulted from the financial stability of a partnership agreement provided the springboard for improved design. In fact, suppliers began to apply JIT techniques to their own production processes and supplier-base farther down the value chain.

Production Batch Sizes Cut. To facilitate shorter production runs, lower inventories and the assembly of all products on a JIT basis, set-up times had to be dramatically reduced. Set-up involved ensuring that all the disks, manuals and packaging were available at the appropriate workstation for assembly. John Douglas, Operations Director, came up with an imaginative and novel approach to eliminating lengthy set-up times. While many exponents of JIT suggested that U-shaped production lines facilitated the process, Microsoft replaced the traditional assembly lines with 15 dual-level carousels or "round-tables" (see **Exhibits 4** and **6**). While operatives assembled from one level of the carousel, individuals who had completed their tasks for that run setup the other carousel for the next production run. In addition to eliminating setups, quality control was facilitated by this approach (e.g., in a production batch of ten units, it became immediately obvious at the end of the process if any disks or manuals were not included in the carton as they would remain highly visible on the carousel). By producing in smaller batches, quality problems were immediately and clearly identified. Within Microsoft the operators at these quality-focused carousels became known as "the knights of the roundtable."

Employee Involvement. The solution to overcoming resistance to change on the shop floor required a radical change in the way individuals were managed. The company identified employees who they felt would be suitable facilitators in the training of operatives in JIT/TQM techniques. Every individual in the organization was involved and flexibility became the byword for operations. To some degree, the process was facilitated by the age profile of the organization, with an average age of 23 years on the factory floor. Employees were now to be paid on the basis of the number of new skills they acquired by way of in-company training. Considerable resources were devoted to education and a library containing the works of Schonberger and other management strategists was opened for all employees. Quality-focused teams were introduced to brainstorm on how the manufacturing process could be improved. The Japanese concept of **kaizen** or continuous improvement was seen as critical to the success of such teams. The impact of such changes were immediately

kaizen
continuous improvement

noticeable: employees wanted to be flexible and champion the production process. A measure of this change was the 3,700 suggestions forwarded to the company's suggestion scheme (see **Exhibit 5**) in the first two years of operation. Richard Schonberger, on a visit to the plant, was later to remark that this was the highest rate of contribution he has observed in *any* western manufacturing plant.

Focused Factories. Wickham Skinner, a Harvard Business School academic, first introduced the concept of focus in manufacturing in the 1970s. He argued that a plant would perform better if it limited itself to a focused number of tasks, processes or products. Brian Reynolds was intrigued with this approach and considered how it might apply in the case of Microsoft. He concluded that a customer-driven approach must form the basis of organising "factories within the factory." The requirements of the marketplace were now to have an impact on the manufacturing process. Since the geographic destinations of the software packages were language-related, four factories within the plant were introduced—Britain and English language products (Euro), Germany, France and the Rest of Europe (multilingual). Each focused factory was now charged with dealing with specific geographic markets and had its own independent manufacturing cells, production equipment (duplicating machines and carousels) and outward shipping bays (**Exhibit 6**). In addition the possibility of extra paperwork and administration was eliminated by extending the concept of focus to suppliers. A printing supplier would now typically deliver to only one focused factory. The national flags of the destination markets were in evidence at focused factory, highlighting the market-driven nature of the approach.

Within months, cost of goods sold had been reduced by 25%, while inventory levels in the plant had been cut by 70%. Simultaneously in a marketplace where time had become a critical issue, manufacturing lead-times were cut to just one day.

The Order Cycle

Prior to the changes made by Reynolds to manufacturing operations, orders were accepted up to the tenth day of each month at the Dublin facility. Production planning techniques such as MRP were used to schedule operations until the final day of the month, thereby necessitating a three week order cycle period. Under the revamped ratebased manufacturing approach, orders are placed by customers on a Wednesday for the forthcoming week. This weekly order was then allocated evenly to each of the next five days with MRP used only for capacity planning, (e.g., for a weekly order of 1,000 units, a daily production rate of 200 units would be assembled on each of the five days of production).

Distribution Channel Structure in the U.K.

At the time of the decision on the location of the U.K. warehouse, Microsoft Ireland shipped product directly to the U.K. subsidiary. From there, Microsoft U.K. would ship to a mix of about 200 distributors and dealers using contract delivery for large distributors and couriers for smaller orders to dealers. Distributors typically carry a wide range of competitive product offerings whereas dealers tend to carry a much narrower product range. Backorder rates were typically of the order of 15%. Approximately nine major distributors accounted for 80% of Microsoft's business in the U.K. The remaining 20% included smaller dealers, educational establishments and original equipment manufacturers (OEMs). A notable feature is that channel structure has been historically based on the computer hardware sector. In the mid-1980s, distributors concentrated on the sale of PCs where high margins were readily obtained. However, this situation changed considerably in the early 1990s as low-cost equipment began to appear on the market. Hardware manufacturers now used more direct forms of distribution to high street dealers as lower cost distribution channels became the norm. Ever narrowing margins on PCs became less attractive to major distributors and their primary focus of attention moved to turnover of software products and ancillary hardware equipment (printers, etc.).

Implications of the Changes in Manufacturing for Marketing

As Brian Reynolds began his analysis of future distribution strategy, he was conscious that there were a number of inter-dependent issues directly affecting channel relationships and warehousing strategy in the United Kingdom that needed to be addressed in his report.

Control of Inventory and Customer Service Levels. One of the major factors that had to be considered was the perceived loss of control by Microsoft U.K. over the entire warehousing function. Concern had been expressed about separating the sales and warehousing functions and the implications this might have for customer service levels in Britain.

Loss of Visibility. In addition to a perceived loss of control, any physical relocation of the U.K. warehouse could potentially eliminate inventory visibility for Microsoft U.K. Warehouse managers and supervisors generally prefer to be able to actually see current inventory levels for all stock-keeping units (SKUs). Some means of providing a "comfort factor" in the event of relocation needed to be examined.

Implications for Channel Participants. Any change in warehousing strategy in the U.K. could effectively eliminate Microsoft U.K. from the operational details of supplying a base of over two hundred customers. Under the existing system, smaller dealers had been content with Microsoft's prices because they were being supplied by Microsoft U.K. and not through a distributor. However, this meant that they had to maintain higher stock levels for anything up to a week. Reynolds recognised that there might have to be changes in this present arrangement with regard to the size and frequency of deliveries, and felt his report should address the impact of such changes on channel members.

Logistical Implications of Rate-Based Manufacturing. Having successfully revamped and redesigned the manufacturing process at Microsoft Ireland, Brian Reynolds believed that there might be some scope for applying the principles of world class manufacturing farther down the distribution channel. He felt that Microsoft could gain a competitive advantage if the benefits achieved with "leaner" manufacturing could be attained in the areas of warehousing and channel strategy.

Market Trends. The Western European Market for software products was estimated to grow at 15% per annum until 1996 (see **Exhibit 7**). The Industrial Development Authority in Ireland has predicted that the dominant market trends during the 1990s will be:

- globalisation of the marketplace
- increasing influence of a small number of very large, powerful companies
- the dominance and influence of the USA, particularly in the product market
- a move toward open systems and standardisation
- changes in users' organisational structures
- emergence of compact disk technology
- impact of advanced telecommunications systems

Furthermore, in the light of the recent phenomenal growth in the sales of Microsoft products, it was clear that any decision on warehousing strategy would have to be capable of handling such demand. In addition, the impact of any decision in relation to the number of channel participants needed to be assessed.

Future Developments in the Channels of Distribution. As indicated earlier, a low-cost channel structure had emerged with regard to the distribution of computer hardware products. The mystery surrounding the use of PCs has gradually evaporated, especially when combined with the emergence of user-friendly graphical interfaces such as Windows. This has led to the emergence of retailers such as Dixons and W.H. Smith. Furthermore Dell Computers, an American PC manufacturer with a presence in the mid-west of Ireland, pioneered direct marketing approaches such as mail order and toll-free telephone ordering.

When consumers purchase a software package such as Microsoft Excel, the company requests that a registration card (to combat piracy) be returned to the sales office. This offers the potential for user registration details to be updated and can facilitate closer liaison and better technical support for the final customer. Simultaneously it provides the software company with the opportunity of informing the customer of product upgrades or new product introductions. In addition, continued growth in the single office-home office (SOHO) sector had been targeted by Microsoft. Meanwhile the emergence of compact disk technology presented both threats and opportunities for Microsoft. Industry analysts have commented that initial growth in this sector will be dependent on large customer accounts with significant data requirements coupled with a greater availability of the supporting hardware.

Future Distribution Strategy. The ramifications of any changes in warehousing policy in the U.K. warehouse raised questions about future distribution strategy for the remaining Microsoft European mainland sales subsidiaries supplied by focused facilities in Dublin. In addition to these considerations, Reynolds believed that his successful turnaround of manufacturing operations with the subsequent savings in cost and inventory levels could have a bearing on the final decision.

DISCUSSION QUESTIONS

1. With the foregoing in mind help Brian Reynolds put together his analysis of distribution strategy for submission to corporate headquarters.
2. Given the tremendous improvements made at Microsoft Ireland thus far, future developments in channels of distribution, and the future distribution strategy, what is the role of TQM?
3. How might a TQM strategy be put to work in this changing environment?

Exhibit 1 Overseas Software Companies in Ireland

Growth Rates

	Year		Growth Rate
	1987	**1992**	
Companies	45	74	16%
Employment	1,500	4,052	34%

Industry Structure

Company Size	Number of Companies	Number Employed
200+	4 (5.0%)	1,824 (45.0%)
50–200	16 (22.0%)	1,275 (31.0%)
41– 49	4 (5.0%)	170 (4.0%)
31– 39	7 (9.5%)	226 (5.5%)
21– 29	10 (13.5%)	250 (6.5%)
10– 19	16 (22.0%)	222 (5.5%)
6– 9	7 (9.5%)	51 (1.5%)
1 5	10 (13.5%)	34 (1.0%)
Total	74 (100.0%)	4,052 (100.0%)

State Aid 1983–1991 £35.5 million
Cost per job (based on employment of 3,525 at the end of 1991) £10,071

Source: *A Strategic Review of the Software Industry of Ireland,* The Industrial Development
Authority, Dublin, 1992.

Exhibit 2 Microsoft Corporation Financial Performance

FINANCIAL PERFORMANCE
Year Ended June 30

	1992	1991	1990	1989	1988
	(In thousands, except employee and per share data)				
For the year ($)					
Net Revenues	2,758,725	1,843,432	1,183,446	803,530	590,827
Cost of Revenues	466,424	372,589	252,668	204,185	148,000
Research and Development	352,153	535,386	180,615	110,220	69,776
Sales and Marketing	854,537	533,619	317,593	218,997	161,614
General and Administrative	89,630	61,996	39,332	27,898	23,990
Operating Income	995,979	649,842	393,238	242,230	187,447
Non Operating Income (expense)	45,286	20,802	17,326	8,566	(3,709)
Income before Income Taxes	1,041,265	670,644	410,564	250,796	183,738
Provisions for Income Taxes	333,205	207,901	131,378	80,258	59,830
Net Income	708,060	462,743	279,186	170,538	123,908
At Year-End ($)					
Working Capital	1,322,759	735,150	533,104	310,131	227,827
Total Assets	2,639,903	1,644,184	105,349	720,598	494,019
Stockholders' Equity	2,192,958	1,350,831	918,563	561,780	375,498
Number of Employees	11,542	8,226	5,635	4,037	2,793
Common Stock Data ($)					
Net Income Per Share	2.41	1.64	1.04	0.67	0.49
Book Value Per Share	8.06	5.17	3.59	2.29	1.55
Cash and Short-Term Investments Per Share	4.94	2.63	1.76	1.22	0.76
Average Common and Equivalent Shares Outstanding	294,218	281,489	268,677	253,103	251,181
Shares Outstanding at Year-End	272,139	261,351	255,824	245,637	241,484
Key Ratios					
Current Ratio	4.0	3.5	3.9	3.0	2.9
Return on Net Revenues	25.7%	25.1%	23.6%	21.2%	21.0%
Return on Average Total Assets	33.1%	33.7%	30.6%	28.1%	31.7%
Return on Average Stockholders' Equity	40.0%	40.8%	37.7%	36.4%	40.3%
Growth Percentages–Increases					
Net Revenues	49.7%	55.8%	47.3%	36.0%	70.8%
Net Income	53.0%	65.7%	63.7%	37.6%	72.4%
Net Income Per Share	47.0%	58.3%	54.5%	36.5%	72.1%
Book Value Per Share	55.9%	43.8%	56.9%	47.1%	54.2%

Exhibit 3 Microsoft Corporation Worldwide Performance

	U.S. Operations	European Operations	Other International Operations	Eliminations	Consolidated
			(in thousands $)		
Net Revenues: Customer	1,492,630	1,008,545	257,550	—	2,758,725
Intercompany	384,773	497,874	14,161	(896,808)	—
Total	1,877,403	1,506,419	271,711	(896,808)	2,758,725
Operating Income	664,396	329,305	10,553	(8,275)	995,979
Identifiable Assets	1,858,156	872,228	288,743	(379,224)	2,639,903
1991					
New Revenues: Customers	974,359	697,729	171,344	—	1,843,432
Intercompany	236,107	326,414	15,626	(578,147)	—
Total	1,210,466	1,024,143	186,970	(578,147)	1,843,432
Operating Income	372,630	280,203	11,772	(14,763)	649,842
Identifiable Assets	1,278,247	578,572	207,739	(420,374)	1,644,184
1990					
Net Revenues: Customers	717,630	363,294	102,522	—	1,183,446
Intercompany	139,827	211,609	19,421	(370,857)	—
Total	857,457	574,903	121,943	(370,857)	1,183,446
Operating Income	269,724	148,879	16,716	(370,857)	1,183,446
Identifiable Assets	865,223	364,356	58,806	(183,036)	1,105,349

Intercompany sales between geographic areas are accounted for at prices representative of unaffiliated party transactions. "Other International Operations" primarily include subsidiaries in Australia, Canada, Japan, Korea, and Taiwan. The majority of export revenues results from OEM distribution in the Far East and Europe and finished goods exports to the Far East and South America.

International revenues, which include both international operations and export, were as follows:

	1992	1991	1990
	(in thousands $)		
European Operation	1,008,545	697,729	363,294
Other International Operations	257,550	171,344	102,522
Export	254,695	187,734	184,433
	1,520,790	1,056,807	650,249
Percentage of Total Revenues	55.1%	57.3%	54.9%

Exhibit 4 Manufacturing Processes with Carousels

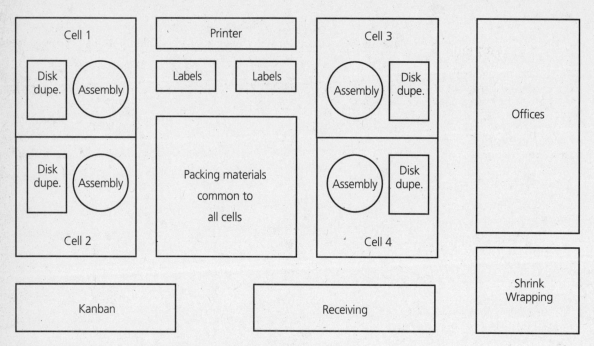

Note: outline layout of manufacturing cell, not to scale

Exhibit 5 Suggestion Scheme

MICROSOFT IRELAND
PROCESS IMPROVEMENT SHEET

Sheet No.

SUBMITTED BY: _____ DATE:_____

_____

ASSIGNED TO: DATE ASSIGNED: _____

VENDOR TEAM	ADMINISTRATION TEAM	FRENCH TEAM
EQUIPMENT TEAM	PSG	GERMAN TEAM
DISK DUPE TEAM	WAREHOUSE TEAM	MULTILINGUAL TEAM
CUSTOMER TEAM	QUALITY TEAM	FACILITIES TEAM
TRAINING TEAM	EURO TEAM	MIS TEAM

SUMMARY: _____

DESCRIBE THE CURRENT PROCESS:

HOW MIGHT THE CURRENT PROCESS BE IMPROVED:

RESPONSE OF W.C.M. TEAM:

IMPLEMENTED   FOR FUTURE IMPLEMENTATION

NOT IMPLEMENTED   FURTHER INFORMATION

FEEDBACK ACKNOWLEDGED BY ORIGINATOR: _____ DATE:_____

Exhibit 6 Plant Layout with Focused Factories

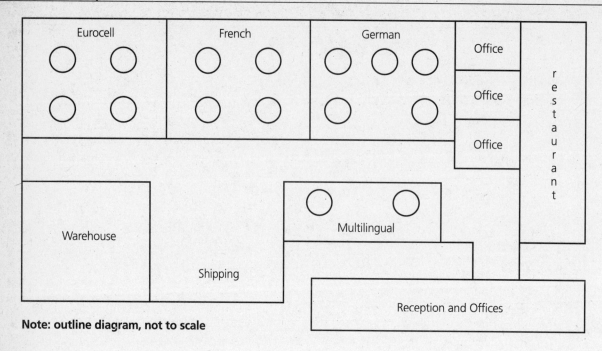

Note: outline diagram, not to scale

Exhibit 7 Market Trends

Forecasts of Western European Computer Software and Services Market ($ billion)

	1991	1996	Growth Rate
Processing Services	9.4	13.3	7%
Turnkey Services	12.3	24.3	15%
Applications Software	9.0	20.8	18%
Systems Software	12.6	21.5	11%
Professional Services	24.7	51.9	16%
Network Services	4.7	11.6	20%
Systems Operations	1.4	3.8	20%
Systems Integration	3.4	8.0	19%
Total (rounded)	*77.5*	*155.2*	*15%*

Industry Sector, 1991

Sector	% of Market
Manufacturing	29
Banking and Finance	20
Distribution	9
Services	8
Local Government	7
National Government	7
Others	20
Total	*100*

Source: Forecast of European Computer Software and Services Market,
Input International Ltd., London, 1991.

PART III

Tools
of
TQM

Quality Cleaners

The owner of Quality Cleaners has decided that a quality improvement program must be implemented in its dry cleaning service. Customers bring clothes to one of five stores or pickup stations. Orders are then delivered to the cleaning plant twice (morning and afternoon) each day, with deliveries of orders being made to the stores at the same time, allowing for same-day service by customer request.

The stores are opened at 7:00 a.m. by a full-time employee. This person is relieved at 3:00 p.m. by a part-time employee, who closes the store at 6:00 p.m.

When the clothes are received from the customer, a five-ply ticket showing the customer name, phone number, due date, and special requests is prepared. One ply is given to the customer as a claim check and the store keeps one ply (to show what they have in process). The clothes and the remaining plies of the ticket are put in a nylon laundry bag for delivery to the plant.

At the cleaning plant the departments are:

Mark-in. Each order is removed from the bag; items are tagged for identification later and sorted into large buggies according to due date, type of garment, and cleaning requirements. The buggies are moved to the cleaning department as they become full. Also at mark-in, garments are checked for spots, stains, tears, or other special handling. The problem is written on a strip-tag (a half-inch wide paper tape) and attached to the garment with the identification tag.

Cleaning. The buggies are emptied into the cleaning machine one item at a time to allow for inspection. The primary items checked are spots and stains requiring special attention and for foreign objects. For example, an ink pen left in a pocket could ruin the whole load. As items are removed from the cleaning machine, they are placed on hangers and moved by conveyor to the pressing department.

Pressing. There are four presses: one for silks, one for pants, and two general-purpose. On an ordinary day, three of the presses will be operating, but which three of the four are operating will depend upon the total demand and product mix that particular day. As items are pressed, they are placed on a conveyor that delivers them to the assembly department.

Assembly. Cleaned items are grouped into customer orders, bagged, and put in the appropriate queue for delivery to the respective store. At this time, two plies (of the remaining three) of the ticket are attached to the order, and

Source: Professor Marilyn S. Jones, Winthrop University, as published in Jay Heizer and Barry Render, *Production/Operations Management,* 4th ed., Prentice Hall, Upper Saddle River, NJ, 1996, pp. 103–105.

one ply stays at the plant to show this order was completed. When the customer picks up the order, one ply will stay on the order.

The store will retain the last ply and pull the corresponding ply from their work-in-process file to show that this order is complete.

Note: Although quality is a larger-than-average cleaning operation, total annual revenues are approximately $500,000. Therefore, any suggestions must be relatively inexpensive.

At present, a majority of the employees are cross-trained to allow for flexibility. **Table 1** indicates the production employees and the positions for which they are trained. A letter *P* indicates the primary duty, or the one the employee performs most often. A check indicates that the employee is also trained in that function.

For example, one day David may only clean; the next day he cleans awhile and then presses pants. This presents a problem in determining who put a double crease in Mrs. Jones's slacks, but the owner believes this flexibility in scheduling is valuable and must be maintained.

DISCUSSION QUESTIONS

1. Design the quality program. Consider the following issues:
   a. Where should inspection(s) occur?
   b. How will accountability be achieved?
   c. What factors (variables, attributes, other considerations) should be checked?
   d. Is statistical process control (SPC) appropriate?
      i. Variable or attribute?
      ii. At what point?
2. What are the cost items for implementing your plan? Give a budget, including equipment, supplies, and labor-hours (divided into types of labor).
3. What records should be kept to measure the success of the program in terms of cost, quality performance, and service to the customer?

Table 1 Production Employees and the Positions for which They Are Trained

| Employee | Cleaning | Presses | | |
		General Purpose	Silks	Pants
David	P	✓		✓
Tasha	✓	✓		P
Len	✓	P	✓	
Mary		✓	P	✓
Betty (part-time)	✓	✓		✓
Mike (part-time)	✓	✓		✓

SPC at the Gazette

Of critical importance to a newspaper is accurate typesetting. To assure typesetting quality, a Quality Improvement Team was established in the Printing Department at the *Gazette* in Geronimo, Texas. The team developed a procedure for monitoring the performance of type over a period of time. Such a procedure involves sampling output, establishing control limits, comparing the *Gazette's* accuracy with that of the industry, and occasionally updating the information.

The team randomly selected 30 of the Gazette's newspapers published during the preceding 12 months. From each paper, 100 paragraphs were randomly chosen and were read for accuracy. The number of paragraphs with errors in each paper was recorded, and the fraction of paragraphs with errors in each sample was determined. **Table 1** shows the results of the sampling.

DISCUSSION QUESTIONS

1. Plot the overall fraction of errors (p) and the upper and lower control limits on a control chart using a 95.45% confidence level.
2. Assume the industry upper and lower control limits are .1000 and .0400, respectively. Plot them on the control chart.
3. Plot the fraction of errors in each sample. Do all fall within the firm's control limits? When one falls outside the control limits, what should be done?

Source: Jerry Kinard, Western Carolina University, as published in Jay Heizer and Barry Render, *Production/Operations Management*, 4th ed., Prentice Hall, Upper Saddle River, NJ, 1996, pp. 141–142.

Table 1 Results of Sampling for Errors

Sample	Paragraphs with Errors in the Sample	Fraction of Paragraphs with Errors (per 100)
1	2	.02
2	4	.04
3	10	.10
4	4	.04
5	1	.01
6	1	.01
7	13	.13
8	9	.09
9	11	.11
10	0	.00
11	3	.03
12	4	.04
13	2	.02
14	2	.02
15	8	.08
16	2	.02
17	3	.03
18	7	.07
19	3	.03
20	2	.02
21	3	.03
22	7	.07
23	4	.04
24	3	.03
25	2	.02
26	2	.02
27	0	.00
28	1	.01
29	3	.03
30	4	.04

Bayfield Mud Company

In November 1994, John Wells, a customer service representative of Bayfield Mud Company, was summoned to the Houston warehouse of Wet-Land Drilling, Inc., to inspect three boxcars of mud-treating agents that Bayfield Mud Company had shipped to the Houston firm. (Bayfield's corporate offices and its largest plant are located in Orange, Texas, which is just west of the Louisiana-Texas border.) Wet-Land Drilling had filed a complaint that the 50-pound bags of treating agents that it had just received from Bayfield were short-weight by approximately 5%.

The lightweight bags were initially detected by one of Wet-Land's receiving clerks, who noticed that the railroad scale tickets indicated that the net weights were significantly less on all three of the boxcars than those of identical shipments received on October 25, 1994. Bayfield's Traffic Department was called to determine if lighter-weight dunnage or pallets were used on the ship. (This might explain the lighter net weights.) Bayfield indicated, however, that no changes had been made in the loading or palletizing procedures. Hence, Wet-Land randomly checked 50 of the bags and discovered that the average net weight was 47.51 pounds. They noted from past shipments that the bag net weights averaged exactly 50.0 pounds, with an acceptable standard deviation of 1.2 pounds. Consequently, they concluded that the sample indicated a significant short-weight. (The reader may wish to verify this conclusion.) Bayfield was then contacted, and Wells was sent to investigate the complaint. Upon arrival, Wells verified the complaint and issued a 5% credit to Wet-Land.

Wet-Land's management, however, was not completely satisfied with only the issuance of credit for the short shipment. The charts followed by their mud engineers on the drilling platforms were based on 50-pound bags of treating agents. Lighter-weight bags might result in poor chemical control during the drilling operation and might adversely affect drilling efficiency. (Mud-treating agents are used to control the pH and other chemical properties of the cone during drilling operation.) This could cause severe economic consequences because of the extremely high cost of oil and natural gas well-drilling operations. Consequently, special use instructions had to accompany the delivery of these shipments to the drilling platforms. Moreover the lightweight shipments had to be isolated in Wet-Land's warehouse, causing extra handling and poor

Source: Professor Jerry Kinard, Western Carolina University, as published in Jay Heizer and Barry Render, *Production/Operations Management*, 4th ed., Prentice Hall, Upper Saddle River, NJ, 1996, pp. 139–141.

space utilization. Hence, Wells was informed that Wet-Land Drilling might seek a new supplier of mud-treating agents if, in the future, it received bags that deviated significantly from 50 pounds.

The Quality Control Department at Bayfield suspected that the lightweight bags may have resulted from "growing pains" at the Orange plant. Because of the earlier energy crisis, oil and natural gas exploration activity had greatly increased. This increased activity, in turn, created increased demand for products produced by related industries, including drilling muds. Consequently, Bayfield had to expand from a one-shift (6:00 a.m. to 2:00 p.m.) to a two-shift (6:00 a.m. to 10:00 p.m.) operation in mid-1992, and finally to a three-shift operation (24 hours per day) in the fall of 1994.

The additional night-shift bagging crew was staffed entirely by new employees. The most experienced foremen were temporarily assigned to supervise the night-shift employees. Most emphasis was placed on increasing the output of bags to meet the ever-increasing demand. It was suspected that only occasional reminders were made to double-check the bag weight-feeder. (A double-check is performed by systematically weighing a bag on a scale to determine if the proper weight is being loaded by the weight-feeder. If there is significant deviation from 50 pounds, corrective adjustments are made to the weight-release mechanism.)

To verify this expectation, the quality control staff randomly sampled the bag output and prepared the chart shown in **Exhibit 1**. Six bags were sampled and weighed each hour.

DISCUSSION QUESTIONS

1. What is your analysis of the bag weight problem?
2. What procedures would you recommend to maintain proper quality control?

Exhibit 1 Bayfield Mud Company

Time	Average Weight (Pounds)	Range		Time	Average Weight (Pounds)	Range	
		Smallest	Largest			Smallest	Largest
6:00 a.m.	49.6	48.7	50.7	1:00 p.m.	49.0	46.4	50.0
7:00	50.2	49.1	51.2	2:00	49.0	46.0	50.6
8:00	50.6	49.6	51.4	3:00	49.8	48.2	50.8
9:00	50.8	50.2	51.8	4:00	50.3	49.2	52.7
10:00	49.9	49.2	52.3	5:00	51.4	50.0	55.3
11:00	50.3	48.6	51.7	6:00	51.6	49.2	54.7
12 Noon	48.6	46.2	50.4	7:00	51.8	50.0	55.6
8:00	51.0	48.6	53.2	1:00 a.m.	49.6	48.4	51.7
9:00	50.5	49.4	52.4	2:00	50.0	49.0	52.2
10:00	49.2	46.1	50.7	3:00	50.0	49.2	50.0
11:00	49.0	46.3	50.8	4:00	47.2	46.3	50.5
12 Midnight	48.4	45.4	50.2	5:00	47.0	44.1	49.7
1:00 a.m.	47.6	44.3	49.7	6:00	48.4	45.0	49.0
2:00	47.4	44.1	49.6	7:00	48.8	44.8	49.7
3:00	48.2	45.2	49.0	8:00	49.6	48.0	51.8
4:00	48.0	45.5	49.1	9:00	50.0	48.1	52.7
5:00	48.4	47.1	49.6	10:00	51.0	48.1	55.2
6:00	48.6	47.4	52.0	11:00	50.4	49.5	54.1
7:00	50.0	49.2	52.2	12 Noon	50.0	48.7	50.9
8:00	49.8	49.0	52.4	1:00 p.m.	48.9	47.6	51.2
9:00	50.3	49.4	51.7	2:00	49.8	48.4	51.0
10:00	50.2	49.6	51.8	3:00	49.8	48.8	50.8
11:00	50.0	49.0	52.3	4:00	50.0	49.1	50.6
12 Noon	50.0	48.8	52.4	5:00	47.8	45.2	51.2
1:00 p.m.	50.1	49.4	53.6	6:00	46.4	44.0	49.7
2:00	49.7	48.6	51.0	7:00	46.4	44.4	50.0
3:00	48.4	47.2	51.7	8:00	47.2	46.6	48.9
4:00	47.2	45.3	50.9	9:00	48.4	47.2	49.5
5:00	46.8	44.1	49.0	10:00	49.2	48.1	50.7
6:00	46.8	41.0	51.2	11:00	48.4	47.0	50.8
7:00	50.0	46.2	51.7	12 Midnight	47.2	46.4	49.2
8:00	47.4	44.0	48.7	1:00 a.m.	47.4	46.8	49.0
9:00	47.0	44.2	48.9	2:00	48.8	47.2	51.4
10:00	47.2	46.6	50.2	3:00	49.6	49.0	50.6
11:00	48.6	47.0	50.0	4:00	51.0	50.5	51.5
12 Midnight	49.8	48.2	50.4	5:00	50.5	50.0	51.9

DecFab, Inc.
Makers of Dental Equipment

DecFab manufactures dental equipment and because of its persistent sales efforts had about 36% of the market in 1980. More recently, DecFab has found its market slipping. The CEO of DecFab was addressing her Marketing VP, John Baldridge, and Andreas Hanson, the Manufacturing VP. "Gentlemen, sales continue to be fairly flat even though we concentrate on the development of new products and provide better services. What's wrong? We have lost market share almost continually during the past eight years so that now we have only about 24% according to our best estimates. What is disturbing is that the greatest share of the markets seems to be picked up by 'off-shore' manufacturers, who, quite frankly, are putting out superb products. Even in those areas where we seem to have possible niches we are facing incredible odds, and, in fact, are losing sales there too. What's wrong, people? We started this company together a long time ago and were riding the crest of a wave for years. We are well known in the trade. But even at the last manufacturers' convention, I sensed that customers were not nearly as interested in our products as they were in foreign manufacturers. John, you heard some of the customers complaining about the quality of our products. I just don't understand it. We were considered to be the best in the seventies. What do you two think?"

DecFab, Inc. has been in the business of making dental drills, hand appliances, and accessories for the dental trade for a number of years. Sue Wilson and her husband, John, started the company in 1953 after they had graduated from Upstate University. John died suddenly from a heart attack in 1980. Sue, who had been closely involved in the company since its start, took over as CEO, and has managed the company extremely well since that time. Andreas Hanson joined the company in the early 1960s with John Baldridge joining shortly after. They were much more involved in the day-to-day activities in the past years than they are today. Company growth has increased sufficiently so that there are now about 125 people working for DecFab. Marketing is generally done through agents who represent DecFab together with several other companies which do not compete with each other. About 60% of the manufacturing is done within the DecFab Operations with the remainder being subcontracted out.

Source: Kenneth D. Ramsing and Timothy M. Bergquist, University of Oregon.

Fairly recently, DecFab has tried to reduce the number of its vendors considerably but with little success. In the past, DecFab let bids for the lowest costs of each of its subcontracted products and subcomponents. Recently, Mr. Hanson has attempted to get a better relationship with a few vendors by giving them more or less exclusive rights. He feels that he has lost some of his credibility with Sue Wilson since she continues to believe they should have many bidders competing to supply the same product.

For a number of years, Andreas Hanson has been taking product samples from the vendors' deliveries for purposes of assuring quality for himself and for marketing. Initially, he did not even know what he wanted to do with the data or how the samples should be taken. He did collect the data at random but beyond that is was pretty "catch-as-catch-can." In more recent years, as he has read more about quality control, Andreas found that he should be mindful of the producer's and consumer's risks when taking simple acceptance samples. In order to save costs in inspection, Andreas decided upon the advice of a friend to set his sample size (n) at 15 and the maximum number of nonconforming (defective) parts permissible (c) at 0. In addition, he set the Acceptable Quality Level (AQL) at 5% nonconforming (0.05) and the Lot Tolerance Percent Defective (LTPD) at 10% nonconforming (0.10). His next step was to develop an Operating Characteristic (OC) curve for his sampling plan.

Over the past several years Andreas has recorded the number of poor quality parts which were observed from samples of incoming parts from the Ajax Company, a subcontractor which produces dental polishing tips under the DecFab name. Andreas was not completely satisfied with the quality of these polishing tips but did not believe he had concrete evidence that the quality was poor. **Exhibit 1** is a sample of the attribute data that he collected from one of his efforts to check the incoming parts.

Another part which the company has subcontracted is a special screw which is made by Delta Machining Company. This is an important screw in that it must fit in a tiny device used by dentists for drilling and cleaning teeth. This device was designed and made by DecFab so that each part, including the screw, would fit together to be used at the high speed of the dental drills. The DecFab engineers set forth very exacting tolerances for each part in the dental drill, including the screw made by Delta. Historically, the process average diameter has been 0.500 millimeter and the process average range 0.200 millimeter. Data from the last eight samples are shown in **Exhibit 2**. The sample size is four.

DecFab has been recently receiving an increasing number of complaints from both dentists and service technicians that the dental drill was wearing out prematurely. The development engineers had carefully reviewed their design drawings to determine if all of the specifications were acceptable. This review revealed no errors or tolerances which were out of specifications. But they were concerned about the drill's failure rate and mean time between failure (MTBF). They had designed the dental drill to work for a minimum of 200 hours before needing service. To check whether this was correct, they took six of the drills off the fabrication line and tested them for 100 hours to determine their reliability. During that time three drills failed (at 15 hours, at 50 hours, and the third at 85 hours) for total unit operating hours for all six drills of 450 hours. Based on discussions with the service technicians, they learned it took an average of five hours to repair the drill on site at the dentist's office.

To help isolate the source of the problem with the dental drill production process, Mr Hanson brought together a "Problem Solving Team" of people from Marketing, Manufacturing, and Engineering to work on the problem. There was some resistance to this approach from the other department heads. Usually, there was little communication between the departments regarding the marketing, designing, and producing of any product. The first step was to develop a flow chart of the production process for the dental drill, including inputs from marketing and engineering. They then brainstormed a cause-and-effect diagram to zero in on the potential problem areas. The team decided to collect some data over the next week regarding the production process. The manufacturing people examined all the problems on the line and tabulated each cause using checksheets. **Exhibit 3** shows the data they collected.

At the next meeting, the team decided that Purchasing, Engineering, and Manufacturing needed to work more closely with the vendors of the parts. Next the team decided to concentrate on the poor machining issue. Therefore, over the next week, they took samples of the particular critical part and measured its diameter, which according to specifications, should be 0.50 millimeter. **Exhibit 4** shows the data they collected grouped by every 0.05 millimeter.

The team also decided to examine dental drills from their major competitor, the Fuji Company. They found that the Fuji Company's drill worked very well. In all the areas which count, their specifications were the same as DecFabs. The only difference found in the five Fuji units that had been taken apart was that their tolerances were significantly narrower than DecFabs. In fact, the Fuji Company seemed to hit the target each time.

For the past several years, Sue Wilson had been trying to establish a stronger commitment to quality but had seemed to find a great deal of resistance among the managers, including John Baldridge. Andreas Hanson seemed more willing to stand behind a total quality management (TQM) program than John, but even he had reservations. Sue was not sure what to do to instill a more quality minded attitude in the company.

DISCUSSION QUESTIONS

Ultimately we want to answer Questions 1 and 2 for Sue. However, using the tools of TQM as presented below may be a fruitful way to develop data prior to answering Questions 1 and 2.
1. How should Sue Wilson develop a total quality management (TQM) program given the conditions which exist in the case? Describe some specific actions she could take to improve quality at DecFab.
2. Describe a course of action for the Problem-Solving Team, in addition to that mentioned in the case.

What will two standard tools of TQM tell the team?
3. Develop a Pareto diagram for the Problem-Solving Team that describes the major causes of problems with the production process of the dental drill.
4. Develop a histogram for the team of the diameter frequency data for the dental drill production process.

What will control charts tell Sue about performance at DecFab Inc. and Suppliers?
5. Develop a P-chart using three standard deviations to help Mr. Hanson determine if the quality of incoming parts from the Ajax Company are poor or not.
6. What does the P-chart tell you about the incoming parts from the Ajax Company?
7. Develop X-bar and R charts for the screw data from the Delta Machining Company, using historical process information to determine the center lines.
8. Does DecFab have a problem with the screw part from Delta Machining Company? If so, why? If not, why not?

What will Acceptance Sampling tell Sue about suppliers?
9. Develop and draw an Operating Characteristic (OC) curve for Mr. Hanson to help with his sampling plan. Assume $n = 15$ and $c = 0$. Find the probability of acceptance (Pa) for p (% nonconforming) of 1, 5, 10, 15, 20, 25, and 30 percent.

10. Determine the producer's risk, a, and the consumer's risk, b, if AQL = 5% and LTPD = 10%.
11. Determine the Average Outgoing Quality Limit (AOQL) for the above sampling plan.

What can we tell Sue about reliability?
12. What is the failure rate for the dental drill, based on the reliability testing?
13. What is the mean time between failures (MTBF) for the dental drill?
14. What is the inherent availability of the dental drill for the dentist?
15. Does DecFab have a problem with the dental drill wearing out prematurely? If so, why? If not, why not?

Exhibit 1 Number of Poor Quality Parts

Observed Number of Poor Quality Parts Recorded in 12 Samples of 2,500 Parts Each

Sample Number	Poor Quality Parts (number)	Proportion of Sample
1	15	0.0060
2	12	0.0048
3	19	0.0076
4	2	0.0008
5	19	0.0076
6	4	0.0016
7	24	0.0096
8	7	0.0028
9	10	0.0040
10	17	0.0068
11	15	0.0060
12	3	0.0012
	p-bar =	0.0049

Exhibit 2 Delta Screw Data

Sample Number	Observations of Screw Diameter in Sample (millimeters)				Sample X	Sample R
	1	2	3	4		
1	0.510	0.630	0.390	0.350	0.470	0.280
2	0.500	0.560	0.420	0.640	0.530	0.220
3	0.680	0.490	0.530	0.620	0.580	0.190
4	0.450	0.330	0.470	0.550	0.450	0.220
5	0.700	0.580	0.640	0.680	0.650	0.120
6	0.480	0.550	0.630	0.660	0.580	0.180
7	0.350	0.400	0.510	0.580	0.460	0.230
8	0.680	0.450	0.700	0.570	0.600	0.250

Exhibit 3 Causes of Problems on the Production Line

Cause of Problem	Frequency
Poor Machining	58
Part Too Large	8
Parts Don't Fit	6
Bad Incoming Part	22
Welds Incorrect	16

Exhibit 4 Diameter of Part and Frequency Within Sample

Range	Frequency
.31–.35	3
.36–.40	2
.41–.45	3
.46–.50	4
.51–.55	5
.56–.60	4
.61–.65	5
.60–.70	6

Westover Electric, Inc.

Westover Electrical, Inc., is a medium-sized Houston manufacturer of wire windings used in making electric motors. Joe Wilson, Operations Manager, has experienced an increasing problem with rejected product found during the manufacturing operation. "I'm not sure where to begin," said Joe at the weekly staff meeting with his boss. "Rejects in the Winding Department have been killing us the past two months. Nobody in operations has any idea why. I have just brought in a consultant, Roger Gagnon, to take a look at the situation and make recommendations about how we can find out what is going on. I don't expect Roger to make technical recommendations—just see if he can point us in the right direction."

Gagnon's first stop later that day was the production floor. His discussions with the production supervisors in the Winding Department indicated they had no real grasp of what the problem was or what to do to correct it. A tour of the winding operation indicated that there were three machines that wound wire onto plastic cores to produce the primary and secondary electric motor windings. After inspection by Quality Control (QC), these windings then went to the Packaging Department. Packaging personnel, Gagnon found, inspect their own work and make corrections on the spot. The problem is that too many windings were found to be defective and require reworking before they can be packaged.

Gagnon's next stop was the Quality Control Department where he obtained the records for the past month's Winding Department rejects (**Table 1**).

DISCUSSION QUESTIONS

1. Prepare an outline for Roger Gagnon's report.
2. What charts, graphs, computer printouts, and so forth might be included in the report?
3. Prepare Gagnon's recommendation, with justification, on one page.
4. Prepare the detail necessary to supplement Gagnon's recommendation and justification so Joe Wilson will understand how he arrived at your recommendations.

Source: Professor Victor E. Sower, Sam Houston State University, as published in Jay Heizer and Barry Render, *Production/Operations Management*, 4th ed., Prentice Hall, Upper Saddle River, NJ, 1996, pp. 101–103.

Table 1 January Transformer Reject Log: Winding Process

Date	No. Inspected	Winder	Bad Wind	Twisted Wire	Broken Leads	Abraded Wire	Wrong Core	Wrong Wire	Failed Electrical Test
1	100	1	1	0	4	1	0	0	1
	100	2	2	1	0	0	1	5	0
	100	3	0	0	0	5	0	0	3
2	100	1	0	1	3	0	0	0	0
	100	2	3	1	0	0	2	3	0
	100	3	0	0	1	6	0	0	0
3	100	1	1	0	0	2	0	0	0
	100	2	0	0	0	0	0	3	0
	100	3	0	0	1	4	0	0	3
4	100	1	0	0	3	0	0	0	0
	100	2	0	0	0	0	0	2	0
	100	3	0	0	0	3	1	0	3
5	100	1	0	1	5	0	0	0	0
	100	2	0	0	0	0	0	2	1
	100	3	0	0	0	3	0	0	2
8	100	1	0	0	2	0	0	0	0
	100	2	0	0	0	0	0	1	0
	100	3	0	0	0	3	0	0	3
9	100	1	0	1	2	0	0	0	0
	100	2	0	0	0	0	0	1	0
	100	3	0	0	0	3	0	0	4
10	100	1	0	0	5	0	0	0	0
	100	2	1	0	0	0	1	0	0
	100	3	0	0	0	5	0	0	4
11	100	1	0	0	4	0	0	0	0
	100	2	0	0	0	0	0	0	0
	100	3	0	0	0	4	0	0	4
12	100	1	0	0	3	0	1	0	0
	100	2	1	0	1	0	0	0	0
	100	3	0	0	0	5	0	0	4
15	100	1	0	0	2	0	0	1	0
	100	2	0	0	0	0	0	1	0
	100	3	0	0	0	3	0	0	3
16	100	1	0	0	6	0	0	0	0
	100	2	0	0	0	0	0	0	0
	100	3	0	0	0	3	0	0	3
17	100	1	0	1	1	0	0	0	0
	100	2	0	0	0	0	0	0	1
	100	3	0	0	0	3	0	0	3
18	100	1	1	0	2	0	0	0	0
	100	2	0	0	0	0	0	1	0
	100	3	0	0	0	4	0	0	1
19	100	1	0	0	2	0	0	0	0
	100	2	0	0	0	0	0	0	0
	100	3	0	0	0	3	0	1	1
22	100	1	0	1	4	0	0	0	0
	100	2	0	0	0	0	0	0	0
	100	3	0	0	0	3	0	1	2
23	100	1	0	0	4	0	0	0	0
	100	2	0	0	0	0	0	0	1
	100	3	0	0	0	4	0	0	3

Table 1 January Transformer Reject Log: Winding Process, concluded

Date	No. Inspected	Winder	No. of Reject Units by Cause						
			Bad Wind	**Twisted Wire**	**Broken Leads**	**Abraded Wire**	**Wrong Core**	**Wrong Wire**	**Failed Electrical Test**
24	100	1	0	0	2	0	0	1	0
	100	2	0	1	0	0	0	0	0
	100	3	0	0	0	4	0	0	3
25	100	1	0	0	3	0	0	0	0
	100	2	0	0	0	1	0	0	0
	100	3	0	0	0	2	0	0	4
26	100	1	0	0	1	0	0	0	0
	100	2	0	1	0	1	0	0	0
	100	3	0	0	0	2	0	0	3
29	100	1	0	0	2	0	0	0	0
	100	2	0	0	1	0	0	0	0
	100	3	0	0	0	2	0	0	3
30	100	1	0	0	2	0	0	0	0
	100	2	0	0	0	0	1	0	0
	100	3	0	0	0	2	0	0	3

Note: Assume that each defective unit was rejected because of one, single defect.

Ajax Sewing Machine Company

The Ajax Sewing Machine Company has just received a large overseas order and has put production on a three-shift basis to meet it. But inventory has fallen to a minimum, and Ajax is considering reassigning its expediters to ensure that critical materials will come in on time.

Four key parts are purchased, respectively, from the Arkwright, Benton, Crowley, and Danielson companies. The four suppliers give rather poor service on deliveries, although they are more than satisfactory in other respects. Ajax, therefore, has made a practice of assigning one of its crack expediters to each of the four accounts.

On the basis of the past five years' experience, Ajax is able to tabulate the average days of delay experienced when each expediter is assigned to a particular supplier, as shown in **Table 1**.

Thus if Jones is assigned to the Danielson account, we may expect Danielson to be eleven days late in making its shipments. If Smith is given this assignment, the delay is reduced to nine days.

An analysis by Ajax management shows that a delay at Arkwright will cost $125 per day; a delay at Benton, $50 per day; a delay at Crowley, $80 per day; and at Danielson, $100 per day.

Ajax has to assign four additional inspectors to handle the increased volume from the four suppliers. The cost of an inspector's mistake is $10 on an Arkwright part, $20 on a Benton part, $30 on a Crowley part, and $40 on a Danielson part.

The four inspectors—Herman, Abrams, Adams, and Johnson—vary considerably in their ability to catch errors. Herman has a 10% chance of letting an error go through in the course of a day, Abrams a 20% chance, Adams a 30% chance, and Johnson a 40% chance.

These estimates are based on the overall records of the four inspectors. However, when the records are analyzed by type of job, we see that Abrams has a bad record on the Benton parts, so that Abrams' chance of making an error on a Benton job is 25%. On a Crowley part, Abrams' record is very good, and the chance of error is only 10% . By the same token Adams has a particularly good record on Danielson-type jobs, with only one chance in ten of making an error.

Source: Gary J. Zenz with George H. Thompson, *Purchasing and the Management of Materials*, John Wiley & Sons, Inc., New York, Seventh Edition, 1994, pp. 606–607.

For the others, the job analysis supports the original estimates. **Table 2** shows the chances of a daily error.

DISCUSSION QUESTIONS

1. How should the four expediters be assigned to minimize delay costs?
2. How should Ajax assign its inspectors to minimize the dollar value of its inspection errors?

Table 1 Days of Delay for Each Expediter

Expediter	Supplier			
	Arkwright	Benton	Crowley	Danielson
Jones	12	40	30.0	11
Smith	24	60	7.5	9
Peters	21	42	20.0	24
Hammond	16	36	12.5	8

Table 2 Chance of Error (%) on the Part of Various Inspectors

Inspector	Supplier			
	Arkwright	Benton	Crowley	Danielson
Herman	10	10	10	10
Abrams	20	25	10	20
Adams	30	30	30	10
Johnson	40	40	40	40

The Mountain States Potato Company

The Mountain States Potato Company is a major potato processor located in a rural section of eastern Idaho. The company exclusively processes dehydrated potatoes. The main plant has recently encountered a significant problem involving its process water. Your analytical skill may solve it.

The plant operates two main processes, granules and slices (see **Exhibit 1** for a process flow chart) and from these processes several different forms of dehydrated potatoes are produced. The processes begin when the potatoes are received and washed on the receiving slab and then flumed to the main plant. Potatoes are also pumped in water between a number of the process steps.

Granules are the main commodity of the instant potato industry and are used for instant mashed potatoes or mixed into a dough for making potato snacks. Granules production involves peeling, washing, and cooking (blanching) the product, mixing it into a sort of mashed potato and drying it to a fine powder. Slices are used in instant potato products such as scalloped potatoes. Slice production involves peeling and washing the product and then slicing, blanching, and drying it.

Since potatoes are similar in density to water, a moving stream of water such as a pump line or "flume" is an economical and efficient way to move potatoes between operations. Most of the steps involve pumping or fluming the potatoes from one step to the next. Flume water is disposed of by using it as irrigation water. The flume water, particularly the water transporting cooked potatoes, picks up a heavy starch load which must be removed before the water is suitable for land treatment. To remove this starch load all process water is gathered and pumped to a clarifier where the setable starch settles out on the bottom as sludge. The sludge is pumped into a small holding tank and picked up by a rotating screen. A vacuum is applied to the screen which draws the moisture out and leaves a filter cake. The cake is scraped off the screen and sent out as cattle feed.

This has been a highly satisfactory solution for disposing of waste since it minimizes waste contamination while maximizing the utilization of the raw

Source: Dr. George A. Johnson and Dr. Joanne Tokle of Idaho State University and Mr. Ed Conn, The Mountain States Potato Company.

Dr. George A. Johnson, Dr. Joanne Tokle, and Mr. Ed Conn
Idaho State University and The Mountain States Potato Company

151

resource. In addition, the revenue has been sufficient to cover the costs of the waste disposal system. If the by-product could not be sold the waste disposal system would represent a significant expense to the company.

THE PROBLEM

Recently, the plant's main customer for the filter cake, a feedlot about 20 miles from the plant, suffered some severe economic losses. The customer's cattle were not gaining weight and the feedlot operator felt the inability of his cattle to gain weight could be attributed to the filter cake. Analysis of the filter cake was begun to see if any recent changes could be readily identified. Normally, ash content should be 2%–3% and solids should run around 11% by weight. The analysis showed high ash content (over 10%) and low solids content (under 8%). Both factors were seen as possible contributors to the cattle-weight problem. The ash content resulted from muddy water entering the system and was easily corrected with some piping changes. The solids were a different problem.

Initially, all that was known of the filter cake system was that historical records showed that the solids had been running in the neighborhood of 11.5% in years past. Presently, the solids were running in the 8% to 9% range. Several additions had been made to the plant in the intervening years which had significantly increased the water and solids volume and the clarifier temperature. What was actually affecting the solids was a mystery, but since the plant needed to get rid of its solids waste if it was going to run, something had to be done quickly. The only practical solution was to determine some way to get the solids content back up to the previous levels. Individuals involved in the process were asked to identify variables that might be manipulated that could in turn affect the solids content. This review turned up six variables believed to potentially affect the percent solids. The variables are described in **Table 1**. Data obtained from monitoring the process several times daily for twenty days are reported in **Table 2**.

DISCUSSION QUESTIONS

1. Develop a statistical model of this process. What conclusions can be drawn from this model?
2. Discuss the effect of outliers on the analysis.
3. Design an experiment to investigate factors that affect solids.

Exhibit 1 Process Flow Chart

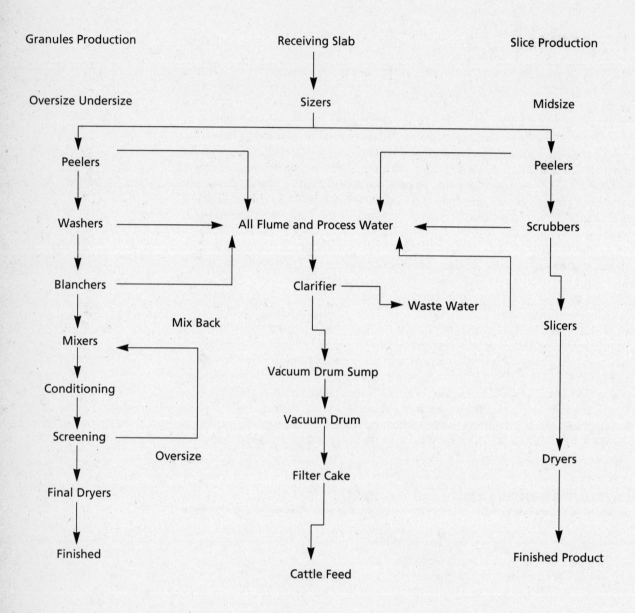

Table 1 Variables Obtained from Filter Cake System

SOLIDS	Percent solids in filter cake.
DRUMSPD	Speed at which the drum was rotated when collecting filter cake. Measured with a stop watch.
VARIDRIV	Setting used to control drum speed. May differ from DRUMSPD due to mechanical inefficiencies.
THICK	Cake thickness measured on drum.
UPPER	Pressure of vacuum line above fluid line on rotating drum.
LOWER	Pressure of vacuum line below fluid line on rotating drum.
PH	Acidity. This indicates bacterial action in the clarifier. As bacterial action progresses, organic acids are produced which can be measured using pH. This is controlled by the downtime of the system.

Table 2 Data for The Mountain States Potato Company Analysis

Obs	solids	ph	lower	upper	thick	varidriv	drumspd
1	9.7	3.7	13	14	0.250	6	33.00
2	9.4	3.8	17	18	0.875	6	30.43
3	10.5	3.8	14	15	0.500	6	34.00
4	10.9	3.9	14	14	0.500	6	34.00
5	11.6	4.3	17	18	0.375	6	36.24
6	10.9	4.2	16	17	0.500	6	31.76
7	11.0	4.3	16	19	0.375	6	34.00
8	10.7	3.9	15	16	0.375	6	32.13
9	11.8	3.6	8	8	0.375	6	37.00
10	9.7	4.0	18	18	0.500	6	36.00
11	11.6	4.0	12	13	0.313	5	45.00
12	10.9	3.9	15	15	0.500	5	50.00
13	10.0	3.8	17	18	0.625	5	46.91
14	10.3	3.8	13	14	0.500	4	57.50
15	10.1	3.6	17	17	0.625	4	60.40
16	9.9	3.8	17	18	0.500	4	53.14
17	9.5	3.5	17	18	0.625	6	34.40
18	10.5	3.8	15	17	0.500	6	33.96
19	10.8	3.9	15	17	0.750	6	35.00
20	10.4	3.9	14	15	0.500	6	35.00
21	10.9	4.0	15	16	0.500	6	34.00
22	11.2	4.4	17	19	0.375	6	34.00
23	9.5	3.8	17	17	0.500	6	33.49
24	10.7	3.9	15	17	0.500	6	33.38
25	10.1	3.8	15	17	0.500	6	41.00
26	10.5	3.8	17	17	0.500	6	36.00
27	10.9	4.0	15	17	0.250	6	34.00
28	15.5	4.3	13	15	0.625	6	41.00
29	13.1	4.0	17	17	0.500	6	35.00
30	11.0	4.0	14	15	0.375	6	36.00
31	12.5	4.2	15	17	0.313	6	37.72
32	11.7	4.2	14	14	0.250	6	36.00
33	11.9	4.4	15	16	0.375	6	36.52
34	11.7	3.4	8	10	0.313	6	38.08
35	17.8	4.3	12	12	0.313	6	38.00
36	11.8	4.5	14	15	0.250	6	33.00
37	10.0	3.7	12	13	0.250	5	48.00
38	10.3	3.7	15	15	0.500	5	48.00
39	9.8	3.8	14	15	0.500	5	47.24
40	10.0	3.7	13	14	0.500	6	37.00
41	10.6	4.1	14	15	0.500	6	33.70
42	11.2	3.9	13	14	0.375	6	38.26
43	10.9	3.7	13	14	0.313	6	38.00
44	11.0	4.1	13	14	0.375	6	37.00
45	11.0	4.1	14	15	0.375	6	38.00
46	11.7	4.5	14	14	0.250	6	36.26
47	11.8	4.4	13	14	0.250	6	37.45
48	12.0	4.2	13	13	0.375	6	38.00
49	11.8	4.6	14	14	0.375	6	36.90
50	11.1	4.0	14	15	0.500	6	37.00
51	11.6	3.9	14	14	0.500	6	37.50
52	11.0	4.0	14	15	0.500	6	36.00
53	11.2	3.9	15	15	0.313	6	35.00
54	11.0	4.2	14	14	0.375	6	37.00

Tom's of Maine

Tom's of Maine, a manufacturer of "natural" personal-care products, was founded in 1970 by Tom and Kate Chappell. The Chappells started their company after moving to Maine seeking a simpler life and a deeper connection to the land. As part of this move, they began using natural foods and products, but were not able to find the natural personal care products they wanted for themselves and their children. So they decided to make and sell their own. (Tom's of Maine considers "natural products" to be those which are minimally processed, derived from natural resources, and free of artificial colors, sweeteners, preservatives, synthetic flavors, and fragrances.) From this simple beginning in the 1970s, the company has grown to become a significant player in the mass market for personal care products. With annual sales of approximately $15 to $20 million, and 75 employees, Tom's of Maine distributes natural, environmentally-friendly products to over 20,000 food and drug stores and approximately 7,000 health food outlets.

Nestled in the picturesque New England town of Kennebunk, Maine, the company is headquartered in a renovated red-brick factory building on the Mousam river. The office area, well lit and open, bespeaks Tom's of Maine's commitment to the environment with abundant, colorful, animal-related artwork. Recycled ingredient containers, transformed into free-standing art by local students, adorn the corridors. Framed copies of the company's mission statement and posters with handwritten excerpts from customer letters also are displayed. A few miles from town, the manufacturing plant is housed in a rustic wooden structure next to a defunct railroad depot. A pleasant minty aroma pervades the inside of the facility in which all Tom's of Maine products are manufactured.

COMMON GOOD CAPITALISM

Tom's of Maine has remained true to the Chappells' original vision to manage their business for both profit and the common good of the community, the environment, and one another. Tom's of Maine strives to integrate the corporate values of commercial success with the belief that companies have a

Source: Jeanne Busemeyer, adapted from Martin Starr, *Operations Management: a Systems Approach*, 1996, Boyd and Fraser (now South-Western College Publishing).

responsibility at all times to the common good of society. Tom Chappell explains that with "common good capitalism," private aspirations or aims (such as what a business owner does with the profits from the business) are accountable to a higher good, a common good. Tom Chappell wants the community in which his company operates to be able to recognize the business as a valuable, contributing presence.[1]

PRODUCT VARIETY

Tom's of Maine manufactures and sells a variety of natural personal care products, including flossing ribbon; alcohol-free mouthwash, anti-perspirant and deodorant, shampoo, shaving cream, and toothpaste—with and without fluoride. Sales of toothpaste account for the majority of Tom's of Maine's total revenue. We will now examine Tom's of Maine's manufacturing process for toothpaste.

PRODUCTION PROCESS FOR TOOTHPASTE

Pre-Production Activities

First the raw materials for the toothpaste must be received. These materials include printed tubes with caps; natural ingredients (including calcium carbonate, fluoride, carrageenan, glycerin, sodium lauryl sulfate, flavors); toothpaste boxes; inner pack wrap; and shipping cartons.

Every incoming raw material is scrutinized against supplier specifications and United States Pharmacopoeia (USP) and Food and Drug Administration (FDA) requirements. The FDA regulates ingredients that alter normal bodily functions, i.e., fluoride in toothpaste and antimicrobials in deodorant. Typical quality control (QC) tests at this stage include chemical assay, microbiology, organoleptic (appearance, smell, taste) and moisture content. QC tests normally are completed within 48 hours of receipt of a sample of the ingredient. If a problem with a one-half pound pre-shipment sample is detected, the sample is rejected, discarded, and the shipment stopped. (To avoid production-scheduling problems if a shipment is rejected, Tom's of Maine generally has a two-week supply of all materials on hand, Lead time to order ingredients is 8 to 12 weeks.) The tubes and boxes are tested against specifications provided by the marketing department to determine that printing and colors are correct.

One problem that may arise at this stage is that the density of the calcium carbonate sometimes doesn't meet requirements. Calcium carbonate is the ingredient that dictates how much water is absorbed in the toothpaste mix, so its density must be right. Testers also must be sure that the pH rate (a scale of acidity-alkalinity) is within a narrow range of specification. If higher than the specification range, the shelf life of the toothpaste will be reduced. Shelf life is 12 to 18 months, depending on storage conditions—the colder the better!

Tom's of Maine holds one week's worth of ingredients in a transition warehouse at the plant; an off-site warehouse about a mile away is for longer-term storage. Materials stored in the off-site warehouse stay an average 40–45 days.

---

1   Tom Chappell, *The Soul of a Business: Managing for Profit and the Common Good*, Bantam, October, 1993.

Liquid ingredients are stored in 55-gallon drums; powdered ingredients are stored in 50-pound bags. No supplies are used without a completed "released for use" sticker which tells the date the supply was tested and released, who analyzed it, and the quantity. This allows Tom's of Maine to trace every ingredient back to its original tester. Ingredients in the transition warehouse are moved 20 feet by forklift into the batch preparation area on an as-needed basis.

Tom's of Maine has close relationships with a few suppliers. The company works closely with suppliers to understand their processes and improvement of them. Target supplier flaw rate (also called the defective rate) is 0.1%. Tom's of Maine shares flaw rate information with suppliers and works with them to improve the rates. When Tom's of Maine first started buying from its tube supplier, for example, the flaw rate was 0.5%. After working closely with them to increase quality, the same supplier has achieved a 0.05% rate, and now supplies all of Tom's of Maine's toothpaste tubes.

Continuous Batch Preparation

Tom's of Maine makes one variety of toothpaste per day, mixing the ingredients in a 300-gallon vat or "change can" weighing 3,6000 pounds The toothpaste ingredients (calcium carbonate, fluoride, carrageenan, glycerin, sodium lauryl sulfate, and natural flavors) are mixed at high speeds of up to 600 rpms for 2 1/2 to 3 hours. This toothpaste mixture is called "slurry." After the mixing is complete the operators scrape the mixing blades to remove as much of the mixture as possible from them; this also facilitates cleaning and preparation of the equipment for the next batch.

Tom's of Maine has ten varieties of toothpaste in all. In a 20-day month, 13 to 14 days are spent on making toothpaste. When filling four-ounce tubes, four batches of one flavor are made in one ten-hour day, which yields approximately 46,000 four-ounce tubes. When filling six-ounce tubes, six vats of the mixture are made, which results in 44,000 to 45,000 tubes in one ten-hour day. Tom's of Maine usually devotes two days per month to making spearmint toothpaste, which is its best selling flavor.

Tom's of Maine has an extensive preventive maintenance program which regularly checks parts and machines. These preventive checks are done during production. While a liquid product (such as deodorant or mouthwash) is being produced, maintenance checks are performed on the equipment used to produce "nonliquid" products, such as toothpaste. When nonliquid products are being processed, checks are performed on the equipment used to make liquid products. A supply of replacement parts is maintained at the factory.

Eleven people are involved in making a batch of toothpaste, including a foreman, a production supervisor, three mechanics (who work alternating shifts from 5 a.m. to 6 p.m., Monday through Friday), one quality assurance (QA) lab supervisor, one lab assistant, three batch mixers and one batch supervisor.

QC Tests on Slurry

After mixing is complete, each vat of slurry is tested for conformity to specs on pH level, density, taste, moisture and FDA requirements for fluoride level. Two taste testers taste the slurry for acceptability. The reject rate on the slurry is below 0.01%. The rework rate on slurry is about 0.25%. QC tests on slurry generally take 10–15 minutes. Results of the chromatography tests for fluoride dispersion (samples of which are taken when the mixing is complete) are not available until after the toothpaste has been inserted into the tubes. This test takes about $1^1/_2$ to 2 hours. Tom's of Maine has only had to reject one batch in 14 years because fluoride was not dispersed evenly throughout the mixture. If a batch is rejected for any reason, the contents are discarded.

Pumping of Vat Contents to Production Line

After the QC tests on slurry are complete, the ingredients are pumped upstairs at a rate of 5 gallons or 60 pounds per minute for continuation of the production process. When all the slurry in the vat has been emptied, the empty vat is moved out of the way and a new vat of slurry that has been prepared off-line is rolled into place. This changeover takes about five minutes.

Four Station Assembly Process

Upstairs in the plant the four assembly stations are set to receive the toothpaste slurry. The empty printed tubes, open at the bottom, have caps already screwed on. The aluminum tubes are lined with a plastic phenolic coating. Without this coating the calcium carbonate would react with the aluminum. Tom's of Maine uses aluminum tubes because they are recyclable. All hand operations in the production process serve a dual purpose: they perform a specific function (such as picking up a tube and placing it in the box) as well as serve as quality checks.

Thirteen people are involved in this serialized part of the production process including a foreman, a production supervisor, three mechanics, one operator at Station I, two operators at Station II, two operators at Station III, one "floater" (who keeps the floor clean, moves boxes, and generally troubleshoots), and one operator and one forklift operator at Station IV.

Stations I through III are synchronized by a conveyor. Operators' idle time is taken up by moving material from station to station, i.e., moving pallets on finished goods to the conveyor which takes them downstairs. The speed of the conveyors used is approximately 30 feet per minute.

Station I. At the first station, a machine operator loads a box of tubes into a magazine that orients the tube. The empty boxes are collected, then sent back to the supplier for reuse. The machine fills each tube and passes each through a series of four crimping stations, which fold the end of the tube three times; the fourth station prints a batch code on the tube. The machine then delivers the tube to a conveyor which moves at 30 feet per minute. Tubes are filled at a rate of 80 to 84 per minute (6-ounce tubes at 80 to 81 tubes per minute; 4-ounce tubes at 83 to 84 per minute). The vice president of manufacturing Gary Ritterhaus refers to these rates as the "quality sweet spots," the processing rates at which a less than 0.01% flaw rate is achieved.

Station II. Two operators pick up tubes off the conveyor and visually check that the crimp is up to code (it is not leaking) and that the printing is okay. One operator loads a magazine with toothpaste boxes; two other operators then insert the tubes into the individual boxes. These operators are rotated once every hour to minimize the adverse effects of repetition and "overuse" injuries. The filled boxes slide off the conveyor into Station III. Air is blown toward the boxes as they slide so that if a box has not been filled, it is blown off the conveyor and onto the floor.

Station III. One operator gathers six toothpaste boxes by hand, stacked in two groups of three boxes. The operator puts the six boxes under a plastic sheet and loosely wraps the boxes with the plastic. The six boxes are then shrink-wrapped together by a machine with a heat chamber. Six-packs are shrink-wrapped at the rate of 13 to 14 per minute.

Station IV. Another operator puts six 6-packs into a corrugated master case, producing a little over two master cases per minute. The batch code is put on the case; then the case is loaded onto a pallet. An operator loads 100 master cases onto each pallet. The master cases are "stretch-wrapped" onto the pallet. Pallets are then loaded onto a conveyor and taken downstairs. From there, a forklift operator moves the pallets downstairs, where they are stored until the truck is loaded, either the evening of the day the tubes are filled or the next morning. The truck ships the pallets to the warehouse the next morning.

Four people work in the warehouse. The product is stored in racks in the warehouse for up to three months. Orders are filled on a "first-in, first-out" basis. The warehouse is arranged randomly, each product marked with a product code. Shelf life for toothpaste is 12 to 18 months. Turnover at retail outlets typically is faster than this. The product is shipped to customers via common carrier.

QC Charts and Checklists

Tom's of Maine uses a variety of QC charts and checklists during the toothpaste manufacturing process. These charts include a "Production Order" and "Toothpaste Manufacturing Checklist" used when the toothpaste ingredients are mixed; a "Toothpaste Checklist" used in preparing the four-station assembly process; a "Fill Report" which is a quality control check used after the tubes are filled; and a record of "Tube Defects Per Day" which records such problems as bad or loose caps, bumps in the tube lining, printing problems, defective liners, or metal shavings.

Forecasts and Production Scheduling

Forecasts for unit sales are generated by Sales & Marketing. Manufacturing looks at the three-month history and considers the Sales & Marketing forecast in scheduling production. Because one marketing strategy Tom's of Maine uses is a revolving product "deal cycle" in which retailers can achieve discounts if they purchase products during specified periods, the company is able to anticipate increased demand and schedule production accordingly. Most retailers use the deal cycle to order product to take advantage of lower prices.

QUALITY EMPHASIS

Producing quality products is a major emphasis at Tom's of Maine. In a discussion of how Tom's of Maine defines "quality," Operations Manager Dave Pierce, Vice President of Manufacturing Gary Ritterhaus, and Public Relations Associate Matthew Chappell cited the following quality concerns:

- Tom's of Maine products must have all natural ingredients that are environmentally safe. The products are packaged in ways which respect nature as well. Consumers are encouraged to recycle the product packaging. Tom's of Maine recycles all of the packaging in which its supplies are delivered.
- All products must be proven safe and effective for consumers. But Tom's of Maine's product ingredients are never tested on animals. To avoid animal

testing, alternative tests are used. For instance, as an alternative to the traditional rabbit eye test for mucus membrane sensitivity, a vegetable protein is used which reacts in the same way as the rabbit's eyes.

- Consideration of customer needs and keeping customers happy is another quality concern at Tom's of Maine. "You don't have a job if you don't have a happy customer" is a common company refrain. Like all health- and environmentally-conscious consumers, users of Tom's of Maine's products are very astute. They demand more information about the products they purchase than the average customer. For this reason, Tom's of Maine includes three panels of product information on its toothpaste packages compared to one panel of information on the average toothpaste carton.

- Customer feedback is solicited on every package. Every letter or phone call Tom's of Maine receives—about 400 per month—is read (or received) and tabulated. Approximately 70% of the letters are positive. All letters are answered by a member of the Consumer Dialogue Team, which is comprised of ten people from all departments in the company. The Quality Assurance and Production Departments receive copies of all complaints.

- Tom's of Maine also strives for a high quality of life for its employees. To this end, there are no weekend or night shifts at the plant and there is frequent rotation on production lines. Employees are members of various teams including the Consumer Dialog Team, Engineering Team, Production Team, Quality Assurance Team, and Scheduling Team. The teams, which are further broken down into task forces, are adaptations of quality circles. Tom's of Maine plans to have all self-managed teams in place in the near future.

- Service to community is an important quality consideration for Tom's of Maine. In keeping with Tom Chappell's theory of "Common Good Capitalism," employees are encouraged to devote 5% of their work time to doing volunteer work in the community. They are given time off—with pay—to perform this volunteer service.

WHAT DOES THE FUTURE HOLD?

Tom Chappell says Tom's of Maine plans to grow at a rate of 15% annually by entering new markets and offering new products every year, while "keeping an eye on the inward or spiritual aspect of how we do things." (Spiritual growth is, unfortunately, not quantifiable.) In 1995 Tom's of Maine introduced several varieties of natural soaps, added two new toothpaste flavors (Wintermint and Cinnamint baking soda), and two new "gentle" deodorants for sensitive skin in Calendula and Woodspice fragrances.

For the near term Tom's of Maine plans to manage growth through continuing to improve productivity efficiencies with faster equipment instead of expanding the production facility or increasing the number of employees and work shifts. Tom's of Maine estimates that production can be doubled in the current facility by using faster machines. For the long term, if continued growth means expanding manufacturing facilities, Tom's of Maine will consider moving to another town, so its influence on Kennebunk will not "overwhelm" the community, according to Tom Chappell. Tom's of Maine also

---

2   *The Wall Street Journal*, Tuesday, May 11, 1993.

hopes to continue expansion into foreign markets. Currently they export their products to England, Canada, and Israel.

You might say that Tom's of Maine was slightly ahead of its time in 1970 in targeting the market for healthier, more environmentally-friendly products. In the 1990s more and more consumers are seeking products that are pure and natural, without chemical additives—a movement partially driven by fear of the environment.[2] Mass marketers such as Johnson & Johnson and Del Laboratories all recently have identified the natural products market as a growth area and are producing such products.

Tom Chappell believes that an emphasis on the science of plants will grow the business. To this end he has brought aboard a pharmacognosist (or specialist in plant chemistry and the medicinal value of plants) to ensure that Tom's of Maine's products remain not only natural but also provide the most efficacious use of natural ingredients for consumers.

DISCUSSION QUESTIONS

1. Discuss how TQM fits into Tom's of Maine's overall strategy and the relationship between strategy and success at Tom's of Maine.
2. Discuss eight dimensions of quality (performance, features, reliability, conformance, durability, serviceability, aesthetics, and perceived quality) with regard to Tom's of Maine toothpaste. Which dimensions do you think are most important to the success of this product and why?
3. Using the tools of TQM identify what happens to toothpaste slurry. Detail its path step-by-step until the finished product is stored.
4. What happens to a 50-pound bag of powdered raw materials? Detail the process and QC steps from receipt of the materials until the empty bag is returned to the supplier.
5. Identify the costs Tom's of Maine incurs with regard to appraisal, prevention, and failure.
6. Identify the various TQM techniques Tom's of Maine employs as related to raw material inspection, work-in-process inspection, and finished goods inspection.
7. What additional TQM opportunities might you suggest for TOM's?

Exhibit 1 Tom's of Maine Sells a Variety of Natural Personal Care Products.

Exhibit 2 The Empty Printed Tubes are Loaded into a Magazine that Orients the Tube.

Exhibit 3 A machine fills each tube and passes each through a series of four crimping stations, which fold the end of the tube three times.

Advanced

Tools

of

TQM

Dynamic Seal (A)

On January 5, 1984, Kevin Lynch, the Manager of Operations for Dynamic Seal, sat at his desk reviewing a letter he had received several months earlier from the purchasing manager of United Aircraft. The letter had, in no uncertain terms, stated that if Dynamic desired to maintain its promising relationship with United, it should begin to place its production facilities under Statistical Process Control (SPC). Toward this end, Mr. Lynch had hired Gordon Jenkins, a manufacturing engineer with quality control experience, and placed him in charge of implementing the SPC system at Dynamic.

COMPANY BACKGROUND

Dynamic Seal was a major producer of mechanical face seals, welded bellows, valves, and stud tensioning systems for a variety of industries. See **Exhibit 1** for some Dynamic Seal products. The firm was founded in 1939 and joined Dynamic Industries in 1968 as a wholly owned subsidiary. For over forty years the company had experienced constant growth. Dynamic's products were found in aircraft, aerospace, marine, military, petrochemical, and power industry applications.

The company began in Readville, Massachusetts, with a small staff of highly skilled engineers and technicians. The company's first development was a patented metal seal used in United's famous Twin Wasp aircraft engine of the late 1940s. In 1984, Dynamic Seal was the largest manufacturer of carbon face seals for all the major jet engine manufacturers in the United States and Europe. Dynamic was also the sole supplier of mainshaft stern seals for every submarine in the U.S. Navy's nuclear fleet.

Dynamic Seal's success was based in large part on its excellent reputation for high quality, innovative engineering, and close tolerance manufacturing capabilities. In 1984, Dynamic had projected sales of over $30 million (see **Exhibit 2**) and had a workforce of approximately 400 people. Dynamic's management organization structure is illustrated in **Exhibit 3**.

Source: Prepared by Joseph R. Carter and Thomas E. Vollmann solely as a basis for class discussion. Copyright © 1984 Boston University and the authors. Revised 1/86.

MANUFACTURING FACILITIES AND EQUIPMENT

Dynamic Seal's main office and production facilities were located in Boston, Massachusetts, and occupied a 120,000 square foot plant. Of this area, approximately 100,000 square feet were devoted to manufacturing-related activities. The fabrication and manufacturing areas were equipped with a variety of machine tools necessary for the fabrication, assembly and testing of a fairly diverse product line. Dynamic's manufacturing process was predominantly a job shop and its equipment varied from very modern computer-controlled machinery to the more traditional (and older) operator-controlled machines.

In the highly competitive, fast growing markets it served, a reputation for manufacturing expertise and high quality was imperative. While the aforementioned aircraft, nuclear, and marine applications allude to the diverse manufacturing skills required, they do not fully illustrate the unique problems facing the production process at Dynamic. Products commonly produced range in complexity from simple aircraft gear-box seals to nuclear submarine mainshaft seals with silicon carbide components 3 feet in diameter finished to tolerances of .00002 inches. They routinely utilize superalloy materials with thicknesses as small as .003 inches. Many of the seals produced by Dynamic sold for more than $1,000. A few product types sold for as much as $10,000 per seal.

QUALITY ASSURANCE

It was the stated policy of Dynamic Seal to "control the manufacture, inspection, and testing of their products to ensure that they conformed to the highest levels of quality specified by the customer." This control was accomplished by ensuring conformance of materials and processes to all applicable standards and to specified commercial or governmental requirements, and was predominantly enforced by vigorous inspection and testing. This policy of 100% inspection resulted in extremely good ratings from their customers.

Dynamic's quality assurance program was administered by an autonomous Quality Assurance Department. This department reported directly to the General Manager and was completely independent of production influence. Dynamic presently employed 35 quality inspectors who were paid an average of $10 per hour including benefits.

MACHINE CAPABILITY

One of the first stages in implementing an SPC program was to ascertain that the equipment utilized for particular operations was inherently capable of producing within the design tolerances. Making this type of assessment was called machine capability analysis.[1] If a machine was incapable of producing within a stated tolerance, placing that machine under SPC would be very impractical.

Gordon Jenkins was most anxious to get started making capability studies. One of his first analyses was of data collected by the operator of the LaBlond lathe (see **Exhibit 4**). These data were also available on a diskette in a format ready for Lotus 1-2-3. The part the operator had machined was a particularly high volume seal housing (403S895). This part had historically shown a large number of defectives. The operator sampled the first 5 parts from 20 different

---

[1] Appendix E is a technical note on machine capability analyses.

lots. He measured the outside diameter (OD) of each sampled part and listed the result on the form provided. The desired tolerance for this particular characteristic was 7.7250 + or − .0005 inches. Gordon was very interested to see the results of a machine capability study for the LaBlond lathe.

$\overline{\text{X}}$ AND R CHARTS

When a machine capability study indicated that a machine was capable of producing to desired design tolerance specifications, SPC called for the establishment of control charts to monitor the production process.[2]

A machine capability study was done for Cincinnati Milling Machine to cut a one-eighth inch wide slot in a particular ring (34164). More specifically, the design specification was 0.125 inches + or − 0.005 inches. A study of the Cincinnati Milling Machine found that it had a standard deviation for this work of 0.001 inches. This means that the natural tolerance limits would be + or − 0.003 inches, well within the design specification.

Ten samples of five parts each were collected at one-half hour intervals during a particular work day (**Exhibit 5**). These data were also on a diskette. It appeared that all was well, because all of the parts were within acceptable limits. Gordon wanted to check this out using SPC.

---

2   Appendix F is a technical note on control charts.

Exhibit 1 Typical Products

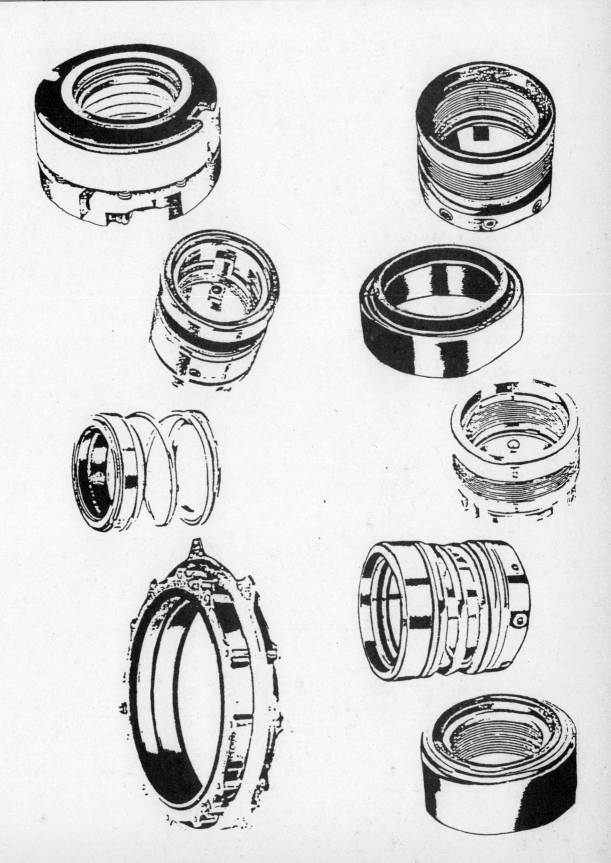

Exhibit 2 Annual Billings (Sales) Data

Year	Billings
1974	7,641,447
1975	8,170,000
1976	8,622,274
1977	10,141,120
1978	13,439,220
1979	17,562,060
1980	21,586,000
1981	23,256,980
1982	24,807,044
1983	27,950,000
1984[1]	30,109,000

1   Projected

Exhibit 3 Organizational Chart

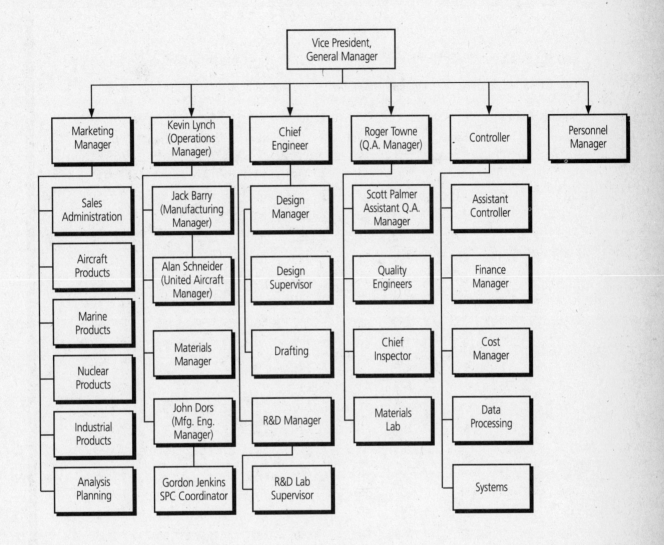

Exhibit 4 Data Collection for Capability Analysis

Part No. & Name *4035895 Housing*   **Char. Measured** *7.7250 ± .0005*

Operation No. & Desc. *#25 Outside Diameter*   **Date**

Sample Data

Item No.	Value	Item No.	Value	Item No.	Value	Item No.	Value	Item No.	Value
1	7.7250	21	7.7252	41	7.7245	61	7.7250	81	7.7255
2	7.7255	22	7.7244	42	7.7255	62	7.7245	82	7.7250
3	7.7251	23	7.7243	43	7.7250	63	7.7252	83	7.7257
4	7.7255	24	7.7240	44	7.7250	64	7.7247	84	7.7250
5	7.7253	25	7.7246	45	7.7250	65	7.7247	85	7.7257
6	7.7250	26	7.7248	46	7.7250	66	7.7250	86	7.7262
7	7.7250	27	7.7235	47	7.7245	67	7.7247	87	7.7250
8	7.7240	28	7.7255	48	7.7247	68	7.7245	88	7.7250
9	7.7238	29	7.7255	49	7.7257	69	7.7249	89	7.7248
10	7.7240	30	7.7246	50	7.7247	70	7.7240	90	7.7250
11	7.7252	31	7.7249	51	7.7245	71	7.7250	91	7.7255
12	7.7255	32	7.7248	52	7.7240	72	7.7255	92	7.7250
13	7.7254	33	7.7256	53	7.7245	73	7.7250	93	7.7250
14	7.7251	34	7.7265	54	7.7240	74	7.7252	94	7.7252
15	7.7248	35	7.7265	55	7.7238	75	7.7260	95	7.7252
16	7.7245	36	7.7255	56	7.7245	76	7.7260	96	7.7254
17	7.7247	37	7.7255	57	7.7240	77	7.7260	97	7.7254
18	7.7245	38	7.7253	58	7.7250	78	7.7262	98	7.7250
19	7.7240	39	7.7245	59	7.7255	79	7.7264	99	7.7250
20	7.7245	40	7.7243	60	7.7250	80	7.7262	100	7.7245

Remarks

1. Changed cutting inserts at 16, 56, 71, 86

2. Sampled first 5 pieces from 20 lots

3. LaBlond™ lathe—work center 306

Exhibit 5 Sample Data for 34164 Ring

Sample	Observation				
	1	**2**	**3**	**4**	**5**
1	0.1261	0.1253	0.1245	0.1249	0.1248
2	0.1259	0.1263	0.1247	0.1240	0.1251
3	0.1239	0.1265	0.1260	0.1257	0.1243
4	0.1225	0.1249	0.1265	0.1248	0.1256
5	0.1259	0.1243	0.1242	0.1257	0.1251
6	0.1255	0.1273	0.1245	0.1268	0.1263
7	0.1251	0.1281	0.1239	0.1245	0.1264
8	0.1288	0.1250	0.1235	0.1240	0.1251
9	0.1240	0.1252	0.1295	0.1262	0.1275
10	0.1233	0.1271	0.1280	0.1291	0.1274

Dynamic Seal (B)

M r. Gordon Jenkins, the Statistical Process Control (SPC) Coordinator, was very concerned with the high cost of rejected materials at Dynamic Seal (see Dynamic Seal [A] for background information). To aid in his analysis of rejected materials, Gordon prepared **Exhibits 1** and **2**, which trace the movement of parts through the organization and show the role of the Material Review Board (MRB) in analyzing rejected materials.

CONTROL OF NONCONFORMANCE

For each part produced there was an Inspection Methods Sheet (IMS) which followed the part through the production process. The IMS described the critical quality characteristics of each part and the measuring tools to be used when checking the relevant specifications. When a part reached an inspection point, a quality engineer referred to the information provided by the IMS in performing his or her job. The specifications on the IMS were frequently tighter than those specified on the blueprint. This discrepancy occurred because customers had a tendency to tighten their requirements over time and blueprints were infrequently updated. Nonconforming material was physically segregated from acceptable material. Relevant information concerning the defective material was placed on a Discrepant Material Report (DMR) and the lot was tagged with a Hold Ticket. A sample DMR for part 4035895 is shown in **Exhibit 3**. The DMR provides a listing of the discrepancies found; the work center that caused the discrepancy; the corrective action to be taken; and the effective date of such corrective action. For in-house manufactured items, this corrective action could range from scrapping the entire lot to reworking each individual piece. For purchased parts, the items could be reworked by Dynamic or returned to the appropriate vendor. The quality engineer who discovered a discrepancy would complete only the top half of the DMR listing the discrepancies found and their cause.

Before any corrective action was taken on a lot, the DMRs (there could have been more than one to a lot) were examined by a Material Review Board (MRB) for their advice and approval. The MRB met each morning, reviewed each DMR, and specified the corrective action to be taken. The MRB completed the

Source: Prepared by Joseph R. Carter and Thomas E. Vollmann solely as a basis for class discussion. Copyright © 1984 Boston University and the authors.

bottom half of the DMR. The MRB was composed of an individual from Manufacturing Engineering, Quality Engineering, Design Engineering, Manufacturing, and an Expeditor. The DMRs were the backbone of the quality control information system. About 80 DMRs were generated each week.

When rework was specified, a special routing sheet or set of operations was required with specific instructions. The work center that caused the discrepancy was not necessarily the same one to correct it. It was very difficult, and in some cases impossible, to determine where a discrepancy actually occurred. A part might go through 5–10 operations before it got to an inspection station. At the inspection station the Quality Engineer would examine the part for several different quality characteristics. **Exhibit 4** shows a summary of operations for part 4035895. As can be seen, this part goes through five different operations at three different work centers before it reaches the first inspection station.

Approximately 25% of all discrepancies were unattributed to any specific work center. There were times when a DMR might not get written for several days after a discrepancy had been discovered. If a problem was discovered in a critical lot, for example, the rework might be done immediately without waiting for MRB approval. The DMR for this lot would be generated several days later. By this time memories had a tendency to fade.

A summary record of all deviations and dispositions was maintained in the Dynamic Summary of DMRs. This report was generated monthly by the Quality Assurance Department. If a Dynamic manager required any other type of quality information, it had to be generated manually. One page from this report for the month of November, 1983, is shown in **Exhibit 5. Exhibits 6, 7,** and **8** contain a condensed summary of the November report for the United Aircraft production cell. This was a separate department dedicated to the manufacture and assembly of 25 high volume mainshaft seals sold to United Aircraft. **Exhibit 6** summarizes the DMR report for the United production cell production area. It lists the numeric designation of each United work center; the type of operation performed at those work centers; the number of DMRs attributed to each during November; and the scrap dollar value generated by each work center. **Exhibit 7** gives a summary of the cause, detection, and corrective action codes listed in the Dynamic Summary of DMRs for November, 1983. **Exhibit 8** provides an explanation of each numerical code. A diskette is also available with a database of more than 350 DMRs collected from the United Aircraft cell. These data are in a format ready for analysis by Lotus 1-2-3.

Gordon Jenkins was interested in studying these data to see if he could find any patterns that would help him reduce the costs of rejected materials.

THE DATA

Gordon Jenkins, the SPC Coordinator, and Alan Schneider, the manager of the United Aircraft cell, spent some time working with the database of DMRs. They found that it was somewhat difficult and time consuming to try to deal with all the data on the diskette. It also was somewhat frustrating in that they seemed to be asking many more questions than they were answering. For this reason, they decided to initially limit their investigation to some selected subsets of the database.

They first decided to focus their attention on a subset of manufacturing work centers. A perusal of **Exhibit 9** led Alan to a particular interest in grinding, so they selected work centers 151, 152, 154, and 157.

The cause codes of interest were also in manufacturing. Gordon and Alan decided initially to restrict their attention to cause codes 309, 310, 312, 318, 324, and 326.

The next subset of interest was part numbers. The database contains 120 unique part numbers, which is a large number to deal with. Gordon and Alan decided to start their analysis with an investigation of five part numbers, 792806, 694085, 4031517, 5004292-01, and 548761.

Gordon felt that analysis of these subsets of data would provide a good foundation on which subsequent work could be built. In particular, by working with only one type of equipment, only focusing on some of the manufacturing related causes, and only tracking down the quality problems with a subset of the part numbers, he and Alan would be better able to deal with a problem of manageable proportions. By working with Alan, analysis could be integrated with appropriate corrective actions. With successful changes made in manufacturing operations, further analyses would be possible, and perhaps some changes in data collection might also occur.

Exhibit 1 Flow of Materials and Inspections Points

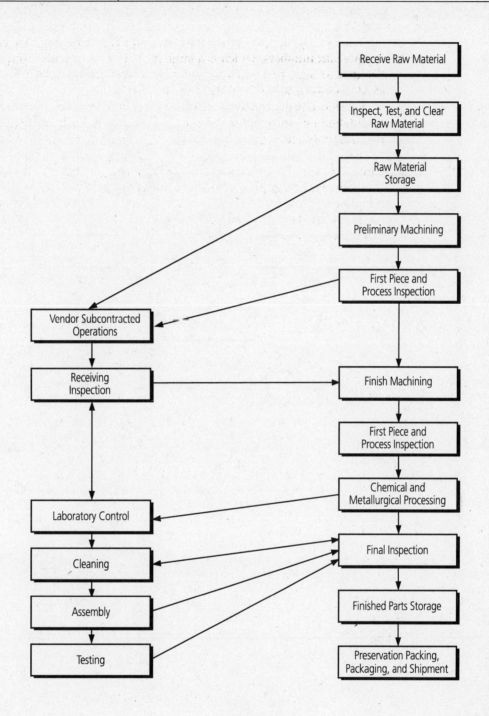

Exhibit 2 Inspection and Material Review Process

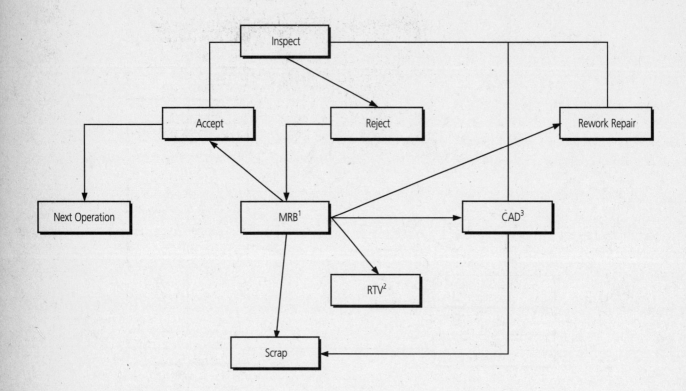

Exhibit 3 Discrepant Material Report

DISCREPANT MATERIAL REPORT — D 78550

4035895	REV. *OK*	OP. NO.	INSP. TYPE — CIRCLE ONE (70)–71–72–73–74–75–76–77–78–79	VENDOR	
MO #*53984*	DASH #	LOT #	INSP. METHOD — CHECK ONE ☒ IMS ☒ 100% ☐ SAMPLING	P.O. #	ITEM #
HOUSING		SAMPLE SIZE	ACC REJ AQL	DATE REC'D	VEND CODE
TED 100	QTY. ACC. 40	QTY. REJ. 60	INSP. BY *W. Kelly*	DATE 10/19/--	REVIEWED BY nc

DWG. DIM & TYPE (LETTER)

LIST DISCREPANCIES	DIS. CODE
A. 21 pieces: .0019 – .0041 over maximum	100
A. 3 pieces: .0055 – .0060 over maximum	100
A. 1 piece: tool mark on surface o.k. to use	200
A. 2 pieces: .0090 over maximum	100
A. 12 pieces: .0035 – .0060 over maximum	100
A. 21 pieces: .0020 – .0021 over maximum	100

CAUSE: ☒ SEAL ☐ VENDOR ☐ OTHER	CAUSE CODE	W/C CAUSE
Combination of comparator and repeatability of LaBlond lathe.	324	306
Parts were good before turning.	350	

CORRECTIVE ACTION: ☒ SEAL ☐ VENDOR ☐ OTHER	C/A CODE	C/A W/C
Machine Repaired	324	306
Not relevant	350	

C/A SIGN *ERF*	EFFECTIVE DATE 10/19/--	FOLLOW UP DATE

COMMENTS:

STD RUN LABOR	STD MATERIAL	TOTAL L & M

QTY. SUBMITTED 100	INSPECTION ACCEPT 40
CUST. M.R.B. 3	REWORK 53
REPAIR ACCEPT	M.R.B. ACCEPT
R.T.V.	QTY. SCRAP 4
DESIGN ENGR. APPROVAL & DATE	
PROD. ENGR. APPROVAL & DATE *Ken Ober* 10\19\--	
Q.A. APPROVAL & DATE *W. J. Chauritte* 10/19/--	
OTHER D	

COMPLETE ON SIG.

Exhibit 4 Dynamic Seal Summary of Operations, 4035895 Housing

Operation Number	Work Center	Description	Setup Time/Run Time
01	191	Issue from Stock	.00/.00 min.
05	315	Process Per Method Print	4.00/.00
10	315	Bore Inside Dimension	2.00/.22
15	099	Heat Treat to Spec 11-22[1]	.00/.00
18	350	Grind Face to Remove Distortion	.25/.04
20	350	Grind Faces to Specifications	.30/.10
21	070	Inspect	.20/.02
25	306	Turn O.D. Faceback of Flange, Turn Hub & Skirt Diameters	2.00/.16
27	306	Bore Inside Diameter	1.50/.14
30	306	Finish Bore	1.00/.11
31	070	Inspect	.00/.30
35	335	Drill 12 .166–.170 Dia. Hole	1.50/.15
40	331	M.11 3 Slots	1.50/.12
45	331	Deburr Corners	.30/.20
50	70	Inspect	.30/.05
55	306	Bore and Chamfer	1.50/.13
57	099	Magnetic Particle Inspect	.00/.00
60	099	Flame Plate Bore[1]	.00/.00
61	071	Inspect	.30/.02
65	152	Grind Coated Bore	1.50/.40
70	151	Grind Chamfer	1.00/.12
72	070	Inspect	.30/.02
75	190	Stock	.00/.00

1   Sent to a vendor

Exhibit 5 Summary of DMRs

Summary of DMRs

Report Date 12/09/83
Time 22.01.23

W/C¹ Cause	C/A² W/C	Part Number	Dollar Value³	Cause Code	Effective Date	DMR No.	Rev. No.	Prod. No.	S.O. No.	Dash No.	Lot No.	P.O. No.	Vendor Code	Item No.	Desc.⁴ Code	Action⁵ Code
0306	0306	CO2T1-BP3	64	324	10/28/83	79305	01	41N	054013					01	100	305
	0306	4012469		315	08/21/83	78911	OC	06A	064425					01	100	304
	0306	4031517	333	310	09/18/83	79403	OK	86A	053984					01	100	304
	0306	4035895		324	05/09/83	78550	OA	86A	062898					02	100	306
	0306	4035895	389	324	05/09/83	78550	OA	86A	062898					01	100	306
	0306	4035895		324	05/09/83	78550	OA	86A	062898					17		306
	0306	4035895		324	05/09/83	78550	OA	86A	062898					16	200	306
	0306	4035895		324	05/09/83	78550	OA	86A	062898					15	100	306
	0306	4035895		324	05/09/83	78550	OA	86A	062898					14	100	306
	0306	4035895		324	05/09/83	78550	OA	86A	062898					13	100	306
	0306	4035895		324	05/09/83	78550	OA	86A	062898					12	100	306
	0306	4035895		324	05/09/83	78550	OA	86A	062898					11	100	306
	0306	4035895		324	05/09/83	78550	OA	86A	062898					10	100	306
	0306	4035895		324	05/09/83	78550	OA	86A	062898					09	100	306
	0306	4035895		324	05/09/83	78550	OA	86A	062898					08	100	306
	0306	4035895		324	05/09/83	78550	OA	86A	062898					07	100	306
	0306	4035895		324	05/09/83	78550	OA	86A	062898					06	100	306
	0306	4035895		324	05/09/83	78550	OA	86A	062898					05	100	306
	0306	4035895		324	05/09/83	78550	OA	86A	062898					04	100	306
	0306	4035895		324	05/09/83	78550	OA	86A	062898					03	100	306
	0306	548761	198	000	09/08/83	79075	OB	83A	063700					04	600	311
	0306	548761	366	309		79611	OB	83A	063699					02	100	327
	0306	548761		309	09/08/83	79075	OB	83A	063700					03	100	311
	0306	548761		309	09/08/83	79075	OB	83A	063700					01	100	311
	0306	548761		309	09/08/83	79075	OB	83A	063700					02	100	311
	0306	175516	128	324	11/02/83	79786	04	41N	057156					01	200	312
	0306	195116-S	74	324	10/28/83	79321	01	41N	056075					01	100	305
	0306	195216-S	51	329		79319	01	41N	056076					01	100	305
	0306	28648		314		78061	01	01E	060901					02	100	301
	0306	28648		314		78061	01	01E	060901					01	100	301
	0306	54601BL		314	06/22/83	78766	00	24K	064516					01	200	301
	0306	54601BL		325	06/22/83	78766	00	24K	064516					02	100	312
	0306	58578-16	56	314	11/08/83	79323	02	41N	057128					02	100	301
	0306	58578-16		314	11/08/83	79323	02	41N	057128					01	100	301
	0306	68153N1		314	10/26/83	79659	03	61E	053429					04	200	325
	0306	68153N1	174	315	10/26/83	79659	03	61E	053429					01	100	301
	0306	68153N1		320	10/26/83	79631	03	61E	053425					02	100	311
	0306	68153N1		320	10/26/83	79631	03	61E	053425					01	100	311
	0306	68153N1		325	10/26/83	79659	03	61E	053429					02	200	311
0306	0306	68153N1		325	10/26/83	79659	03	61E	053429					03	200	311
		TOTAL VALUE	1833													

1 Work center where discrepancy was caused. / 2 Work center where discrepancy was corrected. / 3 Scrap dollar value of discarded piece. Rework costs not listed. / 4 Discrepancy code. / 5 Action code.
N.B. This is only one page from a 69-page report. The report is broken down by work center.

Exhibit 6 Dynamic Seal Summary of DMRs, United Aircraft Cell (condensed), November, 1983

Work Center	Type	No. of DMRs[2]	Scrap Dollar Value
0000[1]	Unknown	28	$1,986
0137	Mill/Grind	0	0
0151	Grind	3	67
0152	Grind	5	656
0154	Grind	3	0
0156	Grind	0	0
0157	Grind	0	0
0160	Misc.	4	0
0180	Misc.	1	0
0183	Misc.	1	171
0185	Misc.	3	100
0306	Turning	40	1,833
0311	Turning	2	0
0315	Turning	0	0
0330	Mill/Drill	4	953
0331	Mill/Drill	14	1,097
0335	Mill/Drill	1	512
0350	Grind	1	384
0410	Turning	11	580
		121	$8,339

1 Work center not listed on DMR

2 Number of Discrepant Material Reports

Exhibit 7 Dynamic Seal Summary of DMRs, United Aircraft Cell (condensed), November, 1983

Cause Code	Freq.[1]	Discrepancy Code	Freq.[1]	Corrective Action Code	Freq.[1]
000[2]	37	000[2]	1	000[2]	37
306	1	100	77	301	10
309	13	200	36	304	13
310	7	250	2	305	6
313	2	600	3	306	19
314	7			310	1
315	9			311	19
316	1			312	8
318	1			324	1
320	6			327	4
324	22				
325	3				
326	1				
327	1				
329	10				
901	1				

1 Frequency of occurrence during November

2 No code listed on DMR

Exhibit 8 Dynamic Seal Code Description

Cause Code

```
                              ┌──────► Dept.
                              │
                          X X X   Reason
                          └─┴──────────┘
                                     ▲
```

Discrepancy Code	Description	Dept.	Reason
100	Dimensional Inspection	1. Engineering	01. Seal Drawing
200	Visual Inspection	2. Mfg. Engineering	02. Customer Drawing
250	Visual (Carbon Chippage)	3. Mfg.	03. Missed Inspection
300	Paperwork	4. QC	04. IMS Error
400	Process (Methods or Specs Not Followed)	5. Inspection	05. Inspection
		6. Contracts	06. RPR Part
500	Chemical or Physical Properties	7. Vendor	08. Supervision
		8. Customer	09. Mfg. Hazard
600	Count	9. Other	10. Unknown
700	Handling		11. Unauthorized Approval of Deviation
			12. Rework
			13. Methods
			14. Incorrect Procedures
			15. Technique
			16. Fixture
			17. Gauge
			18. Handling
			19. ECN Change
			20. Tool
			21. Leakage
			22. Shelf Life
			23. Information Not Transmitted
			24. Machine
			25. Material
			26. Heat Treat
			27. Clearning
			28. Salvage Parts
			29. Other

Corrective Action Codes

```
                              ┌──────► Dept.
                              │
                          X X X   Action
                          └─┴──────────┘
                                     ▲
```

Departments = Same as Under Cause Codes

Action

01. Revise Process, Procedure, or Methods	15. Initiate IMS
02. Revise or Replace Gauge	16. Review Purchase Order
03. Revise or Replace Fixture	17. Review Specifications
04. Instruct Operator	18. Adhere to Procedures
05. Caution Operator	19. Replace
06. Replace Tool	20. Revise Sales Order
07. ECN	21. Engineering
08. Add Inspection	22. Notify Vendor
09. Control Routing	23. Notify Customer
10. Limited by State of Art	24. Initiate Q.C.M.
11. None Required	25. Revise Drawings
12. None Available	26. Repair/Rework
13. Survey	27. Other
14. Revise IMS	

Exhibit 9 Pareto Analysis of Work Center by DMRs

Work Center	DMRs	% of Total	Cum. DMRs	Cum. %
0	52	14.9	52	14.9
152	47	13.5	99	28.4
151	31	8.9	130	37.2
306	24	6.9	154	44.1
160	22	6.3	176	50.4
335	16	4.6	192	55.0
154	13	3.7	205	58.7
331	12	3.4	217	62.2
311	11	3.2	228	65.3
640	7	2.0	235	67.3
869	7	2.0	242	69.3
329	6	1.7	248	71.1
337	6	1.7	254	72.8
664	6	1.7	260	74.5
570	5	1.4	265	75.9
137	4	1.1	269	77.1
183	4	1.1	273	78.2
315	4	1.1	277	79.4
330	4	1.1	281	80.5
338	4	1.1	285	81.7
410	4	1.1	289	82.8
920	4	1.1	293	84.0
99	3	0.9	296	84.8
157	3	0.9	299	85.7
180	3	0.9	302	86.5
351	3	0.9	305	87.4
430	3	0.9	308	88.3
850	3	0.9	311	89.1
870	3	0.9	314	90.0
70	2	0.6	316	90.5
153	2	0.6	318	91.1
305	2	0.6	320	91.7
310	2	0.6	322	92.3
584	2	0.6	324	92.8
642	2	0.6	326	93.4
60	1	0.3	327	93.7
106	1	0.3	328	94.0
116	1	0.3	329	94.3
138	1	0.3	330	94.6
139	1	0.3	331	94.8
178	1	0.3	332	95.1
185	1	0.3	333	95.4
201	1	0.3	334	95.7
226	1	0.3	335	96.0
251	1	0.3	336	96.3
328	1	0.3	337	96.6
340	1	0.3	338	96.8
345	1	0.3	339	97.1
352	1	0.3	340	97.4
354	1	0.3	341	97.7
557	1	0.3	342	98.0
588	1	0.3	343	98.3
610	1	0.3	344	98.6
616	1	0.3	345	98.9
628	1	0.3	346	99.1
710	1	0.3	347	99.4
911	1	0.3	348	99.7
935	1	0.3	349	100.0

Dynamic Seal (C)

Gordon Jenkins, recently appointed Statistical Process Control (SPC) Coordinator at Dynamic Seal had done some preliminary analyses of problems (see the A and B cases for background). He wanted to move ahead on SPC, and he had convinced his boss, Kevin Lynch, that this was a good idea. It was clear to Gordon, however, that SPC had many steps and that SPC was, itself, a part of a larger set of manufacturing issues. Kevin Lynch had set a meeting for February 28, 1984, to review these issues with a steering committee formed to oversee SPC implementation.

As Gordon Jenkins prepared for the meeting, he came up with the following tentative implementation schedule.

A. Education
B. Gather Data
C. Evaluate Machine Capability
D. Evaluate Process Capability
E. Troubleshoot
F. Identify Corrective Action
G. Make Corrections
H. Re-evaluate
I. Apply Statistical Process Control

Gordon was hopeful that the steering committee would agree to this schedule and give him the mandate to go forth.

THE FEBRUARY 28, 1984, MEETING

Statistical process control had been discussed at Dynamic Seal for some time. In December of 1983, a steering committee was formed to oversee the implementation of SPC at Dynamic. Members of the committee were Messrs. Kevin Lynch; Jack Barry, the Manufacturing Manager; Gordon Jenkins, the SPC Coordinator; Roger Towne, the Director of Quality Assurance; Scott Palmer, the Assistant Director of Quality Assurance; John Dors, the Manager of Manufacturing Engineering; and Alan Schneider, the manager of the United Aircraft cell. On the morning of February 28, these men met in the

Source: Prepared by Joseph R. Carter and Thomas E. Vollmann solely as a basis for class discussion. Copyright © 1984 Boston University and the authors. Revised 1/86.

staff conference room to discuss the implementation of the SPC system at Dynamic. The opening comments were made by Kevin Lynch.

> *Gentlemen, I have called this meeting to discuss what I feel will be one of the most successful programs to be implemented at Dynamic Seal. You are all aware of the significant quality costs that are being incurred at Dynamic. I sincerely believe that Statistical Process Control can put an end to these costs. I have instructed Gordon Jenkins to implement the SPC system in the United cell area first. I have chosen the UA manufacturing area for several reasons.[1] First, it is a self-contained, manageable work area. Second, even though United comprises 14% of Dynamic's sales, we have yet to show anything but a small profit. Third, I feel confident we will be receiving another large order from United. I would now like to let Gordon Jenkins outline his implementation plans.*

Gordon Jenkins then put up an overhead transparency with his points A through I, and he explained why this was his plan. The next person to speak was Roger Towne, the Director of Quality Assurance.

> *Kevin, I agree with you that our quality costs in United are out of sight. But, it is the same story everywhere at Dynamic. Instead of just implementing the SPC system in the United area, I think we should pick a particular machine type that produces the largest number of defects and apply Statistical Process Control to that particular machine type throughout the entire plant. In this way we could cure the largest number of defects in the shortest amount of time. Once you have set up control charts for a particular type of machine, such as a lathe, getting control charts for every other lathe should be relatively easy. I have had recent conversations with United and contrary to that letter we received, the implementation of the SPC system is not mandatory as long as our quality level remains high.*

Scott Palmer agreed with Roger Towne.

> *Not only is SPC important to United, but I have heard rumors to the effect that Avco, Sikorsky, and General Electric are all discussing the benefits of putting their manufacturing process under SPC. I feel it is only a matter of time before they approach us in the same manner as United. By implementing the SPC system throughout the plant, we could use that fact to competitive advantage.*

The next to speak was Jack Barry.

> *If SPC can eliminate rework and reduce lead times, I am all for it. We need to get a handle on rework. I must spend one month out of every year just reworking defective parts.[2] And this is just rework I know about. This rework and scrap plays havoc with my material control system. Every time one of my material handlers looks for a particular lot, it is either being inspected, waiting for inspection, or rejected. It is no wonder the end of each month is pure chaos.*

Scott Palmer directed these remarks to Jack Barry.

> *Jack, I appreciate the problems you are having getting your materials on time. But you are mistaken if you think SPC will make a significant difference. My inspectors are just plain overworked. Much of the work we do entails products that will ultimately be used for National Defense purposes. Meticulous records need to be kept. Each lot needs to be inspected whether there are defects in it or not.*

---

1   See **Exhibit 1** for a description of the United Aircraft cell.
2   In subsequent cost analysis, this statement proved to be quite accurate.

Alan Schneider now addressed the impact SPC might have on the workforce.

I am deeply concerned about the effect the implementation of the SPC program will have on my workers. As you are well aware, the UA production area is composed of a group of highly skilled albeit somewhat temperamental machinists. To them machining is as much an art as a science. They are the people who specify the feed rates, the machine speeds, and many of the tools used in an operation. I don't want to alienate them. Even though our relations with the union are cordial, we are inviting trouble if the union gets the impression management is on a witch hunt.

In closing the meeting, Kevin Lynch addressed his comments in particular to Gordon Jenkins and in general to all present.

I thank all of you for your salient comments. We certainly have many issues to address before we can fully implement the SPC system at Dynamic. Our next meeting will be held on Thursday, March 29, 1984 at 1:00 p.m. At this next meeting, Gordon, it would certainly be helpful if you could provide us with a milestone chart detailing phases to be completed and supporting efforts. I am particularly interested in a way to measure the progress of the SPC program. Other areas that will need additional coverage are the implementation area, data gathering, data analysis, software, and identifying responsibilities that will be needed to support the SPC efforts. Of course, don't limit yourself to these areas. Feel free to make recommendations about any phase of our quality control system.

After the February 28 meeting, Gordon Jenkins returned to his office to think about the SPC project. As the day went on, he grew more and more pessimistic about the results of the meeting. It was clear that his goal of receiving a mandate to move forward was not accomplished.

Gordon spent the afternoon thinking about the meeting, SPC, and his future at Dynamic Seal. That evening he tried to talk it over with his wife, but found that he just couldn't explain the problem. The next day he closed his office door and left word not to be disturbed. On a blackboard, he listed all of the facets of the SPC project he found important. Gordon hoped that this process would clarify his understanding and form the basis of a heart-to-heart talk with Kevin Lynch. At the end of the day, the following were some of the items on his blackboard.

- Quality is now largely achieved by inspection—we cull out the bad rather than build them right.
- Our inspectors are not trained in SPC—they are paid less than shop workers.
- I work for Kevin, not for Roger.
- There is a discrepancy between the IMS sheets and blueprints.
- Methods are informally maintained—operators decide on feeds, speeds, tools, etc.
- The SPC requirements of United are better known than those of other companies. Will others be the same or will we need to adapt?
- What is Alan most concerned about? How do I get him on my side?
- Much of the data on the DMRs is incorrect or unclear. How do we change this? What will Roger say if I point this out?
- What does an SPC-based quality organization look like? How do we get from here to there?
- How important is SPC to the top management at Dynamic Seal? Do they understand what it is and the efforts required?
- What role should I play as the SPC Coordinator? How can I be most effective?

Exhibit 1 United Aircraft Cell

United Aircraft (UA) comprised 14% of Dynamic's sales and was one of its fastest growing customers. For this reason, Dynamic made the decision to set up a separate department of equipment and personnel dedicated to the manufacture and assembly of the 25 UA mainshaft seal assemblies (670 total parts). The equipment was located in a separate UA manufacturing area (cell) and was staffed by a workforce consisting of a UA manufacturing manager (Alan Schneider) and 18 highly skilled machinists. Each machinist was paid an hourly wage of approximately $13.

The 25 UA assemblies could be grouped according to three major characteristics. Those characteristics were length of the carbon seal (long or short), wall thickness (thick or thin), and number of slots used to hold the seal in place (three or four). In general, each seal assembly within a particular grouping went through a similar set of operations. The same operation could be done on any one of a number of machines depending upon the tolerances required and scheduling constraints.

The principal measure of effectiveness of the UA cell was the ratio of direct labor costs to overhead. Direct labor costs consisted only of the labor necessary to complete a given amount of work. Overhead cost consisted of setup times, idle times, tooling expenses, and a percentage of the overhead created by support departments such as accounting, quality control, etc. Quality costs, due to the difficulty of attributing them to any particular machine or work center, were not used in the calculation of either direct labor or overhead. According to Alan Schneider, the UA cell manager:

> *Rework costs are especially difficult to measure. I schedule the rework so as to not disrupt my daily production. Besides, much of the rework is done by the original operator before the part gets to inspection. For example, if the operator sees that some of the parts he has produced are defective, he will immediately rework them before releasing the lot to the next operation. In the long run, it saves us time and a good deal of paperwork.*

International Inc.

It was January 1994 and Robert Davis, the CEO for International Inc., was at his office receiving the last year's performance reports. Davis was concerned because the numbers were more unfavorable than those of the previous years. Davis, with the performance reports still in his hand, stormed into Jim Brown, in the General Manager's office. "Jim," said Davis, "could you please explain to me why our company hasn't fared well in the last year?" "Robert," replied Jim Brown in a soft voice, "what do you want me to do? One of the major reasons is that our information group has been very slow to respond to the customer complaints." "Jim, we need some new ideas and a quick solution. Don't try to work by yourself. Ask your staff for their ideas. I think this problem can be resolved. A different approach to handling the complaints may solve the problem. You have three months to solve this problem. I want you to provide me with a detailed report on the steps taken to handle this situation. The reports are due on my desk by March 31, 1994."

BACKGROUND

International Inc. is an exporting enterprise located in the southern part of United States. The company exports computers and computer peripherals to Latin American countries. The company employs 50 people. In the past year, International Inc. had received several complaints from its customers that the service provided by the company had deteriorated. The number of complaints had increased from 15% in 1992 to 35% in 1994. In December, 1992, Robert Davis hired Jim Brown, a reputed quality specialist, to improve the overall performance of the operation. Brown's primary charge was to implement a comprehensive performance enhancement program using total quality measures that would reduce waste, cut costs, and improve system performance substantially.

SEARCHING FOR A SOLUTION

Jim Brown knew that he was now under pressure to search for a feasible solution. He had to act right away. Brown decided to call an emergency meeting of all managers and employees who were directly involved with the problem.

Source: Jaideep Motwani and Ashok Kumar, Seidman School of Business, Grand Valley State University, Grand Rapids, Michigan.

Brown's initial discussions with these managers and employees revealed that the company had many operational problems that affected product quality. However, a key factor that tarnished the company's image, and affected its competitiveness, was the fact that the company's information group was slow to respond to the customer complaints. Brown recognized early on that controlling such delays would have to be addressed at a war-footing priority if the company wanted to keep its customers happy; indeed, if the company had to survive.

The customer complaint correction process was substantially affected by unacceptable long response times arising from computer downtime caused by human and equipment error, equipment damage, anomalies in software, and other abnormalities in the computer system (i.e. hardware or software). In many instances, irregularities in the system caused many problems that resulted in customer dissatisfaction due to late deliveries, inappropriate deliveries, overcharge, lack of credit extension, or losses to the company due to lost customers, remedial steps, and distribution problems.

In order to identify the salient factors and interactions that caused excessive variations, Brown, based on recommendations made by managers and employees, decided to form a task force. The task force comprised of the IS manager, one IS assistant manager comptroller, sales manager, two customer service employees, and Brown himself. The first meeting of the task force was scheduled for February 5, 1994.

PROPOSED SOLUTION

On February 5, 1994, the task force met at Jim Brown's office. Jim asked each member of the team for opinions on how to solve the problem. After extensive discussions and brainstorming, the team felt that implementing the Taguchi's Robust Experimental Design Technique would help solve the problem.

Initial discussions within the team members produced the following list of sequential steps considered essential in order to bring the system response time down:

1. Define the goal of the study in objective terms.
2. Identify critical factors and their interactions (using the brainstorming approach).
3. Select an appropriate orthogonal array that can adequately assess the impact of the factors and the interactions identified in Step 2.
4. Conduct ANOVA and other Taguchi-related analyses.
5. Identify significant factors and interactions. Conduct Non-Linearity analysis.
6. Find the optimal combination of factor levels to minimize system response time.
7. Determine benefits (if possible in dollar terms) of the optimal setting.

The team decided systematically to address each step, one at a time. The team decided that it would take three weeks to perform the necessary experiments. Jack Trent, the IS manager, was asked to collect the necessary data and provide it to the team by February 12, 1994. The task force felt that by obtaining this data, they would be in a position to start the process immediately. The meeting was adjourned.

At 1:00 p.m., February 12, 1994, the task force met for another brainstorming session at Jim Brown's office. As promised, Jack Trent furnished the task force with relevant data concerning the problem. After studying the data carefully, the committee decided to start the process by clearly defining the goal of the study. After about an hour of discussion, the committee agreed on the following definition of the problem. It was as follows:

> *The system response time to correct customer complaints is excessively high. According to several estimates, the average time needed for correction of a complaint is 18 hours with variability of up to 15 hours on the higher side. The task force should identify factors/reasons that are responsible for such excessive delays and variations and suggest measures, including exact process parameters settings, that would reduce the system response time and the associated variations by at least 20%.*

The next couple of hours were spent by the task force to identify critical factors and their interactions. In all, it was determined that eight factors, seven of them having three levels, and one of them having two levels, were significant. Also, there was consensus among team members that there would be a significant interaction between two factors, namely the type of the problem and the information group's familiarity with that problem type. The remaining interactions, 26 in all, were ruled out as insignificant by the team. To facilitate further discussion, factors were assigned alphabet-identifiers (see **Exhibit 1**). **Exhibit 2** provides the system response times under various treatments.

It was now 6:00 p.m. Jim Brown felt that the committee had made significant progress and therefore, decided to adjourn the meeting. The next meeting was scheduled for February 19, 1995.

DISCUSSION QUESTIONS

For the purpose of the case analysis, assume you are Jim Brown. Your job, as the leader, is to make sure that the next five steps are systematically conducted. You want to make sure that the following questions are answered:

1. What orthogonal array should the team select?
2. How many different experiments should be conducted?
3. Compute the S/N ratios and normalized S/N ratios for each trial.
4. Compute the main effects and interactions for each factor.
5. Compute the analysis of variance based on normalized S/N data.
6. Compute the optimal combination of factor levels by investigating the non-linearity of S/N ratios. Also, develop non-linearity graphs for factors and interactions.
7. Develop confidence intervals for the current viability of each factor.
8. Compute the average value of the system response time.
9. What changes would you recommend be made to the operation of the system?

Exhibit 1 List of Factors Affecting System Response Time

Factor Identifier	Factors	Levels		
		Level 1	Level 2	Level 3
A	Method of Recording Complaint	E-Mail	Error-log in the Network	Verbal Reporting
B	Explanation of Problem	Elaborate	Simple	Sketchy: Identify the Failing Module Only
C	User Understanding of the Problem	Good	Moderate	Negligible
D	Information System Group Familiarity with the Problem	Repetitive Problem	First Occurrence of the Problem	Intermittent Problem
E	Type of Problem	Hardware-related	Software-related	Non-identifiable
F	Preventive Maintenance: Frequency of System Shut Down for Daily Backup	None	Twice a Week	Daily
G	Priority Assignment Entity	Information Systems Group	None	User
H	Error Reporting Period	8 a.m. to Noon	Noon till 5 p.m.	After 5 p.m.

Exhibit 2 System Response Times Under Various Treatments

Trial No.	Factor Identifier								Response Time in Hours		
	E	**D**	**A**	**B**	**C**	**F**	**G**	**H**			
1	1	1	1	1	1	1	1	1	4	9	8
2	1	1	2	2	2	2	2	2	4	6	5
3	1	1	3	3	3	3	3	3	17	18	16
4	1	2	1	1	2	2	3	3	18	20	18
5	1	2	2	2	3	3	1	1	5	4	5
6	1	2	3	3	1	1	2	2	12	10	12
7	1	3	1	2	1	3	2	3	33	34	36
8	1	3	2	3	2	1	3	1	16	12	18
9	1	3	3	1	3	2	1	2	24	24	23
10	2	1	1	3	3	2	2	1	15	16	13
11	2	1	2	1	1	3	3	2	6	6	5
12	2	1	3	2	2	1	1	3	18	17	18
13	2	2	1	2	3	1	3	2	30	30	27
14	2	2	2	3	1	2	1	3	30	34	29
15	2	2	3	1	2	3	2	10	8	12	10
16	2	3	1	3	2	3	1	2	24	24	22
17	2	3	2	1	3	1	2	3	34	34	30
18	2	3	3	2	1	2	3	1	18	24	19

Find-It-Fast Files

Find-it-Fast Files (FIFF), a division of Quality Office Systems Incorporated, had been losing market share steadily over the past three quarters. Scott Bantered, the division manager, tired of suffering the humiliating teasing of other division managers, was determined to turn Find-it-Fast around. He assigned a study to the marketing research department to evaluate the perceived competitiveness of the Find-it-Fast products on a price/quality basis with close competitors such as Steelcase, OfficePro and DuraCraft.

The results of this study revealed that Find-it-Fast had lost its quality leadership position in the high price/high quality market segment in the last year (**Exhibit 1**). In particular, there was a significant drop in perceived quality. Disturbed by this finding, Scott consulted with Mark Jensen, the production foreman for office file systems, in an attempt to isolate potential quality problems occurring in the file production process. Upon inspecting several files, Mark concluded that the majority of the quality problems were due to poor performance by the welders, especially on the welds along the back panel of the cabinet, which are a key factor in the sturdiness and durability of the finished product. Currently all file case welding was completed by a crew of welders (eight employees), with experience ranging from 2 to 25 years.

THE FIFF PRODUCTS

FIFF produces a broad spectrum of home and office files. The files differ in the number of drawers (2–5), in width (letter or legal), and in option packages (locks, colors, etc.) for a total of 144 distinct SKUs. The production of all styles of files follows the same basic production process. The file drawers, cabinets and options are produced in separate lines and are brought together in final assembly to produce the 144 possible combinations of options. The drawers and cabinets are produced from coil steel, which is straightened into flat sheet metal, cut, and bent in brake presses into three appropriate shapes. Both the drawer and cabinet lines involve fabrication, assembly, welding, enamel painting, and drying stages before the components move on to the final assembly area.

Source: Darwin J. Davis, under the direction of Professor Vincent A. Mabert, Indiana University.

AUTOMATION OF THE PRODUCTION PROCESS

For the past several months, Scott had been interested in the possibility of automating some of the file production process and improving product quality. It seemed that this current problem with poor welding quality could be a good justification for experimenting with automation. Rather than risk a very large investment in a technology that he was unsure of, Scott decided to invest in mechanical spot welders for just one of the cabinet production lines and to assess the effectiveness of the process before making plant-wide changes.

The five drawer letter-size file product line (5000) represented the most popular files produced by FIFF. The 18 distinct SKUs in the 5000 product line differed only in the option package that they used (**Exhibit 2**). Eager to realize improvements in the quality of the 5000 line, Scott elected to install the automated welding system on the model 5001 cabinet line (the cabinet used in all 5000 products) and possibly to expand the practice to all of the lines if this test proved successful.

The New Welding Technology

After the cabinet components (side and back panels) had completed the fabrication stages of production, they would be secured in a special fixture that was designed to hold them securely in place for the welding operations. The fixture (bolted to a pallet) moved along a conveyor belt to the welding area. A laser eye would sense when the pallet was in the proper position for the cabinet to be welded and trigger a brake that would stop the pallet and hold it in the proper alignment.

The automated spot welders (**Exhibit 3**) were capable of performing two simultaneous welds (by using two pairs of electrodes), one on each side of the back panel of the cabinet. Two of the electrodes would contact the back of the file from the inside (inside electrodes) at the same time that the other two would contact the outside face of the back of the cabinet (outside electrodes) so that each inside electrode was lined up with one of the outside electrodes. Upon contact, electrical current flowing between the two electrodes in each pair would cause a portion of the two sheets of metal being welded to melt, forming a small molten nugget which would then cool and bond the two sheets together.

Upon completing the first pair of welds, the electrodes would withdraw from the cabinet, lower to the proper height for the second set of welds and repeat the same steps once again. This would continue until six sets of welds (12 total) were completed on each file. The purchase and installation of the special fixture, laser eye, brake and welding equipment required an investment of $190,000.

The Test

As Scott Bantered drove to work on the first day that the automated welding process was to be used, he anxiously contemplated the sizeable investment that had been made in automation as well as the possible employee morale problems that could follow. Being somewhat unsure that the new equipment would be a suitable alternative to manual welding, he decided that no welders would be released until the test proved successful and the technology was implemented on all production lines. Rather, the welders would be temporarily reassigned to weld drawer assemblies in other areas of the plant.

Scott realized that this move toward automation could mark the beginning of an exciting new era of market leadership or result in an expensive flop that his ailing division could ill afford. As he passed Boyd Stevens, the quality manager, on the way into the office, he reminded Boyd that he was eager to see a full report of the performance of the new equipment ASAP. The next morning Scott found the report (**Exhibit 4**) of the first day's production on his desk.

Experimentation

Distressed by the less-than-perfect performance of the new welding equipment, Scott called in Albe Wright, a manufacturing engineer, for advice. Albe indicated that there were many factors affecting the quality (quality measured as—does the weld bond the two parts together?) of the welds. Some of these factors included:

1. The style of welding tip used—
   A variety of different spot welding tips were available from different suppliers.
2. How often the file fixture was recalibrated—
   The fixture that holds the cabinet being welded was prone to becoming out of adjustment as it was used repeatedly and needed periodic recalibration.
3. Cleanliness of the metal parts to be welded—
   Before the metal parts were welded, they passed through a solvent bath to remove grease and other impurities. Any impurities that remained after the solvent bath or any residue left by the solvent tended to impede the welding process. A variety of solvents with different characteristics were available for use.
4. The carbon content of the steel being welded—
   Sheet metal purchased from different suppliers had different levels of carbon content even though the material met all purchasing specifications.
5. How often the electrodes were recalibrated—
   The electrode arms must be adjusted periodically so that a proper contact is made when the arms come together.
6. The duration of the electrode contact—
   A longer contact will have a better chance of bonding the parts. If the contact was too long, the metal would overheat resulting in cosmetic damage to the surface.
7. Miscellaneous—
   Humidity, dust, etc. (all can contribute to poor welds).

Albe suggested that some type of experimentation should be performed in order to find good settings for the important factors in order to improve the welding performance.

Experimenting with a single factor would involve holding all other factors constant and trying various settings of the factor of interest to see what worked best. For example, to determine which style of welding tips would be the best to use, one would hold all of the other factors constant (fixture recalibration intervals, solvent, steel supplier, etc.), try each of the styles of welding tips for some reasonable amount of time, and then check the quality of the welds made by each of the different styles of tips to see which style worked best.

A full experiment would consist of all combinations of the factors at different settings (known as treatment levels) so that the best combination could be determined. So for an experiment with six factors with three treatment levels each $3^6 = 729$ experiments would be required. Due to the nature of some of the factors, like recalibration, each experiment would need to span at least one full day to be meaningful. Scott was frustrated with the unforeseen difficulty with the automated process and did not relish the thought of waiting 729 days for an answer to the problem.

Because of the unreasonable time and expense required by such an experiment, Albe and Scott determined that it would be best to choose the three factors that seemed to be the most pertinent and focus on these three factors at two different treatment levels each. After some deliberation, Scott elected to focus on the following factors at two levels (A and B) each:

1. The type of welding tip used
   a. Pairs comprised of two flat tips
   b. Pairs comprised of one flat tip and one domed tip
2. How often the fixture was recalibrated
   a. Recalibrate once per shift
   b. Recalibrate twice per shift
3. Cleanliness of the metal parts to be welded
   (i.e., which solvent to use in the bath)
   a. Use naphtha
   b. Use carbontetrachloride

This experimental design would be comprised of $2^3 = 8$ experiments as shown in **Exhibit 5**. Albe recommended that for each of the next eight production days a different experiment should be implemented and that the day's output should be inspected to find which set of conditions is most conducive to quality spot welding.

Over the next eight days, the eight different welding experiments were conducted by changing welding tips, recalibration frequencies, and solvents as per the instructions provided by Bantered and Wright. During this time, Boyd Stevens supervised the inspection of the output. On July 16, Boyd sent a memo to Scott Bantered detailing the results of the experiments (**Exhibit 6**). As Scott read through the results of the testing, he was somewhat troubled by the fact that the same workers had not been responsible for quality inspections throughout the testing, since some judgement was required in determining a good versus a defective weld. At least he now had some information that should be beneficial in alleviating the problems with the new technology and determining what needed to be done next.

DISCUSSION QUESTIONS

1. Which welding tip, calibration frequency and solvent combination seems to provide the best results in terms of quality?
2. Do you feel the change in the inspection crew in the middle of the experiment has invalidated the study's value? If so, why? If not, why?
3. Given the cost data that follows, is it cost effective to recalibrate the welding equipment more than once per shift?

   Recalibration cost
   (labor and lost production) = $50.00

   Cost of reworking a defective file = $3.50

Exhibit 1 Market Research Report

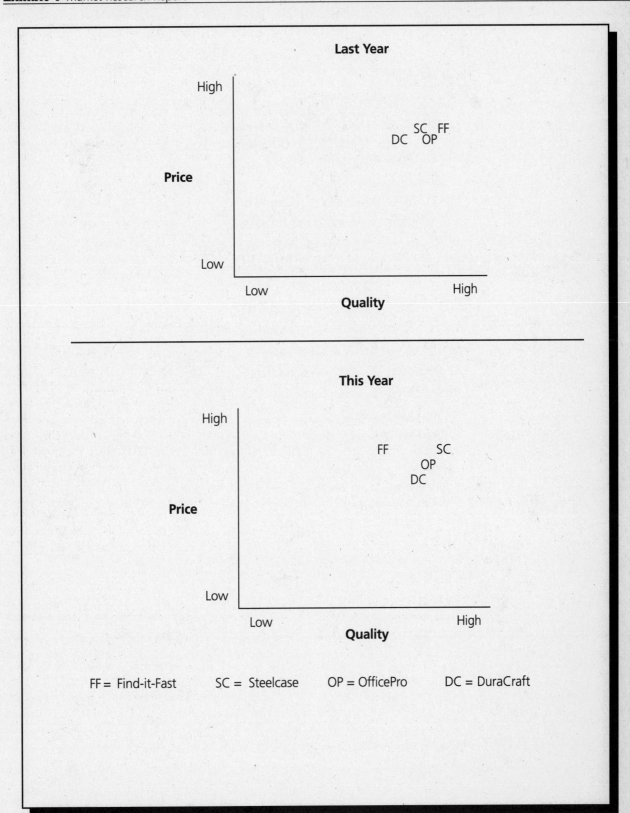

Exhibit 2 The Five Drawer Letter-Size File, 5000 Product Line

Bill of Materials

5000 Five Drawer Letter-Size File (1)

    5001 Cabinet (1)

        8412 Sheet Metal (8 Square Yards)

        3008 Reinforcement Bars (5)

    8125 Drawer Assembly (5)

        8412 Sheet Metal (1 Square Yard)

        8007 Drawer Divider Assembly (1)

            8412 Sheet Metal (1/8 Square Yard)

            2136 Release Bar (1)

            6545 Spring (2)

        8116 Cast Aluminum Handle (1)

        8117 Cast Aluminum Release Mechanism (1)

        8118 Aluminum Label Holder (1)

    5002 Right Drawer Suspension Bar (5)

    5003 Left Drawer Suspension Bar (5)

    5004 Ball Bearing (20)

    lXXX Option Package (1)

Exhibit 3 Top View of the New Welding Process

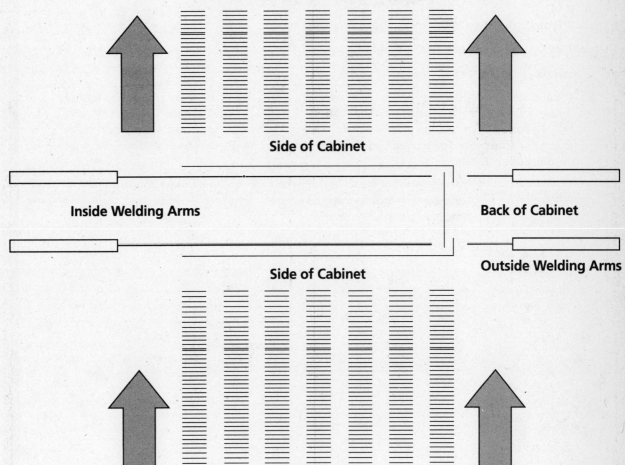

Top View of the New Welding Process

Exhibit 4 Memo

To: Scott Bantered, Division Manager

From: Boyd Stevens, Quality Manager

RE: Inspection of welds

Date: June 21, 19XX

Of the 12 welds to be performed on each of the cabinets, many of the cabinets had one or more unsuccessful welds. To simplify the inspection process our workers simply counted good and bad cabinets where a cabinet with one or more unsuccessful welds was considered bad.

Total production of cabinets	496
Number of good cabinets	411
Number of bad cabinets	85

Exhibit 5 A Full Experimental Design for 3 Factors with 2 Treatment Levels Each

	Factors		
	TIP	**CAL**	**CLN**
Day 1	FF	1S	NPT
Day 2	FF	1S	CTC
Day 3	FF	2S	NPT
Day 4	FF	2S	CTC
Day 5	FD	1S	NPT
Day 6	FD	1S	CTC
Day 7	FD	2S	NPT
Day 8	FD	2S	CTC

Abbreviation	**Factors and Treatment Levels**
TIP	1. The type of welding tip used
FF	A. Pairs comprised of two flat tips
FD	B. Pairs comprised of one flat tip and one domed tip
CAL	2. How often the fixture is recalibrated
1S	A. Recalibrate once per shift
2S	B. Recalibrate twice per shift
CLN	3. Cleanliness of the metal parts to be welded (i.e., which solvent to use in the bath)
NPT	A. Use naptha
CTC	B. Use carbontetrachloride

Exhibit 6 Memo

To: Scott Bantered, Division Manager

From: Boyd Stevens, Quality Manager

RE: Inspection of welds for eight day experiment

Date: June 16, 19XX

As you must realize, this has been a cumbersome project for our small quality team. Due to summer vacation requests which had been granted previously, we were short-handed on Thursday (July 3), Monday (July 7), and Monday (July 14). Since we needed extra help and the displaced welders did not have meaningful work to do, I asked Mark Jensen to assign them to inspecting the cabinets. This worked out well since they were available and familiar enough with the product that we could train them in a short amount of time.

		Factors			Production	
		TIP	CAL	CLN	Total Units	Defective Units
Wed	July 2	FF	1S	NPT	490	127
Thr	July 3	FF	1S	CTC	493	157
Mon	July 7	FF	2S	NPT	512	144
Tue	July 8	FF	2S	CTC	485	54
Wed	July 9	FD	1S	NPT	489	78
Thr	July 10	FD	1S	CTC	525	38
Fri	July 11	FD	2S	NPT	517	62
Mon	July 14	FD	2S	CTC	503	131

Printed Circuit Boards, Inc.

Printed Circuit Boards, Inc. (PCB), like most members of the industry, expected problems with ionic contaminates on the surface of the boards on its new line. As a supplier of boards to the Department of Defense, PCB was required to meet the specifications of MIL-P-28809. However, no specifications had been established for current process capability on this line. Moreover, there was no data on actual performance. Consequently, the need for improvements (reduction) in ionic contamination had not been established. Sam Wentz, as Director of QC and Bob Hunt, Senior Process Engineer, were charged with putting together a team to design and execute an experiment. Their team also consisted of a reliability engineer and two process engineers with extensive printed circuit board manufacturing experience.

Mr. Wentz and Mr. Hunt believed that by deriving answers to the following experimental questions, the plant would be better able to define limits and capabilities of the manufacturing process in relation to ionic contamination.

The following experimental questions were of central concern to the resolution of the problem:

1. What is the average (μ) level of contamination as measured in micrograms per square inch ($\mu g/in^2$) in relation to the printed wiring area (PWAs) produced by the organization?
2. What is the variance (σ^2) of the current PWA contaminate levels?
3. What theoretical distribution should the PWA contamination levels follow?
4. Does the distribution lie within an acceptable range with respect to ionic contamination?
5. What manufacturing variables account for 80% or more of the total observable variation in contamination levels?
6. Which manufacturing variables are "leverage" in nature with regard to ionic contamination?
7. Can the causal leverage variables, and any associated relationships existing between the causal variables be adequately controlled in order to comply with MIL-P-28809?

Source: Mike Carnell, Carnell and Associates, Payson, Arizona; and Gary Cone, Dave Dipre, Mikel J. Harry, Jim Morris, and George Peters. This case is based on actual data.

Successfully answering these seven experimental questions should enhance the organization's ability to better control the process, which will result in increasing product quality and productivity while decreasing costs.

Further discussion of the experiment strategy, design, and analytical procedure is shown in **Exhibit 1** of the attachments. Sixteen variables, as identified in **Table 1** of the attachments, are to be evaluated. Additional figures and tables are provided to assist in analysis.

Exhibit 1 Experiment Strategy, Design, and Analytical Procedures

Stage 1: Validation of the Problem

The first experimental question to be answered was whether or not the existing cleaning process and associated process controls produced boards that met the MIL-P-28809 cleanliness requirements. To facilitate an answer, it was necessary to establish a contamination distribution using experimental data with 95% confidence intervals (μ and σ) to determine the "current" process performance. If the process performed within the required cleanliness range under "worst case" estimates, then no further testing would be necessary. On the other hand, if an unacceptable nonconformance level was observed, then further testing would be required.

The staff engineers collected the data from six boards as shown in **Table 2** to address the contamination level issue prior to any further testing. A 95% confidence interval was deemed appropriate.

Stage 2: Determine Representativeness of Test Board Configuration and Design

This stage was primarily concerned with determining if a statistically significant difference existed between the mean of the experimental test boards (μ_t) and the mean of "commonly used" production board designs (μ_p) in relation to the response measure (μg of NaCl/in^2). This particular procedure allowed inferences back to the general population of board designs and configurations. An alpha risk (α) of .05 and beta risk (β) of .05 was utilized for this stage of the experiment. This step utilized a B vs. C data analysis procedure and followed a "two group comparison" design.

The second objective at this stage of the experiment was to study the effect of component type and density in relation to contamination via One-Way Analysis of Variance (1-way ANOVA).

Subsequently, contamination levels on 30 production boards were compared with eight experimental boards designed for this experiment (**Table 3**). The test board was divided into four quadrants to test for cleanliness. Total test board contamination levels were calculated by averaging the contaminations levels of the four quadrants. Results are shown in **Table 4.**

Stage 3: Isolate the Statistically Significant Variables in Relation to Ionic Contamination

This stage of the experiment was concerned with determining which of the 16 experimental variables identified in Table 1 were among the "vital few" variables versus the "trivial many." The variables (factors) were classified into four heterogeneous groups (**Figure 2**).

A 2^{4-1} Fractional Factorial Group Screening Design was used to structure the four major grouping variables. **Figures 2** and **3** illustrates the testing combinations under a 2^{4-1} fractional factorial group screening design. If more than one group had proved to be statistically significant, then further testing using the group screen design concept would have been conducted.

Variable levels used in this stage are shown in **Table 5.**

Stage 4: Identify all Statistically Significant Main Effects and Interactions Related to the Experimental Factors

This stage surfaced the main effects and interactions existing between the "vital few" variables and highlighted the proportion (%) of observed variation accounted for by each main effect and interaction. A Full Factorial Design was employed. The number of levels (n) and factors (k) selected for inclusion in the full factorial model were based upon the previous stage-wise experimental results. Analysis of variance was utilized to extract all relevant information from the experiment design. Alpha risks on all effects were established at the .05 level (see **Tables 6**, **7**, and **8**).

Stage 5: Optimization of the Response Variable

This stage of the experiment was configured to identify the optimum levels for the vital few variables with known degrees of risk and confidence. It was not performed because adequate control levels were found in Stage 4 for the vital few variables. Further optimization was reasoned not to be cost effective.

Exhibit 1 Experiment Strategy, Design and Analytical Procedures, concluded

Stage 6: Implement Process Controls

Process controls were developed at this point and implemented via the assembly process procedures governing the wave solder and cleaning processes The data of **Table 9** was collected after the process controls were implemented.

Stage 7: Validation of Experimental Results

This particular stage was concerned with validating the experimental results after implementing Stage 6 process controls. This step was achieved using a two group comparison design of a pre-test/post-test nature. The mean of the observed sampling distribution of Stage 1 (μ Stage 1) was compared to the sampling average after Stage 6 (μ Stage 6). An alpha and beta risk of .05 was utilized.

Figure 1 Groups/Factors

GROUPS

	W	X	Y	Z
	A	E	I	M
FACTORS	B	F	J	N
	C	G	K	O
	D	H	L	P

Figure 2 Factorials

FULL FACTORIAL

		D_1		D_2	
		C_1	C_2	C_1	C_2
A_1	B_1	●	●	●	●
	B_2	●	●	●	●
A_2	B_1	●	●	●	●
	B_2	●	●	●	●

2^4 = 16 POSSIBLE TEST COMBINATIONS

2^{4-1} FRACTIONAL FACTORIAL

		D_1		D_2	
		C_1	C_2	C_1	C_2
A_1	B_1	●			●
	B_2		●	●	
A_2	B_1		●	●	
	B_2	●			●

1/2 x 16 = 8 POSSIBLE TREATMENT COMBINATIONS

NOTE: DURING TESTING, THE COMBINATIONS SHOULD BE
RANDOMIZED IN ORDER TO RANDOMLY DISTRIBUTE
UNKNOWN TEST VARIATION

Figure 3 Testing Combinations

(1)	(0000, 0000, 0000, 0000)
WZ	(1111, 0000, 0000, 1111)
XZ	(0000, 1111, 0000, 1111)
WX	(1111, 1111, 0000, 0000)
YZ	(0000, 0000, 1111, 1111)
WY	(1111, 0000, 1111, 0000)
XY	(0000, 1111, 1111, 0000)
WXYZ	(1111, 1111, 1111, 1111)

Table 1 Manufacturing Variables Theorized to Be of Experimental Concern

Rating	Group Rank	Overall Rank	Factor	Description	Experimental Levels Lo	High
A	1	1	A	Time in Boiling Sump	10 Sec.	50 Sec.
A	2	2	B	Time in Cold Sump	10 Sec.	50 Sec.
A	3	3	C	Time in Vapor Zone	10 Sec.	50 Sec.
A	4	4	D	Time in Drying Zone	10 Sec.	50 Sec.
A	5	5	E	Time from WS to Degreaser	30 Min.	3 Min.
A	6	6	F	Agitation Time (Cold Sump)	0 Sec.	10 Sec.
A	7	7	G	Alcohol Spray Direction	90 Deg.	30 Deg.
A	8	8	H	Alcohol Spray Duration	10 Sec.	40 Sec.
A	9	9	I	Alcohol Scrub Time	0 Sec.	30 Sec.
A	10	10	J	Preheat Temperature	220 F	180 F
A	11	11	K	Flux Specific Gravity	940 g/cc	915 g/cc
B	1	12	L	Alcohol Soak Time	5 Sec.	60 Sec.
B	2	13	M	Flux Sprayed on Topside	Yes	No
D	1	14	N	Time from Degrease to IPA	30 Min.	1 Min.
D	2	15	O	Time from Clean to Test	Not Controlled	
E	1	16	P	Degreaser Drip Time	10 Sec.	50 Sec.

A = Very High Importance, Likely to Prove Causal
B = Important; Could Prove Causal
C = Some Concern; Might Be Somewhat Causal
D = Little Concern; Likely Not to Be Causal
E = No Concern; Should Not Prove Causal

Table 2 Production Boards Tested Prior to Conformal Coating

Project	Test Date	Run Date	Board No.	Ser. No.	Board Sq. In.	Sol. Ht.	Start Mohm	End Mohm	Run Time	µg.NaCl /In^2
DKW	050285	050185	2025	D263	46	56	20	8.6	10	9.5
DKW	050285	050185	2025	D261	46	56	20	6.2	10	13.2
TSCOPE	050285	050185	9726	N513	98	135	20	10.2	10	9.1
TSCOPE	050285	050185	9726	N511	98	135	20	6.6	10	14.0
MRS	050285	050185	2691	F1281	36	79	20	12.6	10	11.7
MRS	050285	050185	2691	F1253	36	79	20	13.5	10	10.9

4µg.NACL: N = 6   Sum X = 68.4   Sum $(_i-\overline{X})^2$ = 19.2 $\overline{X}$ = 11.4   S = 1.96

Table 3 Production Boards

Project	Test Date	Run Date	Board No.	Ser. No.	Board Sq. In.	Sol. Ht.	Start Mohm	End Mohm	Run Time	µg.NaCl /In^2
DKW	041885	041785	2021	D260	56	112	20	15.5	5	10.3
DKW	041885	041785	2021	D251	56	112	20	19.5	5	8.2
DKW	042285	041985	2005	D249	56	112	20	14.5	5	11.0
DKW	042285	041985	2005	D250	56	112	20	14.2	5	11.3
DKW	042485	042385	2009	D265	56	112	20	17.0	5	9.4
DKW	042485	042385	2009	D263	56	112	20	15.8	5	10.1
DKW	042685	042685	2001	D262	56	112	20	11.3	10	14.2
DKW	042685	042685	2001	D266	56	112	20	13.2	5	11.6
DKW	042685	042685	2301	D103	56	112	20	11.1	10	14.4
DKW	042685	042685	2301	D107	56	112	20	11.3	10	14.2
TSCOPE	041885	041785	9750	1039	101	202	20	17.9	5	8.9
TSCOPE	041885	041785	9750	1019	101	202	20	18.7	5	8.6
TSCOPE	042285	041985	7237	N196	28	56	20	13.5	5	11.9
TSCOPE	042285	041985	7237	N199	28	56	20	13.2	5	12.1
TSCOPE	042285	041985	6838	N142	90	180	20	14.4	5	11.1
TSCOPE	042285	041985	6838	N146	90	180	20	10.9	5	14.7
TSCOPE	042485	042385	1990	2609	142	135	20	10.1	5	7.5
TSCOPE	042485	042385	1990	2538	142	135	20	13.2	10	5.8
TSCOPE	042485	042385	9753	9830	101	135	20	11.5	5	9.3
TSCOPE	042485	042385	9753	2943	101	135	20	11.2	10	9.5
MRS	041885	041785	1407	F0686	22	22	20	10.0	5	8.0
MRS	041885	041785	1407	F0676	22	22	20	9.5	5	8.4
MRS	042285	041985	2616	F3474	40	79	20	19.7	5	8.0
MRS	042285	041985	2616	F3475	40	79	20	17.8	5	8.9
MRS	042685	042585	2618	F3506	48	90	20	13.3	10	11.3
MRS	042685	042585	2618	F3511	48	90	20	14.4	5	10.4
MRS	050285	050185	6321	F0258	76	112	20	14.2	10	8.3
MRS	050285	050185	6321	F0260	76	112	20	11.5	10	10.3
MRS	050285	050185	2356	F0634	36	79	20	16.7	10	10.5
MRS	050285	050185	2356	F0622	36	79	20	16.0	10	11.0

4µg.NACL:N = 30   Sum X = 309.   Sum $(_i-\overline{X})^2$ = 137 $\overline{X}$ = 10.3   S = 2.1

Table 4 Test Boards

Ser. No.	Resistors µg.NaCl /In^2	Caps µg.NaCl /In^2	IC's µg.NaCl /In^2	Control µg.NaCl /In^2	Total µg.NaCl /In^2
101	6.88	7.94	8.05	7.30	7.54
102	7.13	7.30	7.49	6.29	7.05
103	8.76	9.86	8.76	7.63	8.75
104	8.45	7.89	7.44	6.88	7.66
105	6.72	8.90	7.09	5.92	7.16
106	6.92	7.99	8.64	6.43	7.50
107	7.54	7.44	7.54	6.50	7.26
108	6.68	8.48	6.40	6.76	7.07
X =	59.08	65.8	61.41	53.71	59.99
X^2 =	4.52	4.91	4.32	2.15	2.15
X =	7.39	8.23	7.68	6.71	7.50
S =	0.80	0.84	0.79	0.55	0.55

Table 5 Variable Levels for Stage 3

Overall Rank	Experimental Variables	Experimental Levels Lo	High
1	Time in Boiling Sump	10 Sec.	50 Sec.
2	Time in Cold Sump	10 Sec.	50 Sec.
3	Time in Vapor Zone	10 Sec.	50 Sec.
4	Time in Drying Zone	10 Sec.	50 Sec.
5	Time from WS to Degreaser	30 Min.	3 Min.
6	Agitation Time (Cold Sump)	0 Sec.	10 Sec.
7	Alcohol Spray DIrection	90 Deg.	30 Deg.
8	Alcohol Spray Duration	10 Sec.	40 Sec.
9	Alcohol Scrub Time	0 Sec.	30 Sec.
10	Preheat Temperature	220 F	180 F
11	Flux Specific Gravity	940 g/cc	915 g/cc
12	Alcohol Soak Time	5 Sec.	60 Sec.
13	Flux Sprayed on Topside	Yes	No
14	Time from Degrease to IPA	30 Min.	1 Min.
15	Time from Clean to Test	Not Controlled	
16	Degreaser Drip Time	Repeat of Dry Time	

	Control Variables		
1	Person Executing Cleaning	Ranny Konn	
2	Spray Both Sides Before Cold Sump	Yes	
3	Handling Method	Gloves	
4	Alcohol Brush	Same Throughout	
5	Spray Nozzle Pressure	Normal/Constant	
6	Spray Time in Vapors	1/2 of Vapor Zone Time	
7	Drying Method	30 PSI Air	

Table 6 Manufacturing Variables Theorized to Be of Experimental Concern

Rank	Group	Variable	% of Variation*
1	W	Time in Boiling Sump	
2	W	Time in Cold Sump	
3	W	Time in Vapor Zone	22.0
4	W	Time in Drying Zone	
5	X	Time from Wave Solder to Degreaser	
6	X	Agitation Time in Cold Sump	
7	X	Alcohol Spray Direction	20.1
8	X	Alcohol Spray Duration	
9	Y	Alcohol Scrub Time	
10	Y	Preheat Temperature	
11	Y	Flux Specific Gravity	40.4
12	Y	Alcohol Soak Time	
13	Z	Flux Sprayed Topside	
14	Z	Time from Degreaser to Alcohol	
15	Z	Time from Alcohol to Test	10.2
16	Z	Drip Time at Degreaser	
		Total	92.7

* Percent (%) of observed variation accounted for by a given experimental grouping. This value may generally be thought of as the amount of "leverage" inherent to a particular experimental group.

Table 7 Variable Levels for Stage 4

Rank	Variables	Experimental Levels	
		Lo	High
1	Flux Specific Gravity	940 g/cc	915 g/cc
2	Preheat Temperature	220 F	180 F
3	Alcohol Soak Time	5 Sec.	60 Sec.
4	Alcohol Scrub Time	0 Sec.	30 Sec.
	Controlled Variables		
1	Person Executing Cleaning	Ranny Konn	
2	Handling Method	Gloves	
3	Alcohol Brush	Same Throughout	
4	Spray Nozzle Pressure	Normal/Constant	
5	Flux Sprayed on Topside	No	
6	Time from WS to Degreaser	3 Min.	
7	Spray Both Sides Before Cold Sump	Yes	
8	Time in Boiling Sump	30 Sec.	
9	Time in Cold Sump	20 Sec.	
10	Agitation Time (Cold Sump)	10 Sec.	
11	Time in Vapor Zone	30 Sec.	
12	Spray Time in Vapors	1/2 of Vapor Zone Time	
13	Time from Degreaser to IPA	1 Min.	
14	Alcohol Spray Duration	20 Sec.	
15	Alcohol Spray Direction	30 Deg.	
16	Drying Method	30 PSI Air	

Table 8 Variation Attributable to Stage 4 Variables

Rank	Variables	% of Variation
W	Flux Specific Gravity	60.5
X	Preheat Temperature	28.1
Y	Alcohol Soak Time	0.6
Z	Alcohol Scrub Time	7.8
	Total	97.0

Table 9 Omegameter Results

Date	Bd. No.	Area (In^2)	Vol (ml)	Cont (μg)	Project
20586	2570	41.3	5300	2.6	ALT16
20586	2502	77.0	5000	5.9	ALT16
20586	2599	7.5	2540	8.8	ALT16
20586	2630	10.5	2700	6.3	ALT16
20586	2574	56.3	5500	2.1	ALT16
20586	2590	149.6	11500	0.3	ALT16
20686	9735	104.3	6500	8.1	JSTAR
20686	427	6.8	2600	3.9	ITCS
20686	2590	154.6	11250	0.6	ALT16
20686	2590	154.6	11250	2.3	ALT16
20686	2502	77.0	4900	12.8	ALT16
20686	2570	41.3	5500	2.2	ALT16
20686	2590	154.6	11250	1.2	ALT16
20686	2574	56.3	5400	4.4	ALT16
20786	1558	80.0	11000	0.0	MRS
20786	173	6.5	2500	2.0	ITCS
20786	2570	41.3	5300	3.2	ALT16
20786	2574	56.3	5300	1.8	ALT16
20786	2955	102.5	6500	2.3	
21086	2691	37.8	5500	0.4	MRS
21086	2691	37.8	5500	7.7	MRS
21086	2691	37.8	5500	0.0	MRS
21086	2691	37.8	5500	0.0	MRS
21086	2574	56.3	5500	5.6	ALT16
21086	2570	41.3	5500	2.8	ALT16
21086	2502	77.0	4900	9.6	ALT16
21086	7640	15.0	3500	5.3	
21186	707	32.0	5200	4.1	SEPT
21186	1407	20.3	3400	4.6	MRS
21186	2694	76.5	5600	0.0	MRS
21186	1558	80.0	9500	0.0	MRS
21186	1648	80.8	5600	2.6	MRS
21186	2694	76.5	5400	0.0	MRS
21186	2570	41.3	5500	1.9	ALT16
21186	2590	150.4	11000	1.3	ALT16
21186	2570	41.3	5500	5.8	ALT16
21286	1407	20.3	3300	3.9	SEPTAR
21286	7630	15.3	3700	0.0	APX105
21286	7630	15.3	3700	0.0	APX105
21286	7630	15.3	3700	0.0	APX105
21286	7630	15.3	3700	6.0	APX105
21286	2599	7.5	2600	10.6	ALT16
21286	2590	151.1	11250	3.7	ALT16
21286	2502	77.0	4900	2.3	ALT16
21286	2599	7.5	2600	10.6	ALT16
21286	2574	56.3	5300	0.0	ALT16

Table 9 Omegameter Results, continued

Date	Bd. No.	Area (In²)	Vol (ml)	Cont (µg)	Project
21286	2570	41.3	5500	3.5	ALT16
21286	2599	7.5	2600	8.8	ALT16
21386	6261	76.5	5600	1.9	MRS
21386	6321	72.0	5400	5.7	MRS
21386	6261	76.5	5600	0.0	MRS
21386	2694	72.0	5400	1.7	MRS
21386	1407	20.3	2500	3.9	MRS
21386	6241	312.8	15500	1.1	MRS
21386	2618	46.3	6300	4.6	MRS
21386	6261	76.5	5500	3.1	MRS
21386	7700	13.8	2500	7.7	APX105
21386	7700	13.8	2500	6.7	APX105
21386	2590	144.0	11250	0.0	ALT16
21386	2630	9.0	2500	7.4	ALT16
21386	2502	77.0	4900	4.8	ALT16
21386	2574	56.3	5300	4.7	ALT16
21386	2502	77.0	5400	9.4	ALT16
21386	2599	7.5	2500	10.6	ALT16
21486	1558	80.0	10000	0.0	MRS
21486	1558	80.0	10000	0.0	MRS
21486	2618	45.7	6500	5.5	MRS
21486	2616	36.0	5500	0.0	MRS
21486	1558	80.0	10000	0.0	MRS
21486	2694	75.4	5400	2.3	MRS
21486	2694	72.0	5500	3.5	MRS
21486	2694	72.0	5500	3.7	MRS
21486	7700	15.3	2300	3.5	APX105
21486	2502	77.0	4900	2.0	ALT16
21486	2590	41.3	11250	2.0	ALT16
21486	2570	77.0	5300	4.4	ALT16
21486	2570	41.3	5300	4.4	ALT16
21486	2599	7.5	2500	8.8	ALT16
21486	2599	7.5	2500	8.8	ALT16
21486	2599	148.5	2500	5.3	ALT16
21486	2590	148.5	11250	2.0	ALT16
21486	2599	7.5	2500	5.3	ALT16
21486	2502	77.0	4900	2.0	ALT16
21486	2427	23.0	3800	7.4	
21786	515	76.5	5000	5.1	PPN19
21786	515	76.5	5000	5.1	PPN19
21786	3115	46.6	5400	3.8	PPN19
21786	3141	19.7	3700	6.0	PPN19
21786	3141	19.7	3700	6.0	PPN19
21786	3115	46.6	5400	3.8	PPN19
21786	2356	36.0	5800	7.9	MRS
21786	2356	36.0	5800	0.0	MRS
21786	7700	15.0	2300	0.0	APX105
21786	5718	13.5	2300	5.8	APX105
21786	7700	15.0	2300	0.0	APX105
21786	2570	41.3	5000	6.6	ALT16
21786	2570	41.3	5000	6.3	ALT16
21786	2574	56.3	5400	5.5	ALT16
21786	2599	7.5	2100	6.9	ALT16
21786	2502	77.0	4900	5.0	ALT16
21786	2599	7.5	2100	6.9	ALT16
21786	2570	41.3	5000	6.6	ALT16
21786	2574	7.5	5400	5.5	ALT16
21786	2570	77.0	5000	6.3	ALT16
21786	2502	56.3	4900	5.0	ALT16

Table 9 Omegameter Results, continued

Date	Bd. No.	Area (In²)	Vol (ml)	Cont (µg)	Project
21786	2356	36.0	5800	7.9	
21786	2356	36.0	5800	0.0	
21786	5718	13.5	2300	5.8	
21886	2901	15.3	2500	4.3	SST
21886	2618	46.8	6300	0.0	MRS
21886	2618	46.8	6300	4.2	MRS
21886	6321	75.4	5500	0.7	MRS
21886	6321	75.4	5500	2.0	MRS
21886	2502	77.0	4900	3.4	ALT16
21886	2574	56.3	5300	0.0	ALT16
21886	2590	151.3	11250	0.0	ALT16
21986	9422	104.0	8600	11.9	PPN19
21986	7630	12.5	2000	0.0	APX105
21986	2502	75.1	4900	1.5	ALT16
21986	2574	58.1	5200	1.1	ALT16
21986	2599	6.3	2000	0.0	ALT16
21986	2630	10.3	2300	0.0	ALT16
22086	2901	16.3	3500	16.7	SST
22086	5500	82.5	7100	5.7	SST
22086	2901	16.3	3500	5.5	SST
22086	6241	342.9	15500	2.3	MRS
22086	2616	36.1	5400	0.0	MRS
22086	2694	75.4	5600	0.0	MRS
22086	1558	80.0	9700	0.0	MRS
22186	2616	36.1	5500	0.0	MRS
22186	7902	86.7	6300	3.3	MRS
22186	6261	77.6	5500	0.0	MRS
22186	2502	75.1	5100	1.7	ALT16
22186	2630	10.2	2000	0.0	ALT16
22186	2574	58.5	5300	0.0	ALT16
22486	2694	75.2	5500	0.0	MRS
22486	2694	75.2	5500	0.0	MRS
22486	9735	98.9	8500	0.0	JSTAR
22486	9649	98.9	8500	2.5	JSTAR
22486	2590	146.9	11250	0.0	ALT16
22486	2630	9.0	2000	0.0	ALT16
22486	2502	77.0	4900	0.0	ALT16
22486	2574	58.1	5300	0.0	ALT16
22486	2574	56.3	5300	0.0	ALT16
22486	2502	75.7	5100	0.0	ALT16
22586	2618	46.8	6300	5.0	MRS
22586	6776	31.9	4100	5.3	MRS
22586	6776	31.9	4100	4.5	MRS
22586	1407	19.7	2500	3.9	MRS
22586	9691	98.9	8500	0.0	JSTAR
22586	7630	15.3	2000	4.2	APX105
22586	8856	46.3	6300	5.3	
22686	9117	27.2	3000	4.3	PGSE
22686	1407	19.7	2300	4.6	MRS
22686	7902	86.7	6300	0.0	MRS
22686	1558	80.0	9700	0.0	MRS
22686	1558	80.0	9700	0.0	MRS
22686	2618	46.8	6400	0.0	MRS
22686	1558	80.0	9700	3.2	MRS
22686	2574	56.3	5400	5.0	ALT16
22686	2590	146.9	11250	0.6	ALT16
22686	2502	77.0	4900	9.2	ALT16
22686	1484	283.8	11750	3.5	
22786	11902	75.4	5500	0.0	PGSE

Table 9 Omegameter Results, continued

Date	Bd. No.	Area (In²)	Vol (ml)	Cont (µg)	Project
22786	2618	46.8	6300	0.0	MRS
22786	2599	7.5	2300	3.4	ALT16
22786	2173	24.7	4100	5.3	
22786	6380	34.9	4200	0.0	
22886	1407	20.3	3300	0.0	MRS
22886	3168	165.4	8800	6.0	JSTAR
22886	3198	84.5	8300	1.2	JSTAR
22886	7640	15.0	3000	0.8	APX105
22886	7630	15.3	3000	0.0	APX105
30386	6331	75.4	5500	1.5	MRS
30386	292	112.0	9000	1.3	
30386	1558	114.5	9500	0.0	MRS
30386	2618	46.8	6300	3.6	MRS
30386	7640	15.3	2000	0.0	APX105
30386	1648	78.5	5600	2.4	MRS
30386	7620	14.5	2000	4.6	APX105
30386	2618	46.8	6300	0.0	MRS
30486	22897	15.0	3000	13.3	
30486	9691	104.0	10500	2.9	JSTAR
30486	2590	150.4	11250	6.9	ALT16
30486	380	72.0	7800	0.0	
30486	380	72.0	7700	0.0	
30486	6241	342.9	15500	1.5	
30486	2618	46.8	6300	0.0	MRS
30586	2616	36.1	5500	0.0	MRS
30586	2175	24.7	4100	4.8	
30586	2618	46.8	6400	0.0	MRS
30586	1472	75.4	5600	0.0	
30586	1407	15.3	3000	0.0	MRS
30686	2574	56.3	5300	8.6	ALT16
30686	9589	98.8	8500	2.8	JSTAR
30686	3201	37.0	5500	6.1	JSTAR
30686	304	72.0	7800	0.0	
30686	1243	37.4	5200	0.0	
30686	9913	20.1	3000	0.0	
30786	2694	75.2	5500	0.0	MRS
30786	7640	15.7	2000	0.0	APX105
30786	1558	107.3	9700	0.0	MRS
30786	2618	46.8	6400	0.0	MRS
30786	1407	19.7	2500	0.0	MRS
31086	4312	8.1	2250	0.0	MRS
31086	9796	28.5	4150	3.3	JSTAR
31186	4900	39.3	6000	0.0	
31186	7640	15.7	2000	0.0	APX105
31186	2618	46.8	6300	0.0	MRS
31186	3273	27.1	3500	3.9	PPN19
31186	1648	78.5	5600	0.0	MRS
31486	2618	46.8	6300	0.0	MRS
31486	3198	84.5	8500	0.0	JSTAR
31486	9589	98.4	8500	2.7	JSTAR
31486	7620	14.5	2000	4.6	APX105
31786	7021	137.9	4600	0.3	
31786	7021	137.9	9000	0.7	
31786	3332	23.9	3700	4.4	
31786	3332	23.9	3700	0.0	
31886	2574	56.3	5300	0.0	ALT16
31886	2590	150.4	12500	0.0	ALT16
31886	2502	77.0	4900	4.1	ALT16
31886	2599	7.5	2000	7.0	ALT16

Table 9 Omegameter Results, concluded

Date	Bd. No.	Area (In^2)	Vol (ml)	Cont (μg)	Project
31886	2599	7.5	2000	7.0	ALT16
31986	322	72.0	7700	2.6	
31986	707	32.0	5500	0.0	SEPTAR
31986	707	32.0	5400	0.0	SEPTAR
32086	9725	100.0	8500	0.0	JSTAR
32086	7700	15.3	2000	3.4	APX105
32186	9560	100.0	8500	5.1	JSTAR
32186	8077	100.0	8500	7.2	JSTAR
32186	9671	100.0	8500	0.0	JSTAR
32186	3168	162.0	9000	1.9	JSTAR
32486	6087	72.0	7700	0.0	
32486	6087	72.0	7700	0.0	
32486	6087	72.0	7700	0.0	
33186	6261	76.6	5500	0.0	MRS
33186	2618	46.8	6500	0.0	MRS
33186	1558	109.1	10000	0.0	MRS
33186	2618	46.8	6500	0.0	MRS
33186	2618	46.8	6500	0.0	MRS

$n = 241$

Sum $(_i \overline{X})^2 = 694.5$ $\overline{X} = 2.88$

Sum $(_i \overline{X})^2 = 2408.6$ $S = 3.17$

APPENDICES

A P P E N D I X   A

TQM Problem-Solving Process

PROBLEM SOLVING PROCESS

```
┌─────────────────────────────────────────┐
│  Become Aware of the Problem             │
└─────────────────────────────────────────┘

┌─────────────────────────────────────────┐
│  1.  Use Team Approach                   │
└─────────────────────────────────────────┘

┌─────────────────────────────────────────┐
│  2.  Describe Problem                    │
│      • Analyze existing data.            │
│      • Separate problem.                 │
└─────────────────────────────────────────┘

┌─────────────────────────────────────────┐
│  3.  Implement and Verify Interim        │
│      (Containment) Actions               │
│      • Verify effectiveness of actions.  │
└─────────────────────────────────────────┘

┌ ─ ─ ─ ─ ─ ─ ─ ─ ─ ─ ─ ─ ─ ─ ─ ─ ─ ─ ─ ─ ┐
  4.  Define and Verify Root Causes
│ ┌─────────────────────────────────────┐ │
  │ Identify Potential Causes           │
│ │ • Evaluate team composition.        │ │
  │ • Review and improve the problem    │
│ │   description.                      │ │
  │ • Evaluate each potential cause by  │
│ │   comparison to the problem         │ │
  │   description.                      │
│ └─────────────────────────────────────┘ │

│ ┌─────────────────────────────────────┐ │
  │     Select Likely Causes            │
│ └─────────────────────────────────────┘ │

              ◇
          Is the          * Test each potential cause
│    No   Potential          through experimentation   │
          Cause a            and statistical data
│         Root Cause         analysis.                  │
            ?*
              │ Yes
│ ┌─────────────────────────────────────┐ │
  │    Identify Alternative Solutions   │
│ └─────────────────────────────────────┘ │
└ ─ ─ ─ ─ ─ ─ ─ ─ ─ ─ ─ ─ ─ ─ ─ ─ ─ ─ ─ ─ ┘

┌─────────────────────────────────────────┐
│  5.  Choose and Verify Corrective        │
│      Actions                             │
│      • Evaluate team composition.        │
│      • Evaluate solutions for improved   │
│        Interim Actions.                  │
│      • Evaluate the degree of problem    │
│        reduction or elimination.         │
└─────────────────────────────────────────┘

┌─────────────────────────────────────────┐
│  6.  Implement Permanent Corrective      │
│      Actions                             │
│      • Establish an action plan.         │
│      • Establish contingency plans.      │
└─────────────────────────────────────────┘

┌─────────────────────────────────────────┐
│  7.  Prevent Recurrence                  │
└─────────────────────────────────────────┘

┌─────────────────────────────────────────┐
│  8.  Congratulate Your Team              │
└─────────────────────────────────────────┘
```

1. **Use team approach.** Establish a small group of people with the process/product knowledge, allocated time, authority, and skill in the required technical discipline to solve the problem and implement corrective actions. The group must have a designated champion.

2. **Describe the problem.** Specify the internal/external customer problem by identifying in quantifiable terms the who, what, when, where, why, how, and how many (5W2H) for the problem.

3. **Implement and verify interim (containment) actions.** Define and implement containment actions to isolate the effect of the problem from any internal/external customer until corrective action is implemented. Verify the effectiveness of the containment action.

4. **Define and verify root causes.** Identify all potential causes which could explain why the problem occurred. Isolate and verify the root cause by testing each potential cause against the problem description and test data. Identify alternative corrective actions to eliminate root cause.

5. **Choose and verify corrective actions.** Through pre-production test programs quantitatively confirm that the selected corrective actions will resolve the problem for the customer, and will not cause undesirable side effects. Define contingency actions, if necessary, based on risk assessment.

6. **Implement permanent corrective actions.** Define and implement the best permanent corrective actions. Choose on-going controls to ensure the root cause is eliminated. Once in production, monitor the long-term effects and implement contingency actions, if necessary.

7. **Prevent recurrence.** Modify the management systems, operating systems, practices, and procedures to prevent recurrence of this and all similar problems.

8. **Contratulate your team.** Recognize the collective effort of the team.

A P P E N D I X   B

Reviewing TQM Tools

TOOLS FOR GENERATING IDEAS

Cause and effect diagrams are a way of organizing the potential causes of a problem or the factors that must be successfully executed to achieve a desired outcome. The effect, or outcome, is placed at the right. The important contributing factors (causes) are arranged in logical groupings on the branches of the diagram. Using the four "M's" of manpower, machinery, methods, and materials often provides a good starting point. This chart is sometimes also called a fishbone diagram or an Ishikawa diagram. Traditional brainstorming techniques can be helpful when developing a cause and effect diagram.

A **Pareto Chart** is a special purpose bar chart. It usually shows the number of items that fall into each category from largest frequency to smallest. Frequently, the categories describe the types of defects that are being discovered. The chart is then organized so that the category with the largest number of entries appears on the left. This is followed by the other categories in decreasing order. Such a visual aid makes it easy to see the relative contribution of each type of problem. Periodic use of Pareto charts is an effective way to show progress over time.

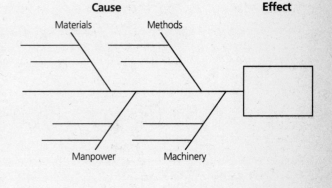

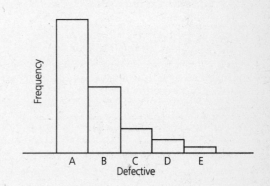

TOOLS TO ORGANIZE THE DATA

Several forms of **flowcharts** to show a step-by-step description of the process can be helpful. They may take several different forms depending on the purpose. (1) A block diagram showing a decision-making process is given as an example. (2) However, a series of movements on a factory floor shown in a flow process chart may also be appropriate. Some flow charts display the activities in a process by also showing the individuals or departments that are responsible for each step.

Data can be organized using a **check sheet**. This is any kind of form that is designed for recording data. In many cases, the recording is done so that patterns are easily seen while the data are being taken. We are attempting to find the facts/patterns of data for subsequent analysis. An example might be a drawing which shows a tally of the area where defects are occurring or a check sheet showing type of customer complaints.

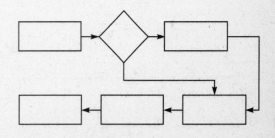

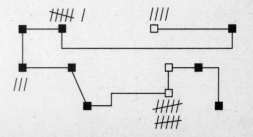

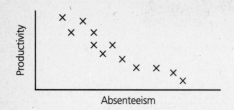

The relationship between two measurements can be shown in a **scatter diagram.** If the two items are closely related, the data points will form a tight band. A random pattern results if the items are unrelated. One way this tool can be used is to evaluate the effect that a process variable has on the quality characteristic of the product.

TOOLS FOR IDENTIFYING PROBLEMS

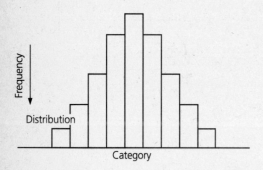

A **histogram** shows the range of values (or categories) of a measurement and the frequency with which each occurs. It shows the most frequently occurring readings as well as the variation in the measurements. Statistics, such as the average and standard deviation, may be calculated to describe the distribution, but it is always important to plot the data, so the shape of the distribution can be "seen." The shape of the distribution may give some insight into the cause of the variation.

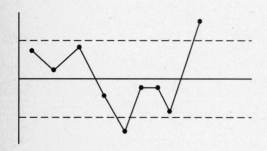

A **time plot** shows measurements in the chronological sequence in which they were taken. This may reveal a pattern which leads to an underlying cause. A control chart is a more sophisticated version of a time plot. It uses calculated limits that are rarely exceeded unless there is a fundamental change (assignable variation) in the process. A **control chart** is a graphic tool for determining the state of control of a process. Control charts assume that plots stay within control limits as long as only natural variation is present and exceed those limits only when assignable variation is present.

Correlation analysis determines the relationship between two variables; an independent variable and a dependent variable.

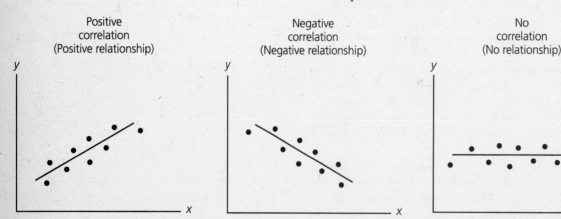

A P P E N D I X   C

Design of Experiments

Experimentation can be used either in the design phase of a product or process or in making improvements in an existing product or process. When working with a product, experimentation is used to make the product the best it can possibly be and to make it most closely fit the needs and tastes of its market. Once the specifications for a product are known, experimentation is used to find the way to most consistently produce the product to meet those specifications.

While experimentation can be used for either a process or a product, the following example will demonstrate the use of experimentation for a product.

EXPERIMENTATION EXAMPLE (FOR A PRODUCT)

Katie Brown, owner of Katie's Cookie Company, a small business which sells homemade cookies, wants to have the best chocolate chip cookie in her cookie market. At the present time, the chocolate chip cookie sold by Gooey Goodies is known to be the market leader. Katie's goal is to improve her chocolate chip cookie so that it is preferred over Gooey Goodies' chocolate chip cookie. She has decided to determine how to improve her cookie through the use of experimentation. The current recipe and specifications Katie uses for chocolate chip cookies are as follows:

Katie's Chocolate Chip Cookies

2 cups margarine	1 Tbsp cinnamon
2 cups white sugar	2 tsp soda
2 cups brown sugar	2 tsp salt
4 eggs	3 cups semi-sweet chocolate chips
2 Tbsp vanilla	2 cups chopped pecans
7 cups flour	

Soften margarine to room temperature (70 degrees). Cream margarine, white sugar and brown sugar. Add eggs and vanilla and mix well. Add flour, cinnamon, soda and salt and mix well. Stir in chocolate chips and pecans. Roll dough into golf-ball sized balls and place 2 inches apart on baking sheet. Bake in a pre-heated 375 degree oven for 9 minutes.

To begin her quest to improve her cookies, Katie will start with a simple question—Should milk chocolate or semi-sweet chocolate chips be used in the cookies?

In order to find out whether consumers in the cookie market prefer milk chocolate or semi-sweet chocolate chips in their cookies, two batches of cookies, one with each kind of chocolate chips, will be baked. The cookies will then be judged by a panel of taste testers. Everything about the two batches of cookies, other than the kind of chocolate chips, must be exactly the same, including the amount of each of the other ingredients, cookie size, and baking time and

Source: Darwin J. Davis, under the direction of Professor Vincent A. Mabert, Indiana University.

temperature. All factors other than the kind of chocolate chips, which is the factor being tested, must be *held constant* so that any difference between the two batches of cookies will be the direct result of the kind of chocolate chips used.

Main Effect

A panel of 20 taste testers whom Katie thinks is representative of her cookie customers will judge the two batches of cookies. Each of the taste testers will compare one cookie from each batch of Katie's cookies with one of Gooey Goodies' chocolate chip cookies (a competitive benchmark) and indicate for each batch whether Katie's or Gooey Goodies' cookie is preferred. The percentage of panel members preferring Katie's cookies with milk chocolate chips over Gooey Goodies' cookies (average effect of milk chocolate chips) and the percentage preferring Katie's cookies with semi-sweet chocolate chips over Gooey Goodies' cookies (average effect of semi-sweet chocolate chips) will be computed. The overall percentage (grand mean) of panel members preferring Katie's cookies over Gooey Goodies' cookies (using both batches of cookies) will also be computed. The difference between the percentage preferring Katie's cookies with milk chocolate chips over Gooey Goodies' cookies and the overall percentage preferring Katie's cookies over Gooey Goodies' cookies is known as the *main effect* of milk chocolate chips (Main Effect of milk chocolate chips = Average Effect of milk chocolate chips – Grand Mean). The main effect of semi-sweet chocolate chips is computed in a similar manner. The main effects of the chocolate chips will be used in making decisions about future cookie production. **Table 1** gives an example of a set of panel results and demonstrates the computation of the main effects.

The main effect of milk chocolate chips is higher than the main effect of semi-sweet chocolate chips. This indicates that Katie's cookies with milk chocolate chips are more highly preferred over Gooey Goodies' cookies than are Katie's cookies with semi-sweet chocolate chips (because high scores are good in this context). The main effects will be considered in making decisions such as whether the cookies with milk chocolate chips are significantly preferred more than the cookies with semi-sweet chocolate chips to make them worth the extra expense of the milk chocolate chips.

Experimentation for Multiple Factors

When experimentation is to be used for multiple factors, such as for two or more of the ingredients in chocolate chip cookies, it is not possible to obtain the desired information by varying each factor individually while holding everything else constant (as was done for the kind of chocolate chips). This is because there may be an *interaction* between the factors. An example of an interaction would be if the best kind of chocolate chips to use depended upon the amount of pecans in the cookies.

Suppose Katie wants to find both the best kind of chocolate chips and the best amount of pecans to use in her cookies to make them better than Gooey Goodies' cookies. This involves two different kinds of variables. The kind of chocolate chips to use, milk chocolate or semi-sweet, is a *discrete* variable, meaning the different options are completely distinct. However, the amount of pecans in the cookies is a *continuous* variable, meaning it can be increased or decreased by whatever small or large amount is chosen. This results in a far larger number of potential pecan amounts than could possibly be tested.

In order to use experimentation to determine the best amount of pecans to be used, the amount of pecans is transformed into a discrete variable by choosing just two different amounts of pecans to work with, one large amount and one small amount. More than two amounts could be chosen, but for our illustration, two will suffice. The experiment now involves two discrete variables.

To find the best kind of chocolate chips and the better of the two amounts of pecans for her cookies, testing two different levels of each ingredient (chocolate chips—milk chocolate or semi-sweet, pecans—two cups or three cups), Katie would have to test two batches of cookies with milk chocolate chips, one with two cups of pecans and one with three cups of pecans, and two batches of cookies with semi-sweet chocolate chips, one with two cups of pecans and one with three cups of pecans. As before, all other ingredients and specifications for the cookies must remain constant. **Table 2** lists each of the batches of cookies. Each of these batches is a separate test setting.

Testing every combination of every treatment level for each factor (as was just done for the chocolate chips and pecans) is called a *full factorial design*. A full factorial design has the benefit of capturing all possible available information but the disadvantage that when even a moderate number of variables are used, large quantities of both time and money can be involved. For example, when seven factors are tested at two levels each, 128 experiments must be run (e.g., for our cookie example, 128 different batches of cookies).

The Size of a Full Factorial Design

The size of a full factorial design is determined by taking the product of the number of treatment levels being tested for each of the factors being tested. Thus, if an experimental design involves two different treatment levels for each of five cookie ingredients, the size of the experiment is $2 \times 2 \times 2 \times 2 \times 2 = 2^5 = 32$, or 32 different batches of cookies must be compared. If experiments are run for 3 levels of sugar, 2 levels of butter, and 4 levels of flour, $3 \times 2 \times 4 = 24$ different batches of cookies must be compared. Notice that when the same number of treatment levels is used for each of the factors, the size of the experimental design is the number of treatment levels used for each factor, raised to the power of the number of factors (two levels for each of five ingredients yields a design size of $2^5 = 32$ experiments). When multiple factors are tested and varying numbers of treatment levels are used for the factors, the size, X, of the experiment is:

$$X = 2^{k2}3^{k3}4^{k4}$$

where:

X = total number of experiments
$k2$ = number of factors with two treatment levels
$k3$ = number of factors with three treatment levels
$k4$ = number of factors with four treatment levels etc.

Partial Designs

In order to save time and money, *partial designs* are often used in experimentation. Partial designs may be set up in several different ways, including a method developed by Dr. Genichi Taguchi. Partial designs do not yield as accurate information as full factorial designs, but they may be worth the trade-off in savings of time and money. Consider an experimental design which tests seven factors at two levels each. The size of a full factorial design would be $2^7 = 128$ experiments while the size of a Taguchi partial design would be just 8. A full factorial design (**Table 3**) and a Taguchi partial design (**Table 4**) for chocolate chip cookies for three factors at two levels each are shown later.

Calculation of the Main Effect for a Partial Design

Once all of the experiments in a partial design have been run, the main effect for each factor can be computed. First the overall average (grand mean) of the experiment results is computed. Then the *average effect* for each factor treatment level is calculated by computing the average of the results over all occurrences of a factor treatment level. The *main effect* of a factor treatment level is the difference between the average effect for the given treatment level and the grand mean (Main Effect = Average Effect – Grand Mean). **Table 5** and **Table 6** demonstrate results for the partial design shown above for chocolate chip cookies and show the calculation of the main effects. To calculate the main effect of the milk chocolate chips, first compute the average of the four experiments (grand mean) and the average of the two experiments which use milk chocolate chips (average effect). The main effect of the milk chocolate chips is the difference between the average effect for milk chocolate chips and the grand mean (Main Effect = Average Effect – Grand Mean). The main effects of the semi-sweet chocolate chips and each of the amounts of pecans and cinnamon are calculated in a similar manner.

After the main effects have been calculated, the best level for each factor can be determined. This is done by choosing the treatment level for each factor that has the best (in this case the highest) main effect. Thus, to make the chocolate chip cookie that has the best chance of being better than Gooey Goodies' chocolate chip cookie, Katie should use milk chocolate chips, 3 cups of pecans, and 1 tablespoon of cinnamon. Notice that this was not one of the batches of cookies that was actually baked.

Note: It is possible that the factor levels that are found to be the best using a partial design may occasionally not be the ones that are found to be best if a full design is run. However, the partial design generally finds the best combination of factors and the savings in time and money may outweigh the risk of suboptimal results.

Table 1 Percent Preferring Katie's Cookies over Gooey Goodies' Cookies

Kind of Chocolate Chips		Main Effect
Milk Chocolate Chips	70%	70 – 57.5 = 12.5% (above mean)
Semi-Sweet Chocolate Chips	45%	45 – 57.5 = –12.5% (below mean)
Grand Mean	57.5%	

Table 2 Full Factorial Design for Chocolate Chip Cookies

		Factors	
		Chocolate Chips	Pecans
Test Setting (Batch of Cookies)	1	Milk	2 c
	2	Milk	3 c
	3	Semi	2 c
	4	Semi	3 c

Table 3 Full Factorial Design for Chocolate Chip Cookies—Three Factors at Two Levels Each

		Factors		
		Chocolate Chips	Pecans	Cinnamon
Test Setting (Batch of Cookies)	1	Milk	2 c	1 T
	2	Milk	2 c	2 T
	3	Milk	3 c	1 T
	4	Milk	3 c	2 T
	5	Semi	2 c	1 T
	6	Semi	2 c	2 T
	7	Semi	3 c	1 T
	8	Semi	3 c	2 T

Table 4 Partial (Taguchi) Design for Chocolate Chip Cookies—Three Factors at Two Levels Each

		Factors		
		Chocolate Chips	Pecans	Cinnamon
Test Setting (Batch of Cookies)	1	Milk	2 c	1 T
	2	Milk	3 c	2 T
	3	Semi	2 c	2 T
	4	Semi	3 c	1 T

Table 5 Results from Taste Testing Panel

Chocolate Chips	Pecans	Cinnamon	Percent Preferring Katie's Cookies over Gooey Goodies' Cookies
Milk	2 c	1 T	65
Milk	3 c	2 T	70
Semi-sweet	2 c	2 T	35
Semi-sweet	3 c	1 T	45
Grand Mean			**53.75%**

Table 6 Main Effects for Chocolate Chip Cookies—Three Factors at Two Levels Each

Factor	Level	Average Effect	Main Effect
Chocolate Chips	Milk	$\frac{65 + 70}{2} = 67.5$	$67.5 - 53.75 = 13.75$
Chocolate Chips	Semi-sweet	$\frac{35 + 45}{2} = 40.0$	$40.0 - 53.75 = -13.75$
Pecans	2 c	$\frac{65 + 35}{2} = 50.0$	$50.0 - 53.75 = -3.75$
Pecans	3 c	$\frac{70 + 45}{2} = 57.5$	$57.5 - 53.75 = 3.75$
Cinnamon	1 T	$\frac{65 + 45}{2} = 55.0$	$55.0 - 53.75 = 1.25$
Cinnamon	2 T	$\frac{70 + 35}{2} = 52.5$	$52.5 - 53.75 = -1.25$

A P P E N D I X   D

Natural and Assigned Variations

Variations occur in the world. They occur in the heights of trees, and people, as well as in dimensions of most other things. These variations occur in manufactured items and in services. Part of the TQM task is to identify and control these variations. These variations are of two types; natural and assignable.

The manager's job is distinguish between these two types of variations, usually with a goal of reducing variations.

Natural Variations occur in virtually all processes and are to be expected. The heights of trees and people are natural variations. The same type of variations occurs for virtually all processes, be they manufacturing processes or service processes. These variations are inherent in a process. The design of the process or the species of the tree determines these variations. To reduce these variations one changes the process. Most variations are the result of the process design. The rule of thumb is that 85% of all variations are due to process design.

natural variations
Occur in virtually all process and are to be expected.

Variations often follow a pattern called a distribution. When these distributions are *normal*, they are defined by two parameters. These parameters are:

First, the mean, μ (a measure of central tendency of the values).
Second, the standard deviation, σ (a measure of dispersion or variation of the values).

When the values are within specified limits, it can be concluded that only natural variations are occurring. When only natural variations are occurring the process is said to be "in control."

Assignable Variations are those variations that can be traced to a specific cause. These causes may be a process or machine that is worn or poorly adjusted. Alternatively the cause may be personnel who are fatigued or poorly trained. The cause may also be material that has changed. When assignable variations are occurring the process is said to be "out of control."

assignable variations
Those variations that can be traced to a specific cause.

Control charts which typically plot the two parameters of the normal distribution (a measure of central tendency and a measure of dispersion) are the standard way to identify when a distribution has changed from naturally occurring variations to assignable variations.

A P P E N D I X   E

Machine Capability Analysis

When determining whether a machine is inherently capable of meeting design specifications of a particular operation, a machine capability study is performed. In essence, this is based on whether the underlying variability of the machine is small enough to accommodate the designated specifications of the particular operation on that part. This is illustrated by example.

A part has an outside diameter that is to be turned to a specification of 1.50000 inches, ± 0.00100 inches. There are four machines that might be used for this operation: A, B, C, and D. A is the most expensive and most accurate, B is next, and so on. Let us say that the inherent accuracy of the four machines is known. We will express these measures of accuracy as the standard deviation for work of this nature. The following measures of accuracy (standard deviations) prevail:

Machine A = 0.00010 inches
Machine B = 0.00015 inches
Machine C = 0.00020 inches
Machine D = 0.00035 inches

The question is, which machines can and cannot be used for this operation? This is the essence of a machine capability study.

The answer is found in comparing the design tolerance for the operation to what is called the "natural tolerance limits" of each machine. The natural tolerance limits are defined as ± three standard deviations of the process. Applying this to our four machines results in the following natural tolerance limits:

Machine A = ± 0.00030 inches, which is well within the design specifications
       of ± 0.00100 inches.
Machine B = ± 0.00045 inches, also well within the design specifications.
Machine C = ± 0.00060 inches, again within the design specifications.
Machine D = ± 0.00105 inches, which does not fall within the design speci-
       fications.

It can be seen then that three out of the four machines are capable of producing this operation within the desired design specifications, but that Machine D is not. This means that if Machine D is chosen to perform this operation, some portion of the parts produced will fall outside the design specifications for purely random causes. Put another way, if Machine D is used it will probably be necessary to cull out some bad parts through inspection. This is necessary not because someone is doing a bad job; the machine is inherently not capable of doing a better job.

Source: This technical note was prepared by Joseph R. Carter and Thomas E. Vollmann for use with the Dynamic Seal Case. Copyright © 1984 by Boston University and the authors. Revised 1/86.

A company might well choose the machine that can do the job at the minimum cost. In this case, the choice would be Machine C. There is no reason to use Machine A or B, which are both more expensive processes.

This example is based on knowing the inherent variability of each machine (expressed as the standard deviation). In most cases this information is not known. It will have to be estimated. This is typically done by analyzing sample information. The analysis can proceed in two ways. The first would be to collect a series of data points and use them to determine a sample standard deviation that would be used to estimate the "population" standard deviation. The second is to collect several samples of size n. In each sample, a range is computed (largest value minus smallest value). These range data can then be used to find an average range. Thereafter, based on tabled values, the natural tolerance limits can be determined.

A P P E N D I X   F

Control Chart Calculations

In controlling dimensions that can *be* measured, the typical approach is to construct two control charts, the $\overline{X}$ chart and the R chart. The $\overline{X}$ chart is used to determine if the mean or average of the variable being measured has changed. The R chart is used to check if the underlying variability of the process has changed.

In the example of Machine C in the machine capability analysis technical note (**Appendix E**), the standard deviation of the process is 0.00020 inches, which yields a natural tolerance limit of ± 0.00060 inches. These would be the control limits if one were to take sample sizes of one piece. That is, the procedure would be to see if a particular part was within ± 0.00060 inches from the desired mean dimension.

There are several statistical reasons why a sample size of one is not appropriate. One in fact takes a sample of *n* pieces, computes the mean or average of these, and compares that to some control limits. The control limits are tighter as the sample size *n* is increased. That is so because the variability in sample means is related to the variability in the population. Specifically, the relationship is:

$$\sigma\overline{X} = \frac{\sigma\chi}{\sqrt{n}}$$

Where $\sigma\overline{X}$ is the standard deviation of sample means, σx is the population standard deviation and $\sqrt{n}$ is the square root of the sample size.

Continuing with the example, if samples of *n* = 5 are taken, the result is:

$$\sigma\overline{X} = \frac{\sigma\chi}{\sqrt{n}} = \frac{.0002}{\sqrt{5}} = 0.000085$$

Control limits are set at the mean dimension, ± three $\sigma\overline{X}$. In this example this would be:

1.5 inches ± 3(.000085)
The upper control limit (UCL) = 1.500255 inches
The lower control limit (LCL) = 1.499745 inches

The procedure would now be:

So much for the $\overline{X}$ chart which checks the mean dimension. The other need is to see if the underlying variability is as believed. (The $\overline{X}$ and machine capability analyses are based on this assumption). One way to do this would be to compute the standard deviation of the five parts in the sample, and compare this to some control limits. In fact the range is used as the measure of variability instead of the standard deviation. It is a less "powerful" statistic, but it is easier to compute.

Source: This technical note was prepared by Joseph R. Carter and Thomas E. Vollmann for use with the Dynamic Seal Case. Copyright © 1984 by Boston University and the authors. Revised 1/86.

Both the range and the standard deviation measure variability in a process. They are related, and **Table 1** provides data based on this relationship.

Other useful data:

$$\sigma X = (A_2 * \overline{R})/3$$
$$\sigma x = \overline{R}/d_2$$

The data in **Table 1** allows construction of an R chart for the example:

Since $\sigma x = \overline{R}/d_2$

$\overline{R} = \sigma x(d_2) = .0002(2.326) = 0.000465$

The upper control limit (UCL) $= D_4\overline{R} = 2.114\ (.000465) = 0.00098$

The lower control limit (LCL) $= D_3\overline{R} = 0\ (.000465) = 0$

This means that the procedure for checking variability is:

> *From the sample of five parts subtract the smallest value from the largest. If this range is less than 0.00098 inches, all is well (with the same statistical proviso as given for X).*

In most cases the underlying process standard deviation is not known. Sample range data can be used to directly determine upper and lower control limits for both the $\overline{X}$ and R charts. This is done by using the formula in **Table 1**.

Table 1 Quality Control Factors

Chart	Central Line	Lower Control Limit	Upper Control Limit
$\overline{X}$	$\overline{\overline{X}}$	$\overline{\overline{X}} - A_2\overline{R}$	$\overline{\overline{X}} + A_2\overline{R}$
R	$\overline{R} = H\overline{R}$	$D_3\overline{R}$	$D_4\overline{R}$

n	A_2	H	D_3	D_4	d_2
3	1.023	0.938	0	2.574	1.693
4	0.729	0.961	0	2.282	2.059
5	0.577	0.970	0	2.114	2.326
6	0.483	0.975	0	2.004	2.534
7	0.419	0.978	0.076	1.924	2.704
8	0.373	0.980	0.136	1.864	2.847
9	0.337	0.982	0.184	1.816	2.970
10	0.308	0.983	0.223	1.777	3.078

A P P E N D I X   G

Control Chart Factors

Sample Size n	X-charts				S-charts				R-charts				Lower Range	Upper Range
	A	A_2	A_3	C_4	B_3	B_4	B_5	B_6	d_2	d_3	D_1	D_2	D_3	D_4
2	2.121	1.880	2.659	0.7979	0	3.267	0	2.606	1.128	0.853	0	3.686	0	3.267
3	1.732	1.023	1.954	0.8862	0	2.568	0	2.276	1.693	0.888	0	4.358	0	2.574
4	1.500	0.729	1.628	0.9213	0	2.266	0	2.088	2.059	0.880	0	4.698	0	2.282
5	1.342	0.577	1.427	0.9400	0	2.089	0	1.964	2.326	0.864	0	4.918	0	2.114
6	1.225	0.483	1.287	0.9515	0.030	1.970	0.029	1.874	2.534	0.848	0	5.078	0	2.004
7	1.134	0.419	1.182	0.9594	0.118	1.882	0.113	1.806	2.704	0.833	0.204	5.204	0.076	1.924
8	1.061	0.373	1.099	0.9650	0.185	1.815	0.179	1.751	2.847	0.820	0.338	5.306	0.136	1.864
9	1.000	0.337	1.032	0.9693	0.239	1.761	0.232	1.707	2.970	0.808	0.547	5.393	0.184	1.816
10	0.949	0.308	0.975	0.9727	0.284	1.716	0.276	1.669	3.078	0.797	0.687	5.469	0.223	1.777
11	0.905	0.285	0.927	0.9754	0.321	1.679	0.313	1.637	3.173	0.787	0.811	5.535	0.256	1.744
12	0.866	0.266	0.886	0.9776	0.354	1.646	0.346	1.610	3.258	0.778	0.922	5.594	0.283	1.717
13	0.832	0.249	0.850	0.9794	0.382	1.618	0.374	1.585	3.336	0.770	1.025	5.647	0.307	1.693
14	0.802	0.235	0.817	0.9810	0.406	1.594	0.399	1.563	3.407	0.763	1.118	5.696	0.328	1.672
15	0.775	0.223	0.789	0.9823	0.428	1.572	0.421	1.544	3.472	0.756	1.203	5.741	0.347	1.653
16	0.750	0.212	0.763	0.9835	0.448	1.552	0.440	1.526	3.532	0.750	1.282	5.782	0.363	1.637
17	0.728	0.203	0.739	0.9845	0.466	1.534	0.458	1.511	3.588	0.744	1.356	5.820	0.378	1.622
18	0.707	0.194	0.718	0.9854	0.482	1.518	0.475	1.496	3.640	0.739	1.424	5.856	0.391	1.608
19	0.688	0.187	0.698	0.9862	0.497	1.503	0.490	1.483	3.689	0.734	1.487	5.891	0.403	1.597
20	0.671	0.180	0.680	0.9869	0.510	1.490	0.504	1.470	3.735	0.729	1.549	5.921	0.415	1.585
21	0.655	0.173	0.663	0.9876	0.532	1.477	0.516	1.459	3.778	0.724	1.605	5.951	0.425	1.575
22	0.640	0.167	0.647	0.9882	0.534	1.466	0.528	1.448	3.819	0.720	1.659	5.979	0.434	1.566
23	0.626	0.162	0.633	0.9887	0.545	1.455	0.539	1.438	3.858	0.716	1.710	6.006	0.443	1.557
24	0.612	0.157	0.619	0.9892	0.555	1.445	0.549	1.429	3.895	0.712	1.759	6.031	0.451	1.548
25	0.600	0.153	0.606	0.9896	0.565	1.435	0.559	1.420	3,931	0.708	1.806	6.056	0.459	1.541

Source: Adapted from Table 27 of ASTM STP 15D *ASTM Manual on Presentation of Data and Control Chart Analysis.* Copyright 1976 American Society for Testing and Materials, Philadellphia, PA.

Cumulative Binomial Probabilities

n	x	.05	.10	.15	.20	.25	.30	.35	.40	.45	.50	.55	.60	.65	.70	.75	.80	.85	.90
9	0	.6302	.3874	.2316	.1342	.0751	.0404	.0207	.0101	.0046	.0020	.0008	.0003	.0001	.0000	.0000	.0000	.0000	.0000
	1	.9288	.7748	.5995	.4362	.3003	.1960	.1211	.0705	.0385	.0195	.0091	.0038	.0014	.0004	.0001	.0000	.0000	.0000
	2	.9916	.9470	.8591	.7382	.6007	.4628	.3373	.2318	.1495	.0898	.0498	.0250	.0112	.0043	.0013	.0003	.0000	.0000
	3	.9994	.9917	.9661	.9144	.8343	.7297	.6089	.4826	.3614	.2539	.1658	.0994	.0536	.0253	.0100	.0031	.0006	.0001
	4	1.0000	.9991	.9944	.9804	.9511	.9012	.8283	.7334	.6214	.5000	.3786	.2666	.1717	.0988	.0489	.0196	.0056	.0009
	5	1.0000	.9999	.9994	.9969	.9900	.9747	.9496	.9006	.8342	.7461	.6386	.5174	.3911	.2703	.1657	.0856	.0339	.0083
	6	1.0000	1.0000	1.0000	.9997	.9987	.9957	.9888	.9750	.9502	.9102	.8505	.7682	.6627	.5372	.3993	.2618	.1409	.0530
	7	1.0000	1.0000	1.0000	1.0000	.9999	.9996	.9986	.9962	.9909	.9805	.9615	.9295	.8789	.8040	.6997	.5638	.4005	.2252
	8	1.0000	1.0000	1.0000	1.0000	1.0000	1.0000	.9999	.9997	.9992	.9980	.9954	.9899	.9793	.9596	.9249	.8658	.7684	.6126
	9	1.0000	1.0000	1.0000	1.0000	1.0000	1.0000	1.0000	1.0000	1.0000	1.0000	1.0000	1.0000	1.0000	1.0000	1.0000	1.0000	1.0000	1.0000
10	0	.5987	.3487	.1969	.1074	.0563	.0282	.0135	.0060	.0025	.0010	.0003	.0001	.0000	.0000	.0000	.0000	.0000	.0000
	1	.9139	.7361	.5443	.3758	.2440	.1493	.0860	.0464	.0233	.0107	.0045	.0017	.0005	.0001	.0000	.0000	.0000	.0000
	2	.9885	.9298	.8202	.6778	.5256	.3828	.2616	.1673	.0996	.0547	.0274	.0123	.0048	.0016	.0004	.0001	.0000	.0000
	3	.9990	.9872	.9500	.8791	.7759	.6496	.5138	.3823	.2660	.1719	.1020	.0548	.0260	.0106	.0035	.0009	.0001	.0000
	4	.9999	.9984	.9901	.9672	.9219	.8497	.7515	.6331	.5044	.3770	.2616	.1662	.0949	.0473	.0197	.0064	.0014	.0001
	5	1.0000	.9999	.9986	.9936	.9803	.9527	.9051	.8338	.7384	.6230	.4956	.3669	.2485	.1503	.0781	.0328	.0099	.0016
	6	1.0000	1.0000	.9999	.9991	.9965	.9894	.9740	.9452	.8980	.8281	.7340	.6177	.4862	.3504	.2241	.1209	.0500	.0128
	7	1.0000	1.0000	1.0000	.9999	.9996	.9984	.9952	.9877	.9726	.9453	.9004	.8327	.7384	.6172	.4744	.3222	.1798	.0702
	8	1.0000	1.0000	1.0000	1.0000	1.0000	.9999	.9995	.9983	.9955	.9893	.9767	.9536	.9140	.8507	.7560	.6242	.4557	.2639
	9	1.0000	1.0000	1.0000	1.0000	1.0000	1.0000	1.0000	.9999	.9997	.9990	.9975	.9940	.9865	.9718	.9437	.8926	.8031	.6513
	10	1.0000	1.0000	1.0000	1.0000	1.0000	1.0000	1.0000	1.0000	1.0000	1.0000	1.0000	1.0000	1.0000	1.0000	1.0000	1.0000	1.0000	1.0000
15	0	.4633	.2059	.0874	.0352	.0134	.0047	.0016	.0005	.0001	.0000	.0000	.0000	.0000	.0000	.0000	.0000	.0000	.0000
	1	.8290	.5490	.3186	.1671	.0802	.0353	.0142	.0052	.0017	.0005	.0001	.0000	.0000	.0000	.0000	.0000	.0000	.0000
	2	.9638	.8159	.6042	.3980	.2361	.1268	.0617	.0271	.0107	.0037	.0011	.0003	.0001	.0000	.0000	.0000	.0000	.0000
	3	.9945	.9444	.8227	.6482	.4613	.2969	.1727	.0905	.0424	.0176	.0063	.0019	.0005	.0001	.0000	.0000	.0000	.0000
	4	.9994	.9873	.9383	.8358	.6865	.5155	.3519	.2173	.1204	.0592	.0255	.0093	.0028	.0007	.0001	.0000	.0000	.0000
	5	.9999	.9978	.9832	.9389	.8516	.7216	.5643	.4032	.2608	.1509	.0769	.0338	.0124	.0037	.0008	.0001	.0000	.0000
	6	1.0000	.9997	.9964	.9819	.9434	.8689	.7548	.6098	.4522	.3036	.1818	.0950	.0422	.0152	.0042	.0008	.0001	.0000
	7	1.0000	1.0000	.9994	.9958	.9827	.9500	.8868	.7869	.6535	.5000	.3465	.2131	.1132	.0500	.0173	.0042	.0006	.0000
	8	1.0000	1.0000	.9999	.9992	.9958	.9848	.9578	.9050	.8182	.6964	.5478	.3902	.2452	.1311	.0566	.0181	.0036	.0003
	9	1.0000	1.0000	1.0000	.9999	.9992	.9963	.9876	.9662	.9231	.8491	.7392	.5968	.4357	.2784	.1484	.0611	.0168	.0022
	10	1.0000	1.0000	1.0000	1.0000	.9999	.9993	.9972	.9907	.9745	.9408	.8796	.7827	.6481	.4845	.3135	.1642	.0617	.0127
	11	1.0000	1.0000	1.0000	1.0000	1.0000	.9999	.9995	.9981	.9937	.9824	.9576	.9095	.8273	.7031	.5387	.3518	.1773	.0556
	12	1.0000	1.0000	1.0000	1.0000	1.0000	1.0000	.9999	.9997	.9989	.9963	.9893	.9729	.9383	.8732	.7639	.6020	.3958	.1841
	13	1.0000	1.0000	1.0000	1.0000	1.0000	1.0000	1.0000	1.0000	.9999	.9995	.9983	.9948	.9858	.9647	.9198	.8329	.6814	.4510
	14	1.0000	1.0000	1.0000	1.0000	1.0000	1.0000	1.0000	1.0000	1.0000	1.0000	.9999	.9995	.9984	.9953	.9866	.9648	.9126	.7941
	15	1.0000	1.0000	1.0000	1.0000	1.0000	1.0000	1.0000	1.0000	1.0000	1.0000	1.0000	1.0000	1.0000	1.0000	1.0000	1.0000	1.0000	1.0000

Appendix H: Cumulative Binomial Probabilities, concluded

n	x	.05	.10	.15	.20	.25	.30	.35	.40	.45	.50	.55	.60	.65	.70	.75	.80	.85	.90
20...	0	.3585	.1216	.0388	.0115	.0032	.0008	.0002	.0000	.0000	.0000	.0000	.0000	.0000	.0000	.0000	.0000	.0000	.0000
	1	.7358	.3917	.1756	.0692	.0243	.0076	.0021	.0005	.0001	.0000	.0000	.0000	.0000	.0000	.0000	.0000	.0000	.0000
	2	.9245	.6769	.4049	.2061	.0913	.0355	.0121	.0036	.0009	.0002	.0000	.0000	.0000	.0000	.0000	.0000	.0000	.0000
	3	.9841	.8670	.6477	.4114	.2252	.1071	.0444	.0160	.0049	.0013	.0003	.0000	.0000	.0000	.0000	.0000	.0000	.0000
	4	.9974	.9568	.8298	.6296	.4148	.2375	.1182	.0510	.0189	.0059	.0015	.0003	.0000	.0000	.0000	.0000	.0000	.0000
	5	.9997	.9887	.9327	.8042	.6172	.4164	.2454	.1256	.0553	.0207	.0064	.0016	.0003	.0000	.0000	.0000	.0000	.0000
	6	1.0000	.9976	.9781	.9133	.7858	.6080	.4166	.2500	.1299	.0577	.0214	.0065	.0015	.0003	.0000	.0000	.0000	.0000
	7	1.0000	.9996	.9941	.9679	.8982	.7723	.6010	.4159	.2520	.1316	.0580	.0210	.0060	.0013	.0002	.0000	.0000	.0000
	8	1.0000	.9999	.9987	.9900	.9591	.8867	.7624	.5956	.4143	.2517	.1308	.0565	.0196	.0051	.0009	.0001	.0000	.0000
	9	1.0000	1.0000	.9998	.9974	.9861	.9520	.8782	.7553	.5914	.4119	.2493	.1275	.0532	.0171	.0039	.0006	.0000	.0000
	10	1.0000	1.0000	1.0000	.9994	.9961	.9829	.9468	.8725	.7507	.5881	.4086	.2447	.1218	.0480	.0139	.0026	.0002	.0000
	11	1.0000	1.0000	1.0000	.9999	.9991	.9949	.9804	.9435	.8692	.7483	.5857	.4044	.2376	.1133	.0409	.0100	.0013	.0001
	12	1.0000	1.0000	1.0000	1.0000	.9998	.9987	.9940	.9790	.9420	.8684	.7480	.5841	.3990	.2277	.1018	.0321	.0059	.0004
	13	1.0000	1.0000	1.0000	1.0000	1.0000	.9997	.9985	.9935	.9786	.9423	.8701	.7500	.5834	.3920	.2142	.0867	.0219	.0024
	14	1.0000	1.0000	1.0000	1.0000	1.0000	1.0000	.9997	.9984	.9936	.9793	.9447	.8744	.7546	.5836	.3828	.1958	.0673	.0113
	15	1.0000	1.0000	1.0000	1.0000	1.0000	1.0000	1.0000	.9997	.9985	.9941	.9811	.9490	.8818	.7625	.5852	.3704	.1702	.0432
	16	1.0000	1.0000	1.0000	1.0000	1.0000	1.0000	1.0000	1.0000	.9997	.9987	.9951	.9840	.9556	.8929	.7748	.5886	.3523	.1330
	17	1.0000	1.0000	1.0000	1.0000	1.0000	1.0000	1.0000	1.0000	1.0000	.9998	.9991	.9964	.9879	.9645	.9087	.7939	.5951	.3231
	18	1.0000	1.0000	1.0000	1.0000	1.0000	1.0000	1.0000	1.0000	1.0000	1.0000	.9999	.9995	.9979	.9924	.9757	.9308	.8244	.6083
	19	1.0000	1.0000	1.0000	1.0000	1.0000	1.0000	1.0000	1.0000	1.0000	1.0000	1.0000	1.0000	.9998	.9992	.9968	.9885	.9612	.8784
	20	1.0000	1.0000	1.0000	1.0000	1.0000	1.0000	1.0000	1.0000	1.0000	1.0000	1.0000	1.0000	1.0000	1.0000	1.0000	1.0000	1.0000	1.0000

A P P E N D I X   I

Baldrige Award Criteria Framework—Dynamic Relationships

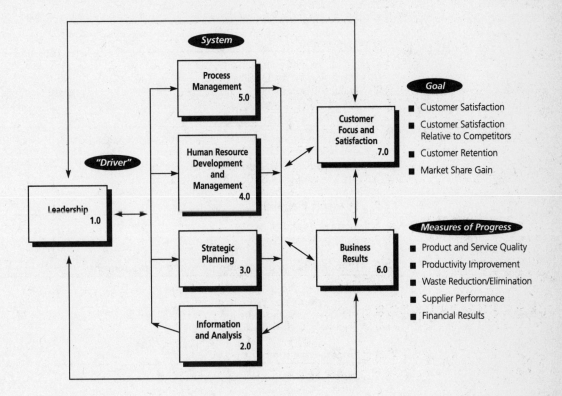

Award Criteria Framework

The core values and concepts are embodied in seven Categories, as follows:

1.0   Leadership
2.0   Information and Analysis
3.0   Strategic Planning
4.0   Human Resource Development and Management
5.0   Process Management
6.0   Business Results
7.0   Customer Focus and Satisfaction

The framework connecting and integrating the Categories is given in the figure above.

The framework has four basic elements:

Driver: Senior executive leadership sets directions, creates values, goals, and systems, and guides the pursuit of customer value and company performance improvement.

System: The system comprises the set of well-defined and well-designed processes for meeting the company's customer and performance requirements.

Measures of Progress: Measures of progress provide a results-oriented basis for channeling actions to delivering ever-improving customer value and company performance.

Goal: The basic aims of the system are the delivery of ever-improving value to customers and success in the marketplace.
    The seven Criteria Categories shown in the figure are subdivided into Examination Items and Areas to Address.

- **Examination Items:** There are 24 Examination Items, each focusing on a major requirement. Item titles and point values are given in Appendix J.

- **Areas to Address:** Examination Items consist of sets of Areas to Address (Areas). Information is submitted by applicants in response to specific requirement of these Areas.

Source: Award Criteria, U.S. Department of Commerce, p. 5.

A P P E N D I X J

Baldrige Examination Items and Point Values

1995 Examination Categories/Items   *Point Values*

1.0 Leadership   90

1.1	Senior Executive Leadership	45
1.2	Management for Quality	25
1.3	Public Responsibility	20

2.0 Information and Analysis   80

2.1	Scope and Management of Quality and Performance Data and Information	15
2.2	Competitive Comparisons and Benchmarks	25
2.3	Analysis and Uses of Company-Level Data	40

3.0 Strategic Planning   55

3.1	Strategic Development	35
3.2	Strategy Deployment	25

4.0 Human Resource Development and Management   140

4.1	Human Resource Planning and Evaluation	20
4.2	High Performance Work Systems	45
4.3	Employee Education, Training, and Development	50
4.4	Employee Well-Being and Satisfaction	25

5.0 Process Management   140

5.1	Design and Introduction of Products and Services	40
5.2	Process Management: Product and Service Production and Delivery	40
5.3	Process Management: Support Services	30
5.4	Management of Supplier Performance	30

6.0 Business Results   250

6.1	Product and Service Quality Results	75
6.2	Company Operational and Financial Results	130
6.3	Supplier Performance Results	45

7.0 Customer Focus and Satisfaction   250

7.1	Customer and Market Knowledge	30
7.2	Customer Relationship Management	30
7.3	Customer Satisfaction Determination	30
7.4	Customer Satisfaction Results	100
7.5	Customer Satisfaction Comparison	60

TOTAL POINTS	**1,000**

Source: Award Criteria, U.S. Department of Commerce, p. 12.